**Praise for *How to Become Famous
in Two Weeks or Less***

"Let's face it, who doesn't want their fifteen
minutes of fame! But the road to getting there can
be as difficult as crawling over broken glass.
Karen and Mel take you on an 'ouch-free' red
carpet ride to the VIP room in this great read,
with lots of laughs along the way."
—ROSHUMBA WILLIAMS
Supermodel

**Acclaim for Melissa de la Cruz's novel *Cat's Meow***

"Grab de la Cruz's debut novel and get swept up in Cat's
whirlwind quest for fame, fortune, and designer outlet stores."
—*Glamour*

"Melissa de la Cruz captures all the nuances of the
New York fashion sillies with wit and accuracy."
—TODD OLDHAM

"A gift-bag of satire, spectacle, and name-
dropping. It's all too fabulous for words!"
—MICHAEL MUSTO

"Melissa de la Cruz has created a rambunctious
first novel that deserves to have its every page
encrusted with sand, its binding ringed with
condensation from highball glasses. At once
calculating and clueless, Cat is a hilarious
Virgil. . . . Writing in the zippy, breathless argot
of *Vogue* and *Vanity Fair*, Cruz pinpoints the
sinister vanities of this air-headed realm while
making it all sound absurdly fun."
—*Los Angeles Times Book Review*

# HOW TO BECOME FAMOUS
*in Two Weeks or Less*

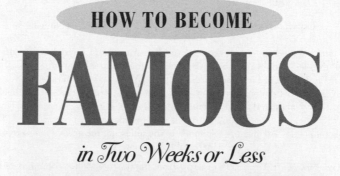

# HOW TO BECOME

# FAMOUS

### in Two Weeks or Less

TANYA BRAGANTI

## by Melissa de la Cruz & Karen Robinovitz

*Ballantine Books* / *New York*

A Ballantine Book
Published by The Random House Publishing Group

Copyright © 2003 by Melissa de la Cruz and Karen Robinovitz

*New York Daily News, L.P.*: excerpts from the Rush & Molloy column dated
November 13, 2002. Reprinted with permission.

*New York Post*: excerpts from "Snaps" dated April 7, 2002, April 17, 2002,
December 1, 2002; "Page Six" dated December 27, 2002, and October 13, 2002.
2002 Copyright, NYP Holdings, Inc. Reprinted with permission
from the *New York Post*.

*New York* magazine logo on page 77 courtesy of *New York* magazine.

www.ballantinebooks.com

Library of Congress Control Number: 2003091517

ISBN 0-345-46294-7

Manufactured in the United States of America

Text design by Liney Li

Cover photo by Tanya Braganti

First Edition: July 2003

1  3  5  7  9  10  8  6  4  2

*For anyone who:*

never got invited to the prom,

always got picked last for teams in gym class,

wondered where to sit in the school cafeteria,

spent most Friday nights in front of the television,

was too afraid to try out for a talent show,

was in the "cool group" but secretly felt like a misfit,

click your heels (make that stilettos) together three times

and repeat after us,

"Fame and fortune await me. Fame and fortune await me."


P.S. And to our families, friends, and Mike (Mel's husband),

who always believed we would become famous,

even if we don't have the guitar-shaped

swimming pools to prove it.

*Come on, shake the covers of this sloth . . . for sitting softly cushioned, or tucked in bed, is no way to win fame; and without it man must waste his life away, leaving such traces of what he was on earth as smoke in wind and foam upon the water.*

—*Dante*, THE INFERNO

*Fame, what you like is in the limo . . .*
*Fame, what you need you have to borrow . . .*

—*David Bowie, "Fame"*

# Contents

# This Foreword Brought to You By ...

Since we were writing a book on how to become famous, we thought it would be excellent — nay, mandatory! — to have a bona fide celebrity write our book foreword. You know, so they could blather on about how great it is to be famous, how they're put on a pedestal, lavished with gifts, but also mention one or two of the perils (oh, the perils!) inherent in the privileged life they lead (no privacy, can't have dinner with anyone of the opposite sex without the media harping on your new love life . . .). We wanted to find someone that you, our reader, could relate to; someone young, pretty, and likable—with blockbuster movie (or television) credits to her name, who would earnestly tell you how great and hilarious our book was.

We rifled through our Rolodexes and came up with the perfect person. A controversial starlet who had appeared in numerous big-budget movies and played a very familiar TV character for years on a major network during a prime-time slot. We had her personal cell phone number, which we procured during a trip to Las Vegas when we bonded with her over blackjack. We called to ask if she'd be willing to do us the honor of writing our foreword and to our delight, she agreed!

(We thanked her with a gift from our goodie-bag stash: candles and bath salts!)

She admitted that she hated to write and asked us to simply interview her on the phone and write it for her. No problem, we thought! We could certainly pull that one off. After three months of stalking her by phone, she finally called us at seven A.M. to give us her quotes. She rambled semi-coherently about fame, fortune, and how she designed her own dresses for awards ceremonies. At one point, she referred to fame as "Christmas on acid." It was a mess, but we endeavored to fix it—editing it here, rewriting it there, chopping it up and rewording it so that it could have some semblance of prose.

But before we even sent her the final draft, we got a call from one of her friends who we happen to be friends with, too. Apparently, our movie/TV star no longer wanted to write the foreword since the lawyer of her high powered, much older Hollywood boyfriend told her it wasn't a good idea. We were shocked. She told us she was "excited" and "flattered" and "honored" to be a part of our project. And we were upset. We sent her a gift, dammit! We called her a dozen times to find out what went awry and tried to salvage the situation. But we never heard back from her. Not even to apologize. Nothing.

Instead, we got an angry call from her manager, someone who was clearly playing the role of the wicked stage mother. She berated us for not going through the starlet's publicist from the get-go. She called us unprofessional and said that the foreword we had written in no way depicts her client. (We faxed a copy to the starlet's publicist after the rejection call to say "See how cute this is. . . . Please convince her not to bail.") We tried to defend ourselves, but no amount of groveling, begging, and pleading would do. The starlet was out. And it was our problem.

"That's Hollywood. Celebrities are like that," we were told by those in the biz. (Later, when the starlet showed up at an awards ceremony in an atrocious dress that was a veritable fashion disaster, we had a good chuckle at the karmic boomerang.)

Our nice editor gave us a month to find another celebrity. But we were panicked—and desperate. This is why they call trying to convince a celebrity to do something "celebrity wrangling." Celebrities are a skittish, difficult-to-pin-down bunch, akin to a herd of stampeding buffalo. Trying to lasso one is an art in itself. We messengered our 288-page manuscript to every publicist, agent, and producer we knew, even to those we just met once, at a party, four years ago.

A call to a certain pretty woman who makes twenty million a picture garnered us no luck. "Sorry," her publicist said before we even finished our sentence, "but she doesn't do things like that, not even for knitting books. And she's *really* into knitting." We were friendly with the manager of a much-married singer/dancer/actress who likes to think she's still "from the block," hoping that she would understand our plight and happily lend her services. But her manager said, "not unless she gets royalties."

So it was on to Plan B. We sent one to the cute star of a racy HBO sitcom, who was hot on the idea until she realized our book "wasn't a novel." We sent one to a very famous former child-actor. His publicist didn't think it was a good idea for him to talk about fame since he was in the middle of attempting a comeback. We received the great news that the edgy widow of a dead rock star was reading our manuscript on her Hawaiian vacation. Unfortunately, we read in Page Six the next day that her trip to Maui ended in her arrest at the airport, so we figured, correctly, that writing a book foreword was the last thing on her mind. At a fancy dinner, we sat next to the famous daughter of a red-carpet maven, who raved about our article in *Marie Claire* and loved the idea of our book. She promised to pen our foreword. We were beside ourselves. She'd gone to an Ivy league college! She could write! But needless to say, we're still waiting. . . .

So alas. We do not have a celebrity foreword. We weren't able to find a famous person who will tell you that our book is funny and smart, sarcastic and honest, a journey through the ups-and-downs of trying and succeeding and trying and failing, in the art of being famous. If you're the kind of person (like us) who gets haircuts that resemble famous people's haircuts, or buys boots because somebody famous bought the same pair, you are out of luck. You'll just have to trust us.

# HOW TO BECOME FAMOUS
## *in Two Weeks or Less*

*Introduction*

# CHASING FAME

*L*ike anyone who's ever stuffed her face full of popcorn while watching Joan Rivers needle celebrities on the red carpet, we have been obsessed with fame and those who are famous for as long as we can remember. We longed for attention—glamorous dresses, standing ovations, and a reason to thank the Academy. Growing up in the suburbs of New Jersey (Karen) and San Francisco (Melissa), we used to transform our bedrooms into theaters and produce one-girl shows with our tolerant parents as our only audience. We wanted to guest star on *Romper Room*, *Sesame Street*, and *The Electric Company* because we believed it would lead to the kind of success that would garner us more than three and a half stars on *Star Search*.

Unfortunately, we couldn't act to save our lives—Karen tried out for countless plays in elementary school through senior year in high school, always landing the part of understudy for a non-speaking role, while Melissa developed an acute attack of stage fright during a kindergarten Christmas performance as the angel of the Lord who forgot all her lines. Moreover, our last names weren't Spelling or Spielberg. We had to face reality: we would never find a place on Hollywood's coveted A-list or land a role as a spoiled virgin on some kind of teen dramedy.

We spent junior high imagining our lives as rock stars. The screaming, frenzied fans! The skintight leather pants! The gravity-defying haircuts! The world tours! The feather boas! The limousine lifestyle! The shopping! It seemed to suit us perfectly. C'mon, we air-guitared and handled fake microphones with divalike aplomb. Multiple karaoke experiences however, confirmed the *unthinkable*—we had the worst voices on Earth! And what good is being a rock star if you're not a lead singer? As much as we longed to be fitted for our own Gaultier-designed cone bras (remember Madonna's, circa "Express Yourself"?), we had to admit that mega, arena-stadium-filling, iconic rock stardom was not in the cards either.

How would we ever achieve our quest for massive recognition? we wondered. The covers of *Vogue, Harper's Bazaar, W, Elle,* and even the JCPenney catalog were closed to us. A modeling agent who visited Melissa's all-girls high school on a talent-scouting trip broke the bad news: she was five inches too short. And at four feet, eleven inches, Karen never even stood a chance at catwalk glory. (Oh, well. We weren't prepared to give up Cadbury chocolate bars!)

We were never going to be famous. So we did the next best thing. We moved to New York City. And a funny thing happened on the way to the subway.

In New York, we soon came to realize, *anyone* could be famous. As we devoured the pages of glossy magazines and scanned the gossip columns of daily metropolitan newspapers at a feverish pace, we discovered a city filled with people we had never heard of but who boasted tons of press clips anyway. This glittery group was invited to the best parties, given gaggles of free clothes, and never had to pay their bar tabs. Oh, sure, some had last names that doubled as condiment brands and hotel chains. Some had powerful husbands. But most had no name and no talent to speak of, other than the ability to look pretty in the right dress.

They were famous simply for being famous. And we wanted to be one of them.

Instead, we wound up writing about them. As journalists we covered the salmon-tartar and caviar-potato circuit, went backstage at fashion shows, survived throbbing champagne hangovers, and perfected the art of talking in patently fake British accents (the better to wrangle invitations with!). We wrote about the rarefied world of private jets, chartering yachts, celebrity dentists, and invitation-only Botox parties. We befriended publicists who had access to the hottest celebrities and the most exclusive shindigs. We rubbed shoulders and thrust tape recorders under the noses of Ethan Hawke, Jason Priestly, Puff Daddy, Marisa Tomei, Will Ferrell, Alicia Silverstone, and many, many more famous people who brushed us off with a gruff, "Oh, there's Alec (Baldwin). I'm going to say hi." (A true story!)

We may have had the dress, the shoes, and the bylines. But we were still on the sidelines. So close, yet so far from our very own stars on Hollywood Boulevard.

# SMALL WORLDS

## Karen

The media is a small industry. Everyone knows everyone—at least by name. I had heard of Melissa de la Cruz a million times. I knew her as the fashion addict (she wrote a style column for a groovy Web site called hintmag.com), who had penned a hilarious novel called *Cat's Meow* about a wanna-be socialite that was a must-read with the catty jet set. When I read the opening line of her book, "I am the type of girl who laughs loudly, smokes incessantly, and is hell-bent on destroying herself, but stylishly," I became obsessed with her.

*She gets it*, I thought. Her book totally encapsulated my bipolar, love-hate relationship with a city where anyone can be the next It girl, the Nazis who man the velvet ropes judge you by your shoes (Manolos, darling), and Page Six (the *New York Post*'s gossip column) is God.

Then I saw her picture in *New York* magazine. She was wearing an insane white silk, one-shouldered top with cartoon-like kittens all over it by Alice Roi, a trendy New York designer. I owned that same shirt! (I found out later that Mel and I bought them from the same store, where they had only two in stock because the owners thought, No way would more than two people want something *this* ridiculous.) I knew right then, I had to be her friend. She was just like *moi*!

At a friend's brunch party, I spotted her at a table across from mine. Wearing gold high-heeled boots with torn "dirty" jeans and a fur-trimmed pink corduroy jacket, she was every bit the cool, brashly funny fashionista I had imagined her to be. She had the whole table agog, laughing heartily while divulging the inside scoop on perhaps the most well-known fashion editrix, who was rumored to be going bald and had her hairpiece fly off during an editorial meeting. I wanted in on that convo!

But I wasn't sure how to introduce myself. I didn't want to seem like a stalking fan. I had devoured all of her pieces. The one she had written about her weakness over giddy indulgences like fur tippets, zipper mules, Victorian jean jackets, and all the superfluous trends of the moment was holding court right smack in the middle of my corkboard in front of my desk. I constantly read it for adjective inspiration when I suffered from writer's block. She might be "just" a writer, but to me, she was famous.

She was *the* Melissa de la Cruz, the girl who did high-profile book readings, traveled to the Hamptons on a chopper, and wrote outrageous stories about crashing her fiancé's bachelor party—while disguised as a man! And she seemed refreshingly laid-back, unaware of her fabulosity. Sometimes, when people reach the limelight, they lose sight of who they are. They think their you-know-what doesn't stink. And they have that constant neck-craning habit of having a conversation with one person while looking over their shoulder to find someone better to talk to. But Melissa didn't project any snobbery.

I decided to approach, and as I walked toward her, she practically leaped off her seat. "You're Karen Robinovitz!" she yelped. Oh, my God. MdlC knew who I was! It was love at first sight! And the rest, as they say, is history.

# MEETING THE $2,500-BOOTS GIRL

## *Melissa*

*I* had been a fan of Karen's for a long time before I met her. Her name was popping up everywhere! I was slightly annoyed. She was a writer too, but she seemed to be living a much, much more fun life than I was. There she was, photographed in St. Bart's on a yacht next to Liev Schreiber in *Harper's Bazaar*. Or else writing for the *Times* about her unorthodox foot laser treatment because of her predilection for wearing four-inch heels. Or else looking foxy in a *Details* spread, wearing nothing but a cat mask and rhinestone underwear at an haute orgy in Soho. The $2,500 Manolo Blahnik knee-high boots she wore in a photo shoot about her "favorite shoes" was the icing on the cake—and more than I could take. "Who is she?" I groaned, throwing the magazine across the room in disgust. Even if I wrote about Manolos, I had never owned a pair.

At a brunch organized by a mutual friend, I finally met my "rival." She was wearing a ripped-up T-shirt with *Karen* playfully spray-painted on the chest, just like a similarly personalized one Madonna was sporting that week on MTV. She had the shortest denim miniskirt I have ever seen, with the waistband and the hem hacked off, so that her Calvin Klein boxers peeked out of the top (and the bottom). On her feet were buttery-soft calf-hugging fringed moccasins, and to complete the outfit, she wore these crazy earrings that looped continuously from one earlobe to the other. She looked fierce, tribal, funny, and over-the-top. She had this huge grin on her face, and when she sat down she pulled out a quilted Chanel bag. Purple. Suede. Gorge.

She kept getting up and taking people's pictures with her disposable camera. She seemed to know everybody at the restaurant but me. And I desperately wanted her to be my friend. I grabbed her elbow as she made her rounds. "You're Karen Robinovitz!"

"Yes, I am." She nodded.

I kept saying it. "You're Karen Robinovitz! *Karen Robinovitz!*"

She didn't seem annoyed by my enthusiasm. I was so excited to tell her I had been following her career from the beginning—from the "Extreme Dating" article, to the wicked profiles of real-life princess parties for three-year-olds, to the televised stints on *Entertainment Tonight* and CNN as a trend expert, to her sex columns about dating moguls in the Hamptons. So of course I blurted out the first thing that came to mind.

"You're the girl who was masturbated by the eighty-year-old sex therapist in *Marie Claire!*"

She blushed, but took it in stride.

We traded e-mail addresses, found out we owned the same silly clothes and were addicted to the same tabloids, and were soon discussing the finer points of Mötley Crüe's biography over "special salsa" at a neighborhood Mexican dive.

It was more than infatuation. It was a meeting of kindred spirits. And we have lived happily ever after ever since.

## *Almost Famous . . .*

Until one fateful Wednesday afternoon, when our editor at *Marie Claire* magazine called to give us our new assignment. "Do you two want to do a story on becoming famous? You'll have two weeks to get famous—be in magazines, get invited everywhere, hang out with stars, and *become a celebrity*," she said.

DID WE? WANT? TO? BECOME? FAMOUS? DUH!!!

For fourteen angst-ridden, exhausting, and thrill-a-minute days, we had to do whatever it took to become a **boldface** name in the annals of celebrity. Fourteen days to navigate the nightlife, host A-list parties, canoodle with a star, get our photographs in the society pages, appear on national television, and score hefty sacks of swag (industry-speak for "free stuff").

We used every ounce of knowledge we had picked up from writing about the famous flock to pull it off. We both wound up in the party pages of the *New York Post*, on the tube, and in obscenely expensive borrowed clothing.

Karen had a birthday party that rivaled Matt Damon's, wearing $2 million worth of Harry Winston diamonds, including the twenty-two-carat ring Whoopi Goldberg had worn to the Oscars, as well as a bodyguard named Lou who was straight out of a Scorsese film! Melissa hosted an intimate dinner at Orsay, a posh Upper East Side restaurant attended by the city's most powerful gossip columnists and spent a glorious week in a five-star resort favored by the likes of Britney Spears!

It took fourteen days to achieve our common goal for the last thirty years, but we did it!

We're *famous*.

Sort of.

This book is our story of begging, clawing, crying, borrowing, cheating, lying, stealing, and bribing our way to celebrity. It is also a guide to claiming your own fame. We provide how-to tips to stardom. Whether you live in New York or Omaha, Milan or Middle America, you can be legendary, the most sought-after kid in town, the one everyone wants to befriend.

So fasten your seat belt, prepare yourself for very little sleep, and get ready for your close-up!

*Days 1–2:*

# A "BRAND" NEW YOU

*A*s a star, it's important to be instantly recognizable, even when you're hiding in plain sight in a baseball cap and sunglasses. What is Gwyneth without her beautiful blond locks? J.Lo without her bodacious butt? Gwen Stefani without her steel midriff bared? Celebrities are like boxes of cereal—packaged and promoted to offer a consistent, bite-size message, so that everything from the clothes they wear to the color of their hair is a reflection of their particular trademark.

The first order of business on your search for the spotlight is to start thinking of yourself as a product, a commodity, and a brand. Witness the golden arches of McDonald's. Every time you see the giant yellow M in the sky, you know you deserve a break today. You, my friend, will need to acquire your own set of golden arches, that certain *je ne sais quoi* that will make people think—even subconsciously—of you every time they see it. The trick is being true to yourself—and possibly coming up with a fabulous stage name (flirt with prestigious identifiable brand names like Kennedy or Rockefeller, or think about adding "Von" or "de" before your last name to give it an upper-crust spin).

You also need to be original. Imitation may be the sincerest form of flattery, but the public can spot a cheap knockoff a mile away (although for some reason boy-band amnesia seems to set in every five years; the success of 'N Sync was spawned from the Backstreet Boys, which in turn was coded from the DNA of New Kids on the Block, which really stemmed from New Edition, a total reproduction of the Jackson Five). Take it from us, the Fame Highway is littered with celebrity roadkill: starlets and also-rans who never elevated themselves from the Blond Clone Army to Hollywood Heaven.

If you don't want to become a bloody mess, discarded like yesterday's trash, your brand must be strong—and likable. In private you can be as quirky, odd, and contradictory as you want. But in the public eye, your brand should always come first. Whether it's the calling cards you hand out at a party, the type of drink you order at a bar, or the kind of car you drive and the esoteric monikers you name your kids (Demi Moore named her three daughters Rumer, Scout LaRue, and Tallulah Belle, for heaven's sake!), you need to adopt a larger-than-life persona and live it to the hilt.

Exhausting? Maybe. But Hugh Hefner didn't become Hef without his silken PJs and breast-implanted accessories.

This chapter will help get you started by teaching you to establish your brand name. We will delineate the types of personas you can adopt (nothing like a little multiple-personality disorder amongst friends). Once you pick your MO, we'll show you how to use it to your advantage and keep up appearances, from creating a business card and letterhead to assembling your own press kit, honing your personal celebrity style, bulking up your social calendar to its desired A-list status, and asking for what you want without making apologies for it (it's called being high-maintenance, and nothing's wrong with that).

Be warned, all of this may come with possible public humiliation, but that's to be expected. Renée Zellweger didn't have us at hello until she made at least a dozen films that flopped, including *Return of the Texas Chainsaw Massacre* in 1994.

## THE BEGINNING: ACQUIRE THE FAME PERSONA

# THE NAKED TRUTH

•  •  •  •  •  •  •  •  •  •  *Karen*  •  •  •  •  •  •  •  •  •  •

*I* was Rollerblading down Second Avenue on a sunny Monday morning. At Forty-second Street I stopped at a red light. I didn't spot any oncoming cars, so I decided to go. The second I started to roll, a Volvo came from out of nowhere and clipped my left leg. I went flying back toward the curb, but I was in so much shock that I got right back up. Hordes of people surrounded me, asking if I was okay. "I'm fine. I'm fine. I have to go to work," I said.

"You're not going anywhere," a woman shrieked in a high-pitched, anxiety-ridden voice that led me to believe she was very concerned. "You've been hit by a car." I looked down. My left leg was bleeding. I thought: *Oh, my God, my leg is bleeding.* Then I thought: *Oh, my God, I can see my leg.* My pants had gotten caught on the fender of the car that hit me . . . and ripped off my body . . . completely! *And I wasn't wearing underpants!* (I know, I know, Mom always says to wear clean underwear in case you get in an accident . . . and I had none!)

I was standing on Forty-second Street during morning rush hour, wearing nothing but Rollerblades and a T-shirt. It was mid-August. No one had a jacket to lend me. I was horrified (though I did sport a very fierce Brazilian bikini wax). I cried, "I'm not wearing any pants!" like a madwoman until the ambulance came to my rescue with a sheet, which I wrapped around my lower half like a sarong.

Twenty stitches and one fat scar later, the story spread far and wide. I once had someone from Philadelphia tell the tale of the "naked blader" back to me! I was a living urban legend. That's when it dawned on me: I could be famous for being naked.

Look at what nakedness did for Sharon Stone's career. Rose McGowan once showed up to the MTV Awards wearing a see-through dress made of silver chains—and a G-string—and the ensemble turned her from Marilyn Manson's girlfriend to an It girl. Even Leo's been photographed nude sunbathing in the Caribbean. And when was the last time you saw Christina Aguilera, Mariah Carey, or Toni Braxton covered up? Since I managed to survive the accident and the humiliation, I decided to brand myself as the girl who doesn't mind being in the buff.

I spent the last six years taking on the most intimate assignments for magazines like *Marie Claire*. For one story, I had to walk around the city streets of New York—topless. (I was photographed for the publication, covering my areolae with nothing but a magazine.) And for another, I had intercourse with my boyfriend in front of a sex coach who was there to improve our technique.

For the record, I do not have a perfect figure. Far from it. But I have always been comfortable in my skin. And doing these kinds of stories has helped me become even more at ease with my body. I built a reputation as the daring writer who likes her birthday suit. Editors assign me their most outlandish ideas, knowing that if it requires me to bare a private part of myself, I'll do it.

Once, an editor asked me to spend a few weeks living in one of those legal brothels in Las Vegas in order to do an exposé. I was all over the assignment . . . until they told me I'd have to sleep with a john. When I said no, my editor was shocked. "Just one," she said, as if that would make it okay. I was upset for a second. I couldn't believe they thought I was *that* kind of girl. Then I realized, *Wow, I really have branded myself well!*

So when a gallery-owner friend introduced me to Alexis Karl, an up-and-coming figurative artist who is known for creating seven-foot-tall oil paintings of naked women, I thought, *Here's my chance for immortality!* "Please let me take my clothes off for you," I begged. She agreed to paint me. I was on my way!

My portrait, which required over thirty-five hours of posing, was shown at the Red Dot Gallery in Chelsea, in New York, in

September of 2002. I was on sale for $8,000—and I will forever be immortalized as the famous naked girl, residing above the sofa in some man's living room!

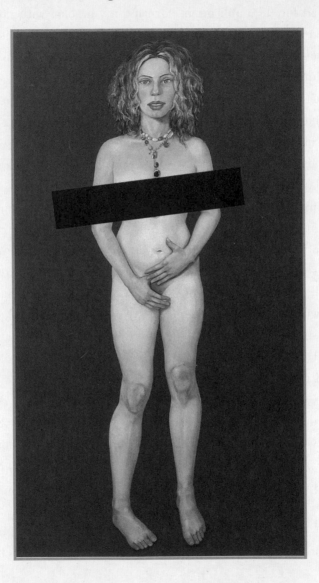

# THE OVER-IT GIRL

. . . . . . . . . . . *Melissa* . . . . . . . . . .

𝒲hen I first got the assignment to claw my way into the lime-light in two weeks, I decided to position myself as the newest in-carnation of species It girl. It girls ran around the city without stockings (even in the dead of winter), danced on tables while breaking champagne flutes, and gave in-depth interviews about the contents of their wardrobes. It was an established nightlife brand—and one I thought I could easily fake my way into—after all, how hard could it be? I'd pop over to some parties, wear some tight clothes, and *boom!* I'd be crowned the latest queen in the It-girl stakes. God knows I can put away the free drinks!

I even found the perfect venue to display my new It-girl per-sona: the aptly named It-girls premiere party for the It-girls documentary starring a whole host of It girls. The film featured the day-to-day lives of two junior socialites, Casey Johnson and Eliza-beth Kieselstein-Cord. Casey and Elizabeth both had bonafide It-girl chops. Elizabeth's last name was a handbag. Casey's was a Band-Aid. She was also a shampoo. And a detergent.

The publicist for the party was nice enough to put me on the list after I sent numerous faxes requesting entry and providing detailed, unimpeachable proof of my journalistic credentials. (I sent her a fawning note on swiped magazine letterhead.)

But styling myself as an It girl was harder than I thought. It girls don't just appear out of nowhere. It girls aren't born.

They're self-made. Plus, the label is commonly bestowed on chicks who don't try so hard—or at least, those who don't look like they do. Just look at Chloë Sevigny, who at eighteen perfected the ingenue's indifferent shrug at celebrity in a fawning profile in the *New Yorker*, which fanned the media fascination even more.

Which leads me to ask, if a girl attends a party and no photographers take her picture, did she even attend?

I would have to make sure my presence was recorded somehow. I begged a good friend who worked at a magazine to put my picture in their party pages. "If you get Patrick McMullan to shoot you next to a celeb at the It-girl party, we'll do it," she promised. So the night before the party, I called social shutterbug Patrick McMullan's office. I groveled on the phone and spent fifteen minutes explaining my situation to Patrick's helpful assistant. She said Patrick would be happy to do it; I would just have to go up to him at the party and brief him on my mission.

Before the party, I spent two hours at a beauty salon getting my hair blown and fake eyelashes glued to my real ones. I put on a Julia Roberts–inspired cutout black top and skinny leather pants. The pants were incredibly tight and stuck to my thighs like sausage casing. I decided I should probably not drink anything so I wouldn't have to go to the bathroom, because who knew if I could zip myself back into them again. My It-girl debut would have to be a sober one. So much for dancing on tables.

I arrived at exactly seven o'clock, as the invitation demanded. There was a line of paparazzi at the front of the restaurant, and several more photographers and camera crew inside. I strutted inside, projecting It-girlish vibes. I telepathically communicated my It status by preening on the red carpet. Sadly, not one photographer looked up. No one took my picture. It was disheartening. And there I was wearing borrowed designer clothes and no bra! Just like a real It girl!

I decided to find Patrick immediately, which was easier said than done, as he was the most popular person there. The man was mobbed. It girls of all stripes were throwing themselves in front of his camera. After all, he was radiating Itness himself, with a television crew from the Metro Channel in tow. I had naively believed that somehow he would just "notice" my fabulous presence and immediately snap my picture. But no.

Storing up my courage, I squared my shoulders and went up to him. "Patrick! It's Melissa de la Cruz!"

He nodded vaguely.

"I need to get my photo taken?"

"Huh?"

"I need to be photographed next to celebrities! I'm doing the It-girl experiment?"

He brightened, "Oh, yeah!"

We grabbed the nearest It girl we could find, and landed Estella Warren, who was also hosting the party and the third star of the documentary. She had recently appeared half-naked and practically mute in the *Planet of the Apes*. She was a model-turned-actress, and most definitely It. Estella looked a bit befuddled upon noticing me posing next to her, but she gamely slung her arm around me and smiled for the camera. Patrick squeezed the trigger. Flashbulbs exploded in my face. I noticed the rest of the paparazzi whispering to each other. Soon enough they, too, were taking my picture with Estella.

For the rest of the evening I squeezed myself next to photographs with both the Band-Aid and the handbag heiresses, mugged next to aloof six-foot-tall models, and followed Patrick around like a pesky stray dog. I met Vera Wang. I was rebuffed by Monica Lewinsky. An editor from *People* asked me who I was. At one point in the evening, Patrick convinced his television crew to film me. He introduced me to his television audience as "a girl who goes to a lot of parties."

In other words, I was an It girl!

I was also exhausted.

Branding myself as the new It girl didn't turn out to be as glamorous as I'd expected. Instead of flitting about like a social butterfly and enjoying myself at a fancy party by guzzling magnum-loads of free champagne, I had spent it as a sweaty and anxious wreck. I didn't even have time to stuff my face with the free hors d'oeuvres. I was too agitated because I had to keep one eye out for the celebrities at all times.

This girl was officially over It.

Until the next week, of course, when I saw my picture in the party pages next to Estella Warren.

"You're an It girl!" the party's publicist cooed on my answering machine. "Congratulations!"

Even friends e-mailed their astonishment at my newly It status.

I scrutinized the picture. My eyes were slits. I had two chins. You could see the outline of my nipples through my see-through shirt. Yikes! But there I was, on the same page as Aerin Lauder and Uma Thurman!

I might have It on the brain, but I loved every minute of it.

# Can't Figure Out What Brand Name Is Appropriate for You?

### TAKE THIS BRIEF QUIZ TO FIND OUT

*1. You're on the red carpet and Joan Rivers is approaching with the microphone. Last season she called you one of the worst dressed. Your reaction is as follows:*

**A.** You send your assistant to tell Joan you are not available for interviews. You give her a dirty look when you pass by and cozy up to another reporter right in front of her. You also do your darnedest to make sure everyone in your circle ignores her, too.

**B.** You are nothing but charming. You smile sweetly and kill her with kindness as you tell her Mr. Gesquiere designed your fabulous dress himself.

**C.** You're too high to even make it down the red carpet.

**D.** They couldn't pay you enough money to go to such a morally decrepit, corrupt zoo where no one boasts an ounce of individuality or intellect! But you're happy to thank the academy from your ranch in Carmel.

**E.** You just can't wait to show off your new implants. You happily pose for the camera, revealing your plunging backline (and new butt tattoo) that's so low, the censors are having an anxiety attack.

**F.** Joan who?

*2. It's been an hour, and your helicopter has not yet arrived to whisk you off to the Hamptons for the weekend. Your reaction is as follows:*

**A.** You lose it and maliciously scream at—and threaten to fire—a heliport administrator who is not under your employ. Don't they know who you are?

**B.** You say, "Damn those silly flying things that are never on time. Oh, well." You put your bicycle in the back of a taxicab and make it to the beach in time for the clambake.

**C.** You chalk it up to another exhibition of the unfairness of the world. You always get the short end of the stick, even if you have the largest home on Dune Drive.

**D.** They couldn't pay you enough money to go to such a morally decrepit, corrupt zoo where no one boasts an ounce of individuality or intellect! But you'll RSVP to P. Diddy's "all-white" July Fourth party anyway.

**E.** You keep chewing your gum—and blow bubbles (or something else)—while waiting. The guy who's carrying your baggage is kind of cute. . . .

**F.** Where are the Hamptons?

*3. You're on the front page of a tabloid as a result of canoodling with someone other than your significant other. Your reaction is as follows:*

**A.** Fire your publicist (it's probably her fault this got into the press) and hire her rival, who issues a public statement of denial. And you slap a $10 million lawsuit on the paper.

**B.** Buy a copy of the magazine for a good laugh.

**C.** Deny the allegations, as you were only examining your fear of intimacy. The relationship was your therapist's idea, after all.

**D.** Read all about it from behind bars after punching the photographer who snapped your picture.

**E.** Lie to your boyfriend and tell him it was nothing. Really, you only did it to get the role.

**F.** Think, *That's odd . . . I didn't know that plushies were considered cheating.*

# THE QUIZ KEY
### FIND OUT WHICH BRAND IS RIGHT FOR YOU

• **If you answered A to all of the above, you're "the Power Girl."** That means you're the fireball who can get things done. Here's how to be the diva: Never leave without your cell phone, trusty two-way pager, and Palm Pilot. Tell friends to call during important appointments so you come across as busy and have to hang up on them. Vice versa, when important people call and you're watching E! with a friend on her couch, say you're in the middle of an important appointment and hang up on them too. Constantly fiddle with your BlackBerry, even if you're just sending yourself love letters. Raise your voice a few dozen decibels. You want everyone around you to know what you're saying at all times. Even if you're just supersizing your fries to go. Warning: You may make a lot of enemies, but who cares . . . you're famous.

• **If you answered B to all of the above, you're "the Holly Golightly."** That means you're eccentric, stylish, and seemingly wealthy—even if you are about to be evicted because you can't pay rent or can't afford dinner unless your date is paying. You're dolled up at all times—in the pouring rain and on a Sunday-morning trip to the grocery store, where you wear an old prom dress over jeans. You do quirky things like name your cat "Cat," go to black-tie parties barefoot, and travel by bicycle with a banana seat. You invite ten people for drinks and two hundred show up to dance on your roof. Your date of choice: the Tortured Artiste.

• **If you answered C to all of the above, you're "the Tortured Artiste."** That's right, you're a misunderstood genius. You're always working on your novel, which you never seem to finish. You adore Japanese Noh theater, French New Wave, and

Italian noir. You carry a copy of Jack Kerouac in your bag so you can skim it during off hours while you're stocking new tapes at the Blockbuster. Oooh. *American Pie 2!*

- **If you answered D to all of the above, you're "the Grumpy Recluse."** You've got a chip on your shoulder the size of a memoir. Complain about never having privacy even when you're always out in public. Don't let people take photos of you—hold your hand up in front of the camera and pull a Sean Penn. Jackets are worn over the head. Drinking your own urine is optional.

- **If you answered E to all of the above, you're "the Bimbo."** You need little more than a large cup size and an unapologetic desire to show them off. Take cues from Pamela Anderson, who was discovered because of her short shirt while watching a football game. Sure, she was cute, but she attained her A-list status only after pumping her chest up to triple Ds. Perfect your voice, which should either be deep and breathy or high and squeaky. Call people "baby," "honey," and "doll-face." Giggle.

- **If you answered F to all of the above, you're "the Weirdo."** This persona usually comes after you've tried and failed at any of the above identities. It is the brand to acquire after making a series of mistakes. Once you're here, it's okay to take everything one step too far. Consider investing in an oxygen mask, which should be worn at all times, and travel with your chimp, Bubbles. Warning: this is only for advanced levels of fame.

- **Double Take:** If you're afraid to take on any of the above personas by yourself, don't worry. Whether you're wholesome and sweet, like the Olsen twins, buxom and recovering from bulimia like the Playboy Playmates, the Barbie twins, or bad to the bone on the tennis court like the Williams girls, famous people make a bigger impact when they come in twos. If you don't have a sister, rope your best friend into pretending to be yours. Dress similarly. Go everywhere together. You'll be easier to remember when there are more than one of you. If you err toward the wild side and you're built with a killer body, your brand may be best showcased as "the hot-blooded, hard-partying hotties who hit nightclubs, wearing almost nothing." Repeat every night until gossip columnists start spreading nasty rumors about you.

## YOUR FAME PAPERS

# A CORRESPONDENCE COURSE

### *Melissa*

*I* opened the box skeptically. "What is it?" I asked my sister as I poked at the tissue I found inside. I distinctly remembered having asked for a gift certificate from J.Crew for my twenty-third birthday.

"They're note cards."

"Huh," I said, taking one out. "What do I do with these?"

She rolled her eyes. "They're for, you know, *correspondence*."

This was in 1994, when penning letters was hardly obsolete, but only nerds who wanted to trade *Star Wars* action figures were on-line. I hadn't written a letter since 1984. I rifled the box. Inside, there were fifty ivory eighty-pound-card-stock note cards from Smythson of Bond Street, the posh stationery store in London where celebs and socialites get their monogrammed stationery. Emblazoned on the top was my full name, *Melissa Ann de la Cruz*, and on the bottom it proclaimed, *New York City*.

"I didn't put your whole address in because you move all the time," she said diplomatically, refraining from mentioning that my frequent change of residence was due to the fact I seemed to always get stuck with roommates who preferred to live in darkness rather than change lightbulbs, brushed their teeth in the bathtub so that it left an oily blue ring on the tile, and left hairballs of unknown origin in the refrigerator.

I put the box away. Correspondence? Was she serious? Who the hell would I write to?

Later that year, I almost sold my first novel. The editor who turned it down was intrigued enough to ask to buy me a drink at a bar downtown. He was charming and encouraging. The next day I took out one of my monogrammed note cards and thanked him for a pleasant evening. He returned the favor by sending me a thick engraved note card of his own, thanking me for my note and complimenting me on my "beautiful note cards." Thus we began a correspondence.

Thrilled with my stationery success, I began to use them for everything. I was a zealous pen pal. I imagined myself as a heroine of an Edith Wharton novel. I even learned the proper etiquette for their use—never write on the back of the card (so gauche), and draw a small vertical line through your first name (so says Tiffany & Co.).

MELISSA ANN DE LA CRUZ

# Le Stationery!

NEW YORK CITY

I thanked hosts for dinner parties, and relatives for presents I received, and I sent greetings with them the year I forgot to buy Christmas cards. I stuck them on birthday presents. Friends marveled. "They're so thick! They're so *classy*," they shrieked. My note cards never failed to impress. I garnered a well-deserved reputation as the slightly old-fashioned girl with the fabulous note cards. My mailbox was soon stuffed with similarly thick, ivory-colored monogrammed cards from gratified and very polite acquaintances.

Then the inevitable happened.

I was down to my last note card. There it sat, lonesome in the box, covered in well-worn tissues. I scribbled a witty aperçu to a friend who had bought me drinks the night before.

I mailed it off with a heavy heart.

Then I switched on my computer and e-mailed a dancing hamster to forty of my closest friends.

# CARD-CARRYING MEMBER
# OF THE CLUB
### *Karen*

*I*mage is everything, especially in the media circle, where people shun you if you're carrying last season's handbag (God forbid). When you start thinking of yourself as a commodity, everything has to have your personal mark, whether it's your signature Chanel red lipstick or your business card.

After three years of using the "Oh, no! I left my cards in my other handbag. I switched bags before I left this morning" excuse when people asked me for the card I didn't have, I decided it was time to make a solid investment in a piece of paper that would give the impression that I'm sophisticated, cool, and far from cheap.

I asked a graphic designer friend to help me source the perfect paper—one with girth and strength, the kind of tree by-product that says I'm durable, tough, expensive, but not pretentious. I sampled all the traditional card stock—sixty pound, eighty pound, one hundred pound. Nothing was good enough. I wanted something different, something no one had seen before, something that would make a bold statement, something no one would want to throw away. There's nothing worse than flimsy paper.

We came across mat board, which is traditionally used for matting drawings or photographs. It was hard, thick, strong, and practically unbendable. It was a bit more than I wanted to spend, but I rationalized the purchase by telling myself that my card would be an extension of myself. I am my own corporation and I want to dazzle people when I hand it off.

I went simple with the design scheme because I wanted the paper to speak for itself. I chose letters that resembled old-school-type writing fonts and had it pressed in, so it looked almost engraved. It said nothing more than my name, address, e-mail, and phone numbers, and yet it said so much more. It was chic, modern, minimalist, fabulous—everything I wanted my card (and image) to be.

The second I saw the mock-up printed, I thought, *Who's not going to hire me to write a story when they see this?* I was *in*, even if it cost $1,600 for a thousand cards! But every penny I spent was worth it. Once, I went into an art gallery and the owner, whom I had never met, saw my card and said, "I have one of your cards. It was given to me as an example of good fonts from one of my artists" (and that artist was also someone I had never met, who had gotten my card from someone else who passed it on as "inspiration"). The card has become my signature, the piece of me that I leave behind wherever I go.

# DESIGNING YOUR CALLING CARD

As a famous person, you are constantly promoting yourself. You need standout business cards and matching stationery to remind people of your brand even when you're not around. Splurge for special paper—the thicker or more colorful, the better. Keep the fonts and design consistent so people will automatically associate it—or anything like it—with you. Hand them out to everyone you meet—the nail salon manicurist, the hostess at the diner, the Gap salesperson of the week—and then everyone will start knowing you as "the girl with the cool card."

Your card should include the following:

- Your name, whatever you answer to at the moment.
- Your address. Unless you're a Holly Golightly, in which case it should read, "Traveling."
- Phone, fax, and mobile numbers. You need to be reachable at all times.
- Watermarks, logos, or some kind of symbol that represents you, be it a Chinese character for danger or your family crest (even if you just created it for the sake of the card).

What to avoid putting on a calling card:

- Cheesy lines and mottos.
- Your job title. You never want to limit yourself to one thing.
- Your photo. This is not a yearbook!

# GETTING YOUR ASSETS TOGETHER

*A*s a famous person, there are some things you'll need—a sample tape of you on television (even if it's a home recording), a headshot, a bio. We call them your vitals. We had to organize these things, and you'll need to, too.

# REEL LIFE

· · · · · · · · · · *Karen* · · · · · · · · · ·

*I*n the past, people have asked me if I have a "reel," which is a videotape of a television appearance in order to show producers or behind-the-scenes types that you know how to work the camera without looking like an eyesore. The only reel I had was an abomination. I was on a panel of relationship experts, commenting on the Darva Conger fiasco after the premiere of the show *Who Wants to Marry a Millionaire*. Every time the camera caught a glimpse of me, I got really uncomfortable and began to shift my eyes furiously back and forth, as if I were watching a tennis match between Agassi and Sampras. At the same time, I nervously played with the sleeves of my sweater, which were too long. And at one point I even hoisted myself up on my chair to sit Indian-style. It was my first television appearance and I'm sure the producers of the show prayed it would be my last. During my *Marie Claire* challenge, I was determined to get a better reel. The hard part about getting on television is that you either have to have experience (and a good reel) to get a gig—or do something that most people wouldn't dream of doing (like eat a pile of gnats, walk on a tightrope fifty feet in the air, or live with eight strangers in the house to see what happens when people stop being polite).

A dermatologist friend was doing a segment on *Entertainment Tonight*. The bit? Women who have Botox parties. I had actually written an article about the rampant trend of uptown girls who gather at their dermatologist's office—after hours—for sushi, gossip, and Botox. But I never thought I'd be the subject of this sort of thing—only the reporter. When he asked me if he could give me a shot of the wrinkle-paralyzing toxin on national television, I reluctantly agreed. I might not have needed Botox, but it was for my career—and the *Marie Claire* challenge— dammit! I put on my favorite Balenciaga ensemble for the appearance, did my hair and makeup, and went into his digs to do the deed.

When the TV crew arrived, I chatted it up for the camera with the rest of the girls, all there for the shoot. I threw in witty sound bites about how Botox has become the new Tupperware party and that it's no more invasive than, say, getting your hair highlighted. They loved me. Until I propped myself up on the doctor's chair and got ready for the money shot. For the record: I'm very squeamish about needles. The second the good doctor came close to my forehead, I squirmed and freaked out, turning my head away. The director yelled, "Cut," and we tried again. Four takes later, the segment producer asked the doctor if someone else could be featured. There went my reel. And the furrow in my brow is even worse than it once was.

# ASSEMBLING A PRESS KIT

A press kit is a marketing tool that is used to sell a product, person, place, or thing. It is sent out to all media people in order to inform them of something hot, trendy, new, or exciting. Like your card, it should represent your brand name. The design, font, paper, layout—even the folder, envelope, and stamp—should blend in a uniform manner, making it instantly recognizable. It's all a part of your brand, which means you've got to package it right, because a good press kit will get you noticed, which will potentially lead to press attention.

Here is what you need:

• A glossy, flattering 8-by-10 photo. The glossier and the more flattering the better. Just make sure it still sort of looks like you and not your overprocessed twin.

• A short biography of your achievements and career and personal highlights. For example, career highlight: Calvin Klein crashed my birthday party; personal highlight: Calvin Klein crashed my birthday party.

• A list of your assets: celebrities you know, contacts in high places, your certification for erotic dancing.

• A "reel," which is a videotape of you. It's important to show people you look good on camera, even if you're just being filmed by a boyfriend who knows his way around a camcorder.

See Step IV, Managing the Press Machine, to find out what to do with your press kit once you have one.

# JUST SHOOT ME

## *Melissa*

· · · · · · · · · · · · · · · · · · · · · · · ·

$\mathcal{S}$pring 2001, I had to get my picture taken because I needed an author's photo for the back of my upcoming book, *Cat's Meow*, a comic novel about a wanna-be socialite (shameless plug here!). At the same time, many of my magazine editors were asking for a photograph of me to put on their contributors' page (in the *front*) of the "book." But the only flattering photographs I had of myself were from a wedding I attended two years ago or at the bar of the Four Seasons restaurant. The first one showed a parking lot in the background, not the most glamorous of venues. In the second, I was blond (and drunk). Neither was acceptable.

I called my friend Eva, a fashion photographer who specialized in striking pictorials involving avant-garde clothes and drag queens. She agreed to take my portrait one afternoon at her apartment in the Flatiron District. All I needed was a glossy 8-by-10, which would entice readers to pick up my novel and show magazine editors that my face would not cause readers to upchuck their Caesar salads. Being attractive was suddenly a real component to an author's career. I once overheard a book editor lament about an author she had just signed: "The book is great, but I'm afraid we're not going to get a lot of coverage. The author is quite hideous."

GULP.

I prayed Eva would save me from such a terrible fate.

Eva was finishing lunch when I arrived. Her loft was just like her—stark, all white with black accents. Eva is six feet tall, platinum-haired, skinny, and wears only black clothing. She even has a German accent. She looks like a Dieter cliché, except she's got a sense of humor about herself. One Halloween she and her friends went as the group from *The Matrix*. Let's just say they didn't even need costumes.

"Let's go up to the roof," she said. "I want to portray you as a true New York author."

The roof was unfinished and full of tar. There were several muddy puddles coagulating in spots. Pigeons flocked everywhere. I stood stiffly next to gargoyles and looked over the roof moodily. Eva took shot after shot, clicking her tongue angrily. "Casual. More natural. C'mon!" she directed. "Open your eyes. Wider. Wider! Chin down, eyes open! No! Too much! Now you look scared!"

It was July and it was hot. I felt sweat beading on my forehead as I attempted to give her what she wanted. After an hour of trying, we looked over the digital pictures in dismay. My dress had bunched at the waist and the wind had whipped my carefully blown-out shag in all directions. The roof looked like a disaster zone.

I didn't look like a New Yorker. I looked like a dork.

Eva sighed. "Let's do some inside. Maybe with props."

I had explained that I wanted to be depicted as a fun-loving, *AbFab* kind of gal, someone who shopped a lot. Eva gave me Jackie O sunglasses and stuffed two shopping bags with tissues. She clicked away. I pretended to throw my head back in laughter. I whipped the glasses off my head and struck a coquettish pose. I swung the shopping bags energetically. We looked over the proofs. Instead of a socialite, I looked like a bag lady in Jackie O sunglasses holding two crinkled shopping bags. When I laughed, I looked demonic. Not to mention chubby.

"Hmmm. No props," Eva decided.

I stood in front of the white wall, nervous that we would never get a good picture of me. From childhood I have always been terrifically unphotogenic. My nose always looked too big and my hair always stuck out in feathered clumps. I despaired. Magazine editors would never put my face in the contributors' page, and I was sure my career was destined for disaster. I imagined potential *Cat's Meow* buyers recoiling from the mere sight of my face, banishing my book to remainder-bin hell. All because I couldn't live up to the beautiful-authoress standards that model-turned-authors like Candace Bushnell and Jennifer Egan embodied. Damn their skinny asses!

Eva suddenly had a brilliant idea. She got up on a stool and started shooting my face from a bird's-eye-view angle. "C'mon, give me a *twinkle* in the eye!" she ordered. I grinned up at her, desperately *twinkling*, my face poised between a smile and a smirk. We looked at the photos. Seen from above, my face looked much thinner. Only one of my chins was showing! And Eva had captured a true side of my personality.

Perfect. Two years later, I'm still using that photo for everything. It's on the back of my book. It's graced the contributors' pages of many magazines. And it's here, too.

The all-important book jacket photo.

EVA MUELLER

## CLOSET CASES

## DRESS TO IMPRESS

• • • • • • • • • *Karen* • • • • • • • • •

"*W*hat the hell is that, a postage stamp?" my father snapped as he looked at my dress on the eve of my thirtieth birthday. When I turned thirty (April 2002), I decided to celebrate with a bang and throw a party. A party had the added benefit of fitting into our *Marie Claire* challenge. I wanted to wear something that would scream, "Look at me! It's my party!" My friend Elisa Jimenez is a designer who dresses Sarah Jessica Parker, Marisa Tomei, Courtney Love, and Cameron Diaz. I know her through mutual friends, and I've always died over her clothes. They're nymph-like, raw, deconstructed, and rock-star fabulous. I invited her to my party (she's a "reach guest"), and after receiving my invitation, she called me and offered to make me a couture dress, sculpted for my body. No one gets that kind of treatment! It was my first celeb perk!

We spent a day at a fabric store to pick out the material. I sifted through velvet, lace, stretch jersey, but nothing would do. I wanted something borderline insane, something I could get away with once—and then toss in the photo album of crazy outfits, like the oversize and massively unflattering sequined Dallas Cowboy jersey that I had to have for my best friend's sweet sixteen (boy, was that a mistake!).

Then I found it—a bubble-gum-pink swatch of spandex with a loud zebra print, embellished with splashes of leopard spots. I know it sounds gross and tacky. It kind of was, but in the best possible way.

"Can I do this?" I asked Elisa sheepishly.

"You'd better!" she said. "You're only thirty once. Set your intention to be the goddess!"

"That's not a dress! That's a postage stamp!"

RONNIE ANDREN

I was a little nervous that it would be too . . . I don't know . . . ugly! But at the same time, that was the very thing that attracted me to it. I went for it. Why not? At least it would be a show-stopper, and no one else would have anything like it (or dare to wear anything like it, I should say). She turned the creation process into a ritual that involved aromatherapy and a prayer. And with a few measurements taken by hand (I was three palms long and two palms wide), Elisa morphed one yard of spandex into a sexy, skin-baring halter dress that hung a mere four inches longer than my crotch.

Looking back, I don't know who I thought I was, wearing such an itty bit of a thing, but I did feel pretty amazing in it all night.

Once I had the dress (or loincloth, if you will), I needed accessories. The true mark of celebrity is in the karats. Diamonds, that is. The stars are known for borrowing the most exquisite jewels. The year before my birthday, I wrote a heartfelt piece about the retiring eighty-something-year-old longtime designer behind Harry Winston's most spectacular jewels. So I called my H. W. contact to ask if there was any way I could borrow some baubles for my party. "We wouldn't do this for ordinary people," she said. "But we'll do it for you, as long as we provide a bodyguard." A bodyguard? Um, yes, please! I went to the magnificently sparkling Harry Winston salon and drooled over twenty-two-karat diamond rings, lavish pink diamond watches, and so many glimmering things that I was nearly blinded. We pored through trays upon trays of pieces that had just returned from the Oscars.

I chose the pink sapphire ring that Whoopi had worn to host the event in 2002, the diamond Y-shaped necklace starlet Lisa Marie had recently borrowed, a flower bracelet Caroline Murphy wears in their recent ad campaign, a $100,000 pink watch, and a subtle pair of four-karat diamond studs on a wire. The total: $2 million! And for one glorious night, it was going to be mine— all mine! Lou, a dapper, gray-haired man who looked like he just stepped off the set of the Sopranos, delivered the rocks before my party and followed me around all night to make sure no one pulled any funny stuff.

The jewels. The dress. The bodyguard. It was madness! A photograph of me in the dress and the diamonds wound up in the

*New York Post* party pages days later. And *Women's Wear Daily*, the fashion trade newspaper that everyone in the apparel industry calls "the bible," wrote a gossip item about it, calling me K.Ro! For weeks, ex-boyfriends, old friends from high school, and everyone I had ever encountered in the New York area called to tell me that they saw me in the diamonds and the dress, confirming, once and for all: It's not who you are . . . it's what you wear that counts . . . even if your father doesn't approve of the getup.

## A TRIP TO THE WEBBIES

*Melissa*

*J*n 1999, the Web site I had founded with several friends was nominated for a Webby Award in the fashion category—the "online equivalent of the Oscars," or so the producers of the show claimed. It was the heyday of the dot-com boom, and we were feeling flush, even if our little Web site was only run out of a studio apartment, half the people on the masthead were imaginary, and we couldn't afford to fly all four of us to San Francisco (we drew straws to see which two could go).

I was confident we would blow the competition away and be called up onstage to give our thank-yous, so I made sure to select an outfit I thought would be eye-catching enough. During one of my many trips to lower Manhattan's fabled designer discount outlet, Century 21 (where Missoni sweaters and

*Mel and Lee at the Webbys!*

hand-beaded John Galliano gowns were sold for a pittance of their original prices), I found the dress. It was designed by Walter van Beirendonck, one of those kooky Belgian iconoclasts who ran a notorious ad campaign that featured hairy "bearlike men" (a gay fetish for very big, very hairy men that is exemplified by the stroke rag titled, aptly enough, *Bear*). Van Bierendonck was known for out-of-this-world clothing (rubber pantsuits dotted with decorative pacifiers, for instance) and was very popular with Japanese club kids (the only people on the planet who would wear rubber pantsuits with decorative pacifiers).

My dress was two layers: a short red hooded minidress underneath a floor-sweeping, stiff red tulle material with puffed lines that circled around it. It looked a bit like a tiered wedding cake, and it made me look like I was wearing a glass tumbler. I loved it! I wore it with the hood up and my oversize Chanel sunglasses. I looked like a very fashion-forward Jedi knight.

"What are you trying to go for?" my mom asked, amused, when she saw me. "*Star* magazine's 'Would you be caught dead in that?' "

"What are you supposed to be, a spaceman?" the chauffeur of our rented (white) limousine asked as Lee and I piled into the mirrored interior.

"Do you think it's too much?" I asked Lee, the site's editor-in-chief (and the winner of the other long straw).

"Are you kidding? It's fucking fabulous!"

Of course, he himself was wearing eye makeup and sporting a faux-hawk. An assymetrical jacket with unfinished threads and a tear down the middle to show off his tanktop, which read "Fashion Victim," topped off his ensemble.

As we walked into the auditorium, the photographers immediately started snapping away. I was gratified by all the attention and knew I had picked my ensemble well . . . until I heard one of them hiss, sotto voce, that my outfit was "Pretentiousssssss!" All night I felt like a pompous heel in a stupid dress. Even the sight of all the free food at the after-party didn't make me feel any better. I barely touched a sushi roll. I had lost my appetite and my confidence.

But three months later, my spaceman outfit and I made our debut in *Paper* magazine's "Cultural Sushi" party page, and I was soon receiving congratulatory phone calls from as far away as the East Village.

*Pretentiousssss, my famous ass!*

## TOP IT OFF!

A friend of ours was shopping at Bergdorf Goodman. For fun, she tried on a gigantic floppy fedora that no one in their right mind would actually wear. Suddenly Steven Tyler, the lead singer of Aerosmith, came up to her and said, "That's a great hat. It looks so good on you." She bought it on the spot. She figured, if Steven Tyler gave her the thumbs-up, how could she pass on it? She walked home with her huge hatbox, all proud of herself, feeling fabulous. Then stress hit. Where on Earth would she ever wear it?

As luck had it, she was working for an event planner who was producing the MTV Music Awards after-party later that month. Our friend was granted a ticket to the soiree. It was her fedora opportunity. She couldn't wait to wear it.

But at the show, Steven Tyler went onstage wearing the same hat! And all night long our friend was known as the girl who wore the same hat as Steven Tyler . . . even though she saw it first! She was famous that night . . . but for wearing someone else's hat! Hey, whatever works.

## MAKE A STYLE STATEMENT

Establish a focused personal style that will set you apart from everyone else. Liz Hurley took off her clothes in a host of B-movies for years before she got noticed for putting on a Versace safety-pin dress for the premiere of *Four Weddings and a Funeral*, her then-boyfriend Hugh Grant's movie. She stole the spotlight that night. Everyone wanted to know who she was and what she was wearing. So whoever said you can't judge a book by its cover was sadly mistaken. In the fame game, clothes are everything. Here are some style concepts that may turn you into the next Liz Hurley:

• **Headgear.** Everyone notices people who wear hats. Newsboys, fedoras, berets, top hats, veils, cowboy hats, pillbox hats. It doesn't matter what you fancy, just get one.

• **Monochromatic dressing.** Be the person who is always in one color, head to toe (black not included, because that's too generic). All white (in the winter!) works, as do shades of red, orange, blue, yellow, turquoise, green, and pink. It might be a bit loud and obnoxious, but it will bring you some well-deserved attention.

• **Makeup for men.** That's right. MAC Cosmetics aren't just for girls, and wearing them doesn't make you a sissy (unless that's the look you're going for). It worked for Nick Rhodes, Nikki Sixx, and KISS. A much-photographed dandy in New York is constantly in the New York *Times*'s Styles page. His signature? Painted eyebrows, rouge, and a beauty mark. Very Boy George–chic. We approve wholeheartedly.

• **Hair color.** Model Linda Evangelista was just a run-of-the-mill catalog cutie until she cut off her hair and began to change her color every three months. The cover of *Vogue* followed, as well as a $10,000-a-day paycheck. Be creative and get brash with hot pink locks, flaming red streaks, a touch of blue. When people question your motives, tell them it's what all the models are doing in Paris.

• **Go ethnic.** Discover your roots with authentic saris and bhindis, obis and Chinese flip-flops (with socks for winter), or whatever signifies your heritage. If you don't have a fashion-friendly heritage, just borrow one. Every blond actress has discovered cheongsams; why don't you?

• **Consider a cane.** That's right. A cane. Paint it colorfully. No one will ever forget having a conversation with the girl with the cane. People will give up their seats for you. You'll get sympathy and fame. Nothing like killing two birds with one stone.

• **Extreme eyewear.** If you think they look too big and too bold, get them. Never take them off. Take a cue from the late famed fashion editor and Old Navy spokesmodel Carrie Donovan, who wore hers to everything—even black-tie affairs.

• **Get wacky.** Over-the-top shenanigans will get you infamous, rather than famous, but what's the difference, really? Dress as a clown for a charity benefit. Go to dinner wearing white makeup and act like you're trapped in a box, mime-style. Or make like Björk and wear a dress that resembles a swan, complete with feathered bum, beak, and a purse shaped like an egg.

## FIND A SIGNATURE SOMETHING—AND STICK TO IT!

# A COPYCAT FINDS HER STRIPES

· · · · · · · · · · *Melissa* · · · · · · · · · ·

*J* have hair lust. I can never resist copying a famous person's iconic haircut. At various points in my life, I've sported the Lady Di, the Bo Derek, the Winona Ryder, the Jennifer Aniston, and the Meg Ryan. I always believed that if a certain haircut worked for the biggest star of the moment, it would also work for me. I was usually wrong. I even dyed my hair platinum blond during a retro Marilyn Monroe phase. (And take it from me, blond locks and Asian coloring should never be attempted outside of Tokyo's Ginza district.)

But I kept hope alive. When I was sixteen, I decided I wanted to look like Siouxsie Sioux. I was going through a punk period. I craved ratted, matted, curly hair—slightly spooky and bad and brave at once. I begged my mother to give me a home perm. Three hours later, I was "Weird Al" Yankovic.

Luckily, in 1994 I had my hair cut into a choppy seventies shag, and while it has varied slightly in length, it's still the same cut I received all those years ago from the Frederic Fekkai salon (I no longer go to the salon, but the cut has been easy enough to replicate at, say, Fantastic Sam's). Like Anna Wintour (*Vogue's* editor-in-chief) and her perennial bob (a 'do she's had practically since birth), I've found a style that works for me. It's become my signature.

Even when I get it cut a little too short on the sides, otherwise known as Flirting with the Mullet, people always assure me it looks just like My Hair. Today, I look in the mirror and I don't see a famous-person wanna-be. I see myself. And I guess that's enough (at least my hairstylist says so). Although I've considered trying the Beyonce Afro! Groovy, baby!

# KARENTINIS

• • • • • • • • • • *Karen* • • • • • • • •

*I*'m a candy addict. Gummy Bears, Swedish Fish, Tootsie Rolls, anything I can get my mitts on. At a trendy bar one day, I asked for a "Yummy Gummy martini." The bartender looked at me as if I were crazy. "You want what?" he said, raising his eyebrows in horror.

"It's a martini made with Gummy Bears and a splash of cherry," I replied, as if it were the most normal request in the world. He didn't have Gummies, but luckily I did. I forked over a few red squishy bears and was sipping happily in no time. Two people next to me wanted what I was drinking and I was gracious enough to share my confectionary treats. I did the same stint for a few weeks, every time bringing my own Gummy Bears and chatting up the (very cute) bartender.

He said that other people had been requesting them since I started coming in and making such big "yum" noises as I drank up the pink chilled liquid from my cocktail glass. I brought him a few bags of bears as a gift and soon after, "Yummy Karentinis" were on the menu. I may not have been famous yet, but my drink certainly was!

## DESIGN A SIGNATURE DRINK

Anyone can have a glass of pinot grigot, but *you* . . . you can get away with saying, "I'll have the usual—sauvignon blanc with a splash of soda, a bit of cranberry juice, and two round ice cubes, please." (Send it back if the cubes are square!) A signature drink will make you unique and make you appear to have control over every aspect of your life, including your taste buds. Be consistent and never falter with the order. Who knows? You might even inspire a trend.

Some things to consider when creating a signature drink:

• Color. Are you a pink, a red, an orange, or a blue curaçao? Choose one that fits your personality and flatters your complexion.

• Ease of order. You don't want the bartender hunting down an obscure liqueur legal only in Russia. It should be quirky without being fussy.

• Taste. Try out some concoctions at home before making a commitment to this beverage, because once you do, it's yours forever. It has to be good enough that everyone will want a sip.

## WHAT'S FAME WITHOUT HUMILIATION?

# JUDGE ITO'S DOPPELGANGER

• • • • • • • • • • **Melissa** • • • • • • • • •

Like many freelance writers, I'll say yes to everything. Yes, I'll cover the transsexual protest at City Hall. Yes, I'll try to get thrown out of the nightclub to see what happens when you spill a drink on a celebrity. Yes, I'll dress as a man to crash my fiancé's bachelor party.

I always thought I would be famous one day, but I never thought it would be because I was the spitting image of Judge Ito in drag. But I'm getting ahead of myself. Mike and I were getting married. My editor at *Marie Claire* knew I was looking forward to the wedding. But other than a matching set of crystal bowls, she had something more in store for me. She asked me to crash his bachelor party disguised as a man and report back on what I saw. I was game. Mike and I both shared a goofy sense of humor, and he knew I did strange stunts for magazine work. I knew he would forgive me when he found out.

Unlike other brides who frown on the bacchanalian practice, I am nonchalant about the thought of seeing my fiancé with another woman's boobs in his face. Boys will be boys, and I'm just not the jealous type. Plus, I knew Mike would laugh the whole thing off when he found out—he's not one to take these things too seriously. At least, I hoped so. What *really* concerned me was the whole "undercover" part—the prospect of becoming a man

Mel or Ito?
You be the judge!

was terrifying to my sense of vanity. What if I made a horrifyingly ugly man? What if instead of having a fabulous Hilary Swank moment, I became dumpy "Pat" from *Saturday Night Live*? My fears were realized when I put on my costume—brown trousers, brown shirt, and brown jacket—I looked like the UPS man. But the worst was yet to come. When the makeup artist was through with me, I was the spitting image of Judge Lance "OJ" Ito.

The strip club was located in the bowels of Times Square; a neon sign in front of the club even advertised a free buffet dinner! I walked inside, feeling nervous and out of place. When Mike and his friends entered, I hid myself behind my overpriced bottle of Bud. I was amazed he did not immediately come over and say hello. I thought that for certain he would divine my presence through psychic intuition. The whole ESP between couples thing. We did have a close call, though—he walked right by me on his way to the bathroom. For the most part, I survived watching sexy women wearing almost nothing bend over and show him their backsides, but it didn't help that every five minutes or so, a stripper would ask me if I wanted a "private dance" myself. Or that when I retreated to the ladies' room, which doubles as the strippers' dressing room, two matrons with hefty ham-sized arms shooed me out. "Oh, no, you don't, mister! You don't belong here!"

"You don't understand—I'm a girl!" I pleaded.

"Well . . . what do you know?" they asked, chuckling.

"You look like Pat," one of them said. "On *Saturday Night Live?*"

A week later I broke the news to him. "You were the weird Chinese pervert with the goatee?" he asks, roaring with laughter. "Oh, my God! That's hilarious! We kept sending girls over to you to give you a lap dance! At one point we would have paid for one! That guy looked so creepy! That was you?"

I wrote the story, and it was published in May. Then the media maelstrom happened. Our phone began ringing off the hook. *Good Morning America* wanted us. "Diane loved the story," the producer cooed (as in Sawyer!). I did radio interviews for stations as far away as North Carolina. *Inside Edition* wanted to make us the "headline feature" for a story. But I was hesitant about it—wasn't that some sort of tabloid show? But this was during my two-week get-famous stint for *Marie Claire*, so I said yes to every opportunity that would lead to some kind of public display.

The television crew took over our apartment. (Neighbors asked if we were shooting a movie, or maybe an episode of *Blind Date*.) The producer of the segment advised us to say "strippers" a lot in the interview. I was apprehensive, but figured no one I knew watched *Inside Edition*. It was broadcast at twelve noon, when my friends and colleagues were at work, or at one A.M., when they were asleep.

I was so wrong.

Mike's family spotted us on TV at the hospital—they had just checked in Grandma, who had had an accident. Apparently they were all in the waiting room when *Inside Edition* blared "Bride disguised as a man crashes bachelor party!" and the zooming graphics revealed Mike and me, looking sweaty under the klieg lights. Then they ran a photo of me dressed as a man next to a photograph of Judge Ito. They were in shock and hysterics. (Luckily, no one had to pull the shock paddles out and scream, "Clear!" for Grandma.)

*Inside Edition*, we soon learned, had a huge following. Mike's boss caught it. My cousins in Los Angeles, Toronto, and Chicago saw it. So did many of my fashionista friends in New York. We couldn't live it down. I even acquired the nickname "Undercover Bachelor."

The story has even made me an international phenomenon. Weeks later, an Australian publicity agent called. The story had been published in a magazine Down Under and had caused quite a stir. Would I be interested in telling my story via satellite? Of course I said yes.

# THE SHIRT
# OFF MY BACK

### Karen

*TimeOut New York* magazine was doing their annual naked issue and they asked me to roam the streets topless for a day—just to see what would happen. Going topless, which is defined by New York City law as baring the breast from the areola down, is technically illegal in New York. There are, however, some loopholes around the rule—when it's for entertainment purposes or a part of a protest.

The assignment could have landed me in jail. Most of my friends told me not to do it.

But I'm not one to back down from a challenge. I have to admit, a part of me liked the fact that the editor called me because she thought I was just outrageous and daring enough to do it. I thought the mission, while embarrassing and risqué, would be a hoot, a practical joke. No one would take it seriously, I rationalized when I agreed to write the piece. Furthermore, breasts are nothing more than skin. How scandalous and horrible could being topless on Eighth Avenue be?

On D-day (or B-day, I should say), I began on Central Park's grass beach, sunbathing without my shirt. Two other women were doing the same, and no one batted an eye. Feeling disappointed, I actually stood up to toss a Frisbee with a friend. This garnered massive attention. Before I had a chance to return to my horizontal position, I received a round of applause from a group of frat-boy types. One of them came over and asked me if I wanted to hang out with him and his buds. At that point, I slipped my tube top up my torso and packed up my stuff to go.

"Suddenly shy?" he asked.

"Only with you," I replied.

I felt like such a piece of meat. (I know, I know—I was half-naked, but still . . . ) Next, I made my way downtown to the Christopher Street pier, an area usually rich with drag queens. A well-built transsexual told me I had cute little "teats." A butchy lesbian asked me if I was making a political stand for equal rights (men can go shirtless but women can't?). And I spotted a young mother shielding her toddler's eyes from my appearance, as if there were something horribly awry with my body ("I am not an animal," I wanted to say, but I refrained). I was making a scene. And I felt proud . . . until a grandmother waved her finger at me and told me my display was disgusting. I apologized and covered up immediately.

The article, accompanied by a photo of me holding a magazine over my chest area, ran the following week. And was I wrong, thinking that no one would see it! My phone rang off the hook. My friends cracked up. "Only you!" they laughed lovingly. My friends' parents even called me.

Days—even weeks—later, the comments didn't stop. (My dry cleaner even mentioned it!) But instead of people saying, "You're so funny," they started scolding, "I can't believe you did that," or "Not the smartest move." I took a step back to think about things. Here I was, a journalist, trying to build a solid reputation for good work. . . . Who would take me seriously after reading a story about my parading around town, exposing myself, doing something illegal?

The negative comments didn't go away. In fact, they got worse. A month after the incident, they kept on coming. I started to regret having done the story. Especially when a high-powered colleague called me and told me that everyone in her office saw it and decided my image was too wild and that they didn't want to work with me—for at least a little while.

I couldn't believe it. They didn't want to work with me! Me? Wild? I didn't even drink, I told her. I may have the guts to be naked in public, but I'm wholesome at heart! But the truth didn't matter. What did was the fact that I was suddenly infamous. I was devastated. I cried my eyes out for hours. When I was first approached with the story, I got so excited to do something crazy, something that would get me recognized, that I totally lost sight of myself and my real goals. My harmless hoax backfired.

It's like eating a piece (or ten pieces!) of cake when you're on a diet. You go for that second of pleasure, and afterward you're left with a few extra pounds on your body that take weeks—even months—to work off. As awful as the backlash of my breast exposure was, my posthumiliation circumstances were actually blessings in disguise. I was forced to decide how I wanted to be known—as the crazy exhibitionist (and damn proud of it) or as a serious writer (who's not as much fun). I am going for option B . . . but not until I write about my experiences at a tantra workshop!

# NOTORIOUS!

One of the fastest ways to fame is infamy and making a spectacle of yourself. Being an outrageous person often leads to instant celebrity status. Be warned: A little infamy is dangerous. People won't likely forget the stunts you pulled anytime soon. If that doesn't bother you, here are some things to try:

- Stand on street corners singing and dancing, wearing nothing but underwear, cowboy boots, and a cowboy hat. A guy known as the Naked Cowboy does this near Times Square in New York, and he landed a movie deal.

- Publicly picket random, inconsequential things you don't agree with. Do this at coffee shops, parks, and while you're doing errands. After a while, people will get so used to your shenanigans that they may even go as you for Halloween. Come on. You're not really famous until you're a Halloween costume, after all.

- Consistently go out dressed to the hilt, with toilet paper hanging out of your pants. It will get you loads of looks and attention. Just act surprised when people tell you about the faux pas, remove the TP, and put it back when you round the corner.

- Don't be afraid to indulge in a little insider trading. You might wind up in jail, but you'll get your heyday in the papers before they cart you off.

## BUSY, BUSY BEES

## "NOW I KNOW WHY
## BENJAMIN DUMPED JULIA."

• • • • • • • • • • *Karen* • • • • • • • •

*D*uring my two-week fame fling for *Marie Claire*, everything about my beloved homebody ways had to change. To be famous, you have to go out around the clock. It's important to be seen. It makes you come off as popular if everyone invites you everywhere. As a journalist, I get invited to tons of parties. Publicists and event planners want writers at their galas in order to try to get press in magazines. But I typically don't RSVP to many things. Mostly because I like to hit the sack by ten-thirty P.M. (I'm no good on less than eight hours of sleep.)

All of that had to be different if I was to successfully elevate my profile. I booked—and double-booked—my calendar solid and forced myself to navigate the nightlife with Clint Eastwoodian skill. My first night, I went to a much-publicized dinner at the Hudson Hotel, a chic midtown hotel owned by Ian Schrager, the guy who brought us Studio 54. I finagled my way onto the guest list through a friend, who was working the door. I didn't know a soul in the room—except for an emerging R&B singer named Kelis, whom I had interviewed the previous year for British *In Style* magazine. Although she was engaged in what appeared to be a serious conversation with supermodel Heidi Klum, I had to approach her and say hello. It was either that or continue fidgeting by the bar, which would bring me no fame to speak of. Both women were as friendly as can be, and they informed me of a party for some film premiere. I found out where it was and made a beeline for the bash.

I figured, if I arrived early, I'd have no problem getting in. When I showed up at the club, the doorperson didn't seem anxious to grant me an entrance. I kept telling her I was on the list. I dropped whatever name I could think of. "Just get Katy. She'll tell you." And just as I was about to leave in defeat, a random guy with a British accent and a shaggy 'do came to my rescue. "You can let her in. She's with me," he said, flashing a gleaming invitation. Apparently he saw me chatting with Kelis and Heidi and assumed I was "one of them." I walked across the room diagonally, a tip I once heard Donald Trump mention in an interview, and said hello to anyone I made eye contact with. By my third catwalk, the Brit asked me to go with him to a birthday party for some major film producer at Lot 61, a groovy club nearby.

*Film producer!* I thought. This was my chance to get discovered. I went to the party with him and held my own at a table of agents and managers. It all seemed so fabulous. And while no one offered me a movie deal, I was dragged to an after-hours event at an underground club where I had to ask for the rabbi to get in. It was wild—dancing on tables, live music, and a room in the back where people were being very badly behaved.

My whole week was like that. I hit a Burberry party to launch the baby beauty product line, two restaurant openings, the film premiere for the new Stephen Dorff film, dozens of things for the Tribeca Film Festival, a store opening for Ferragamo, some kind of charity event for Robert Kennedy, Jr., a cocktail party at Bendel's to launch a clothing line, and a birthday affair for an upcoming hotelier in Las Vegas (that lasted twenty-four hours!). I used my press credentials to guide me as I jockeyed two to three parties a night.

During the day, life was no calmer. I fielded calls from publicists and event planners, all of whom wanted me to show up to their parties. I scheduled two or three lunch meetings a day with clothing designers, store owners, restaurateurs—all of whom had heard of me through friends of friends or industry people who had heard about the fame game. I didn't have to worry about gaining weight, as I didn't really eat, even though I really wanted to. Instead I just pushed the food around my plate, the way most waifish stars do.

It was mayhem. I was losing my mind (and killing my feet). I hadn't talked to my two best friends in days. My parents were wondering if I was dead or alive (I didn't have a second to return their calls). And I had bags under my eyes the size of Samsonites. But I was excited, too. I felt wanted, needed, desired, and famous! Until my (then) boyfriend bitched, "You know how celebrities are so caught up in themselves? Well, that is what's happening to you. Now I know why Benjamin (Bratt) dumped Julia (Roberts)." Ouch. Had I let things go to my head? I wasn't sure, but it was nine P.M. and I was late to the dinner party that I was hosting! I had no time to discuss!

# IT'S MY PARTY?

*Melissa*

$O$nce we inked our book deal (this one), Karen and I thought it would be a great idea to throw ourselves a smashing event to celebrate the occasion. We decided to work with Full Picture PR, the event-planning firm that specialized in outrageous, over-the-top extravaganzas, like the *Victoria's Secret* runway show. They helped us make one of the most important decisions—the date when the party was to be held. November 25.

"Does that work for you?" they asked. Karen and I nodded. It was late September, and November 25 would give us enough time to secure space, sponsors, and a press plan for promoting our party.

I was so excited about the party—and all the attendant details—I rushed home and spilled the news to my husband. "And we're inviting a thousand people . . . and *tons* of models . . . and *all* these places want us to have it there . . . and everything's for free! And there'll be buckets of champagne . . . and Karen and I will get couture gowns to wear . . . and—"

"When is it?" Mike asked.

"November twenty-fifth."

"November twenty-fifth?" he asked incredulously.

"Uh-huh."

"That's my birthday!"

Oh, no. In all my excitement, I had completely forgotten the importance of that date. My husband's birthday. And it was too

# PADDING YOUR SOCIAL CALENDAR

A vital aspect of your new image is that you're busy. Very, very busy. Your social calendar must be packed at all times. It doesn't matter if "I'm booked" means a night of Must-see TV and take-out Chinese with your cat. The busier you *seem*, the busier you will become. Here's how to pull off the busy routine:

- Book your schedule a week to three weeks in advance.

- When people ask to make plans, never commit, and put them off for at least a week. People want what they can't have, and if you're busy, people will make time for you.

- Attend every event you've been invited to when you're new to the scene. However, once you make a name for yourself and become recognizable—pick and choose your events carefully. You don't want to develop a reputation as a social slut, one of those party perennials who'll attend the opening of an envelope.

- It's all about spin—if you're going to the movies, say you're attending a screening; if someone asks you to bring music to a party, say you're the DJ; and if you're throwing a party for an artistic-minded friend, say you're hosting a benefit as a patron of the arts.

late to change because it was the only date in November that worked for everybody, since the month of October was out of the question (early October was too soon, and late October meant we'd be competing with all the Halloween parties), and Full Picture was planning the Victoria's Secret show on November 14 (and they wanted at least a week between that and our event), and we couldn't move it to November 26 because Karen was leaving for Florida for Thanksgiving that day. And we couldn't have it in December because, well, we were planning to write about it in our book and our manuscript was due December 1.

"I can't believe you're going to have your book party . . . *on my birthday*," he said to me in disgust.

One day, I know he'll forgive me. I hope.

## DEMAND, DEMAND, DEMAND!

# TAXI!

· · · · · *Karen* and *Melissa* · · · · ·

When we started our famous assignment for *Marie Claire*, our editors gave us an expense account of $300. On the first day we blew the entire budget—on taxicabs! Celebrities do *not* take the subway, we cried, begging our editors for more cash. How were we to convince the world of our fame if we were forced to travel with the masses, underground, on—gasp!—public transportation? Subways are not conducive to high heels, we argued. And what about the germs? No, we were not getting on the 6 line! It would tarnish our budding images. It was bad enough that we couldn't afford a limousine or at least a car service, but not taking a taxi was out of the question, we said, reading them the diva act. We were a little afraid to be so high-maintenance— scared that if we were too self-important, they'd threaten, "You'll never work in this town again!" But our demands got us exactly what we wanted—more green for taxicabs! As God is our witness, we'll never ride the subway again.

## BALANCING THE HIGH-MAINTENANCE ACT

Don't worry about coming across as high-maintenance, because famous people are, in fact, high-maintenance. It demonstrates that you know what you want and how to ask for it without apologies. Being a little annoying—or even rude—goes a long way:

• Request the newest car (in black with tinted windows) in the fleet when using a car service. You will not dare sit your precious bum down in a ratty old Lincoln "Townhouse." Besides, the new cars are the same price—or $5 more.

• Demand the best table. If no available tables will do, tip the guy at the club or restaurant to bring a table from the back to place in the center of the room. It works for Graydon Carter, editor-in-chief of *Vanity Fair*.

• Never walk into a full elevator. You like your personal space. A notorious actress once demanded this. Keep in mind that if you choose to do this, you might be waiting in the lobby for a long, long time.

- When shopping, ask for the biggest, most private dressing room. Maybe they'll even close the store for your spree. They did for Imelda Marcos. You might just incite a populace to revolution, though.

- Choose an M&M color to hate. Stick to it. Van Halen didn't become Van Halen until they had flunkies weeding out the brown M&Ms from their dressing rooms.

- Is there a perfume that you want? Request to have it spritzed in your quarters. J.Lo can't travel without smelling Barney's Route du Thé anywhere.

- The toilet. Bathed in flowers? Lit by candles? Take a cue from Barbra Streisand. Wherever you park your posterior, make sure it lives up to your standards.

*Days 2–5:*

# THERE'S NO SUCH THING AS BAD PUBLICITY, DARLING

*I*f you want to be famous, you're not allowed to hide your light under a bushel. Blow your own horn, people. And blow it loud! You have to be heard to be seen. But the real trick to bold-face status is to find someone whose voice is a bit louder than yours—and have that person become your mouthpiece.

The secret to stardom lies in the hands of a chatty publicist, a person whose sole purpose is to make something or someone famous, to talk them up to the behind-the-scenes media powers-that-be, as well as noteworthy imagemakers, trendsetters, and tastemakers. A publicist is one who's paid to make you look good, to make sure you know what to say when people ask for your opinion, to make sure people ask for your opinion, and to secure you the right placement in photos, magazines, television, and newspapers.

A publicist will throw you parties and get you into all the right events. And the best part of what a savvy publicist does is simple: he or she will make your name a household one and turn your brand into an enterprise. A publicist. Never leave home without one! How do you think Jennifer Lopez became J.Lo?

These days, everyone has a flack. Dentists, bikini waxers, dermatologists, SAT tutors, even publicists have their own publicists. A good PR person doesn't have to be an NYC–power girl who charges $10,000 per month, but anyone with a natural knack for marketing, persuasion, and making people listen. A good publicist can be anyone who knows a lot of people in some of the right places.

So you can see why it's a vital part of the fame game. Hire a PR guru immediately. And if you don't—or can't afford one— you must learn to become your own. It's called acting, which shouldn't be such a problem, considering that fame is nothing without it. This chapter gives you the inside scoop on the PR world: how to find a publicist and negotiate fees, what to ask for and what to expect in return, the importance of the PR-driven party, and time-honored secrets of how to be your own publicist.

# CALLING ALL FAVORS!

## IT'S WHO YOU KNOW
## THAT COUNTS

### *Melissa*

*I* didn't think I needed a publicist. I felt confident I would be able to attract enough "heat" on my own in order for my visage to be plastered all over town. I was a published author, after all! Didn't that count for something? But being a published author in a town where teenage heiresses wear dresses made of Saran Wrap is like being a nun at an orgy. Nobody pays attention. My strategy got me absolutely nowhere. Oh, I was able to wrangle some party invitations on my own, but after three days of storming the most exclusive events in town, my press clippings–meter stood frozen at zero.

Feeling slightly more desperate as the days went by, my anonymity loomed like a lead balloon over the whole giddy enterprise. I was especially piqued when I received Karen's invitation for her thirtieth birthday party with an RSVP line to PR powerhouse Harrison & Shriftman. Eeek! It was time to call in the professionals!

I decided to contact my friend Norah Lawlor, the head of Lawlor Media Group, a publicity firm that represents luxury-lifestyle accounts. Norah, a six-foot dynamo with a rash of untidy, rocker-chick hair, had a throaty laugh and a no-nonsense approach to the bang-up, slash-and-burn, take-no-prisoners world of New York glitterati nightlife. At twenty-two, as the publicity agent for Stringfellows ("When it was still a nightclub for rock stars instead of a strip club for yuppies") she had jetted to Malcom Forbes's legendary party in the Caribbean, and was the woman behind the prized guest lists at the most elite clubs in the city—including Eugene, where P. Diddy liked to hold court in the VIP room.

Norah had been nice enough to throw me my book party the year before. I had mentioned during one of her intimate dinner parties at a new restaurant she was repping that my first novel was coming out, and on the spot, she offered her services. My publisher had already advised me that their book-party budget was nonexistent, so I was thrilled. Norah arranged for my party to be held at Eugene's front room, a vast expanse of white columns and airy ceilings. She brought in Moët & Chandon to donate splits of champagne (the fashionista drink of choice) and invited three hundred of the city's indomitable party faithful to fete me and my novel. I knew I had "made" it when I spotted New York's most enterprising gate-crasher, nicknamed "Shaggy" by none other than Page Six, hogging hors d'oeuvres and clutching a copy of my book to his chest.

Unfortunately, Norah wasn't returning my calls. A week after the fame game had begun, I finally received a breathless message: "Melissa, I'm back in town; I'm so sorry I couldn't get in touch with you earlier—I was away in LA for the Oscars . . . but let me put something together for you now." Norah chided my earlier efforts, and told me that just being *seen* at high-profile events isn't enough; what I needed to do was *create* one. She decided to go straight to the source—the journalists who decided who was in or out in New York—and to entertain them at a private "media dinner," where they could meet me in person.

In rapid succession, Norah had recruited Jared Paul Stern of Page Six to host my party, and personally invited a dozen powerful journalists from *New York* magazine, the *New York Observer*, the *New York Post*, the *New York Daily News*, *Gotham*, Fox News, *Vanity Fair*, and *Allure* to attend an intimate dinner for me at Orsay, the swanky Upper East Side restaurant favored by socialites like Pat Buckley and Nan Kempner.

Norah also put together a phenomenal goody bag of Oscar-worthy caliber: haircuts and hair products from the fashionable Prive salon at the Soho Grand Hotel, dinners for two at Chango, facials at Warren-Tricomi, a full bottle of Bacardi rum (not just the little airline-sized ones that are par for the course in most goody bag loot), and the pièce de résistance, free airline tickets on Jet Blue to fly *everyone* to stay at the Mercury Resort, a five-star hotel in Miami favored by the likes of Will Smith.

"Pretty hot, no?" she asked, leaning back in satisfaction as we reviewed the guest list. "You're going to be big!" She grinned.

Thanks to Norah's help, my dinner party generated scads of press hits. It was written up everywhere from Page Six to Chic Happens to Fox411.com. My picture ran in *New York* magazine, *Gotham*, the *New York Post*'s party column, and *Ocean Drive*. I was amazed. It took only one phone call to a publicist, and I was already on my way to becoming Somebody.

# PLEADING FOR PR

· · · · · · · · · · *Karen* · · · · · · · ·

*I* barrel into Harrison & Shriftman, a top publicity, special
events, and marketing firm. They are famous in New York, Miami, and Los Angeles for doing the most exclusive parties—
runway shows for Oscar de la Renta, major film premieres
(*Charlie's Angels* and *Bridget Jones's Diary*), store openings for
Jimmy Choo, huge bashes for Mercedes-Benz, and the kind of
galas that Courtney Love and Leo DiCaprio attend. As a journalist, I have covered Harrison & Shriftman events ever since I
began my career. I know the impact of their fab invitations
firsthand. The second anyone receives one, they automatically
RSVP. My goal? To convince them to produce my thirtieth-
birthday bash (and get it press)—for free! The challenge? They
never do personal parties, unless you're, say, Matt Damon (they
did *his* thirtieth birthday party). My plan of attack? Work my
charm and—okay—beg.

After I pleaded my case in their gleaming, sun-drenched
white-and-chocolate-brown offices on a Monday afternoon, they
miraculously agreed. It probably didn't hurt that I've been
friends with Lara Shriftman, one of the company's principals,
for six years! Lara, known as a master planner, called her event
production team into the conference room to begin. I watched in
amazement as she delegated. "You, find a space. You, secure the
liquor sponsors. You, get a DJ. You, get food donated. You, design invitations. You, work on press." Minutes later, a tri-

umphant employee hooked me up with the hottest spot in town, Bungalow 8, which is a very chic nightclub where you need a private key to enter (Carrie Bradshaw even had trouble getting behind the velvet ropes of this place on an episode of *Sex and the City*) and Kevin Spacey is often seen.

They persuaded the owner, an often-photographed It girl called Amy Sacco, to lend me the use of her space gratis. (I had been to her club, but didn't own a key . . . yet!) Faxes and e-mails went out at light-speed, and within a half hour, everything was sealed—a Krispy Kreme doughnut cake, M&Ms special-ordered in pink (to match my dress), a DJ who specialized in disco (my favorite), over fifty pounds of candy from Economy Candy, an old-school candy store on the Lower East Side of Manhattan, and loads of alcohol from Christiana vodka, Piper-Heidsieck, and Guinness. All donated because my party was pitched as a high-profile, A-list event with a guest list of "imagemakers and tastemakers." The reason everyone gave so generously? When a good publicist throws a party, people write about it. And when people write about, it generates press for everyone who donated their bounty. And for me, it would lead to fun, fun, and even more fun.

This was huge! I was told I could invite two hundred of my closest friends. (I didn't even have two hundred close friends.) Before I knew it, word spread about my party. People I hardly knew started calling me to ask if they'd be invited. Hours after I left the H&S headquarters, I bumped into a friend, who said, "I heard about your party! Congratulations," planting a hug on me. She was so excited, you'd think I'd won an Oscar! I was contacted by PR people who represent hairstylists from Warren-

Tricomi, a posh salon always mentioned in *Vogue*, and makeup artists from *the* Bobbi Brown. They wanted their peeps to doll me up for my debut.

Amy Sacco offered me her VIP bathroom suite to get dressed before the big night. My parents decided to fly to New York from Florida for the affair. And the next day, when I was fabric shopping with Elisa Jimenez, we bumped into Sasha Lazard, a superhot girl-about-town who had just released a new techno-opera album. I told her about the party and before I knew it, she agreed to perform! A free, private concert for my three-oh! Life was getting better by the second.

I even heard that Betsey Johnson's flack called to see if the designer herself could come to the bash. And the night of the party? Well, Calvin Klein was there, along with Tara Reid, Estella Warren, model Devon Aoki, and music mogul Damon Dash. It was jammed! But sadly, a dozen of my closest friends were turned away at the door! (I didn't find this out until I got home and listened to my answering machine.) It was then that I realized—I've come a long way since my bowling party last year!

# HIRING A PUBLICIST

- Do your research to find a publicist who's right for you. Befriend the yellow pages, your Better Business Bureau, and scan all of the magazines for a person, place, or thing that is written about everywhere. Then call that company or person's corporate office to find out who does their PR. Hire that person immediately.

- There are many types of PR agencies, including those that handle only corporate accounts, fashion clients, beauty products, special events, and personalities. Ideally, you want to work with someone who handles luxury-lifestyle clients.

- Ask around. Did a friend have a launch party for something? If so, did she hire a publicist? Personal references are key.

- Get the publicist's references and previous press clippings (bounties of his or her work) to prove that they can make some magic happen.

- Find out which "power people" your publicist has relationships with and how they will benefit you.

- Negotiate fees. Most publicists charge a monthly retainer fee, during which time they will do everything they can to promote you and your brand. See if you can do a three-month trial, or try to get away with paying for PR upon delivery (i.e., a certain amount of money for press coverage upon publishing).

- Barter. Some PR agents will trade services with you. Say you have something worthy to give, like clothing you design or photographs you've taken; find out if they'll exchange your hard work for theirs.

# STOP THE PRESS!

## REALITY BITES!
## I'M NOT GOOD ENOUGH
## FOR PAGE SIX!

*Karen*

*I*n New York society, there is one barometer of fame, and it's called Page Six. Page Six is the gossip column of the *New York Post*, a newspaper I happen to write lifestyle and fashion features for regularly. Page Six provides the grittiest, dirtiest, most scintillating dirt in town. Their reporters take no prisoners. They, after all, were responsible for Monica Lewinsky's unfortunate nickname, "Portly Pepperpot." Some of their tidbits have even gotten people suspended without pay—or even fired—from their jobs (the one about the well-known seemingly conservative news reporter who posted a television personal advertising his bondage fetish and homemade "tickle toys," along with his "pleasure-seeking" lifestyle, comes to mind)! Page Six can be your biggest nightmare when you're sleeping with someone's husband, entangled in a high-profile custody battle, or the center of any kind of scandal (no matter how big or small), but it can also be your best friend. Especially if you have a movie, book deal, or new job to plug. Why? Because everyone from film moguls and models to political heads and publishing execs read it.

Page Six is the second home for the likes of Gwynnie, Bill Clinton, and pretty young society things who wear pretty short skirts. Whether or not you want Page Six status, being a Page Sixer, as regulars are often called, is a symbol that you have arrived. Call it a debutante ball of sorts. Of course, I wanted in— sans scandal and humiliating moniker. I hoped that the news of my birthday party would grant me an entrance. So I called one of the Page Six reporters with whom I was friendly. I figured it would be a no-brainer. She was invited to the event, and witness to guests such as Calvin Klein, Tara Reid, Estella Warren, and music mogul Damon Dash. How could she not give me a little love? I thought. I called her confidently to ask for a favor. Before I could even finish my sentence, I got rejected. Brutally.

I was informed that I was not at Page Six level. Not at Page Six level! Why wasn't I good enough? I was an accomplished writer! I had a book deal! And I was one of the *Post*'s own, for God's sake! What would I have to do, I wondered—break up a happy, high-profile marriage, throw a tofu pie at a celebrity wearing fur, rob Saks Fifth Avenue, date Ben Affleck? When I told a PR friend my plight, she shook her head and scolded, "You have to have a publicist make that call, not you!" I looked in the mirror in disgust. I had become the very thing I have always despised: a press whore! I wanted it so badly that I personally called the gossip column and asked them to gossip about me. That might just be the lowest depth of misery. The cardinal rule of celebrity is that the famous ones never call to get their own press.

Although my birthday party pictures and story ran in a different section of the paper, I still felt like such a fool, especially the morning after my party, when I spotted *Melissa's* name in Page Six in **boldface**.

GOTHAM

THE LIFE AND
DEATH
OF FIN...
TED AM...

SEX, SKIN...
AND
SW...

SUNDAY
NEW YORK POST
LATE CITY FINAL
50¢
www.nypost.com 50¢

— Mostly sunny, 47-52 — Weather: Page 62 ★ ★

Buddy pictures (clockwise from above): Chris Meloni of "Oz" and Chris Rock buddied up in a banquette at the Supper Club after viewing "Topdog/Underdog"; writers Michael Musto and Melissa de la Cruz nuzzled platonically at Orsay; and Katrina Boorman and Nell Campbell both found mad hats to wear at the City Opera Thrift Shop gala.

Pans and pics (from left): Jon Favre..., budding Orson Welles, debuted "Dinner for Five," an Independent Film Channel series, at the Cutting Room; Ja Rule, generally a gent, faked some attitude for our lensman at Flow; and the Post's own Karen Robinovitz, in a made-to-measure frock for her birthday bash, mugged with editor Jason Nixon (Hamptons, Gotham and L.A. Confidential) at Bungalow 8.

For the latest photos of your favorite stars: Check www.pagesix.com

*Mel made the "Scene" in New York magazine.*

**WOLFF: THE CITY'S NEW NEWSPAPER WAR**

cue

*New YORK*

*Queer As Folk's*

## Scene

**GAY LIFE NOW**

# Welcome to the Fame Gam

Melissa de la Cruz and Jared Paul Stern at Orsay for a party in De la Cruz's honor.

t his issue takes on... permutations: F... ty of Hilary Sw... takes aim at the... Speaking of fame, in mo... *Marie Claire* magazine had com... York City journalist as the... guests. The mission: to... One participant, Karen Robinovitz, has written for this maga... larly to the *New York Times* and *Marie Claire*. The other, Melissa ... *Cat's Meow*, a send-up of a fashionista's life in New ... m. The PR-savvy duo, teeth bared, set out ... s, and photo-ops as they possi-

experime... Chelsea. thing in l... **Arthur Fl...** being ho... as he squ... **Schneide...** snag som... maybe te... to time."... was worr...

## EYE SCOOP

**ROMAN CANDLES: Sid and Mercedes Bass** will be

Academy in Rome's annual benefit on Monday night at Cipriani. The honorees include: **Hon. Corinne Boggs, J. Carter Brown** and **Lord Jacob Rothschild**, who will be receiving the Academy's Centennial Medal. Rothschild also will be in town to publicize his book, "Waddesdon Manor," about his art- and antiques-filled English estate in Buckinghamshire. The baron has been doing the p.r. rounds lately — he even spent a morning signing copies at Hatchard's in London's Piccadilly.

**JUST CALL HER K.RO:** If you haven't heard the name **Karen Robinovitz**, don't worry, you will — at least if Marie Claire has anything to say about it. Robinovitz, a freelance writer, kicked off her "How to Become a Celebrity in Two Weeks"

...room floo... *tre*, I cringed. Wound... the paper smiling away, chain... A few nights later, I was invited to par... Melissa de la Cruz at Orsay, and I figured that I fl... play the fame game for both. Melissa, it turned out, is an absolute delight and the evening's guests—including Michael Musto, Jared Paul Stern, the *Daily News*'s Colleen Curtis, and the *Observer*'s George Gurley, among others—were fascinating dinner companions. Besides the blinding, constant flashes from the numerous photographers in attendance, the evening was a smash. I'm only hoping that one of those images doesn't make it into the papers.

The nerd within is chuckling away.—J. OLIVER NIXON

P.S. Speaking of fame: Don't forget that May celebrates someone who should *really, really* be famous, dear old Mom. Happy Mother's Day!

d somehow I, these women's ge. k-off party at the a birthday up the pped uptown for a hat Karen knew such asked me to pose with d certainly be cuttin the evening's *raison d'e* ay morning there I was in

With *Marie Claire* contestant #1, Karen Robinovitz, and Amy Sacco at Bungalow 8 (ABOVE LEFT), and (BELOW) with *MC* contestant #2, Melissa de la Cruz, at Orsay.

*I'm in WWD!*

*GOTHAM MAGAZINE*

# CHIC HITS THE FAN

* * * * * * * * * * *Melissa* * * * * * * * * *

$\mathcal{T}$wo of my oldest friends are Ben Widdicombe and Horacio Silva, the brains behind the notoriously bitchy "Chic Happens" on-line gossip column. "Chic Happens," as most in the fashion world know, is the most-read scandal sheet in the trade—the kind of gossip column that asks, "Which executive producer of a fashion show asks her minions to calm her down by making dolphin noises?" "Chic Happens" also broke the hilarious news about the existence of avant-garde photos of supermodel sphincters that included a portrait of Kate Moss's "chocolate starfish." I called Ben and briefed him on my assignment—to garner as many press hits as possible in two weeks—and beseeched him to make me a Chicster. "Sure thing, doll," he promised. The next day, I read, with pleasure, my first entree in "Chic Happens":

> It seems *Cat's Meow* writer Melissa de la Cruz couldn't be getting more fashion attention lately if she turned up to a bar mitzvah in a bacon bikini. She chewed up the *It girls* bash in a slinky Alvin Valley outfit, and was noted in the *New York Post*'s Page Six as giving style tips to Mark McGrath and Suzanne Vega at the Volvo party the night before. God knows they need it.

I called Ben immediately. "I love it!" I gushed. By "Chic Happens" standards, it was a total wet kiss. I felt duly honored. The next week, however, the worm had turned. I clicked on the latest installment of "Chic Happens" to find with satisfaction that my dinner party at Orsay had merited the lead. I was on a roll! Scrolling down, however, I began to feel impending doom and dread. Instead of being another PR coup, the column mocked my inability to stay inside my low-cut designer blouse, and worse, loudly trumpeted an embarrassing scandal from my past!

CRUZ CONTROL

Novelist and fashion writer Melissa de la Cruz was having trouble with her double-sided breast tape this week at a dinner at upper-crust uptown restaurant Orsay, hosted by *New York Post* columnist Jared Paul Stern. But it wasn't just cleavage that was revealed over steak frites and chardonnay. De la Cruz is writing an article in *Marie Claire* magazine about how to become famous in two weeks. However, it's not the first time the Filipina import has made a grab for the limelight. De la Cruz has previously passed herself off in New York as the niece of former Philippines first lady Imelda Marcos—a claim that holds about as much water as a porcupine's condom. The Six Degrees of Separation scam caught up with her at a table that included writers and editors for the *New York Observer*, *Daily News*, as well as *New York* and *Hamptons* magazines. No word on whether she really is Halle Berry's twin sister.

When I first moved to New York, as a gawky eighteen-year-old from South San Francisco (which was famous for its Hollywood-like sign on its tallest hill: *South San Francisco: The Industrial City*), I was immediately intimidated by my sophisticated and cosmopolitan peers at Columbia University. It seemed everyone I met had gone to prep school with a Kennedy, was Audrey Hepburn's goddaughter, had an uncle who executive-produced *The Godfather* or a mom who had hung out with Jack Kerouac. It was my first brush with the East Coast establishment. Next to these well-connected sophisticates, I felt like a geek all over again. And this was college, the great equalizer, or so I was told.

I desperately wanted to appear as soigné as everyone else. But I had no clue as to how. It happened on a whim—someone was telling a story that mentioned Imelda Marcos, and I suddenly blurted out that I was her niece. That captured their attention. Everyone wanted to know inside details on the coup, the palace, whether "we" still had our millions. I was able to spin a clever tale from remembered news reports and my own imagination. The story grew to campus-wide proportions, especially after I accepted a call from my "aunt" during my crowded birthday party in my dormitory suite. I was suddenly as popular as the girl in our class who had starred in *Uncle Buck* with John Candy.

Years later, I was still dining out on the story that I was indeed, related to the world's most famous shoe shopper. During my dinner party at Orsay, I had laughingly confessed to Ben the truth as we lingered over drinks at the end of the evening. I never dreamed he would tell the world! And now it was staring me in the face. I was outed as a faux Marcos! A crass, social-climbing liar! No better than Andrew Cunanan, Versace's killer, who used to tell people he was related to Corazon Aquino!

I called Ben in desperation. "You've got to take it down!" I begged.

"Mel," he barked, "it's 'Chic Happens'; if you're going to be in the column, we've got to go a little rough on you. It's not personal! I think it's hilarious!"

All week long I fielded amazed calls and e-mails from friends who were still under the impression I was Filipino royalty, asking if the item was true. If only I had a publicist who could have smoothed over the whole thing—a bulldog who could call a press conference and deny, deny, deny! I badly needed a spinmeister who could lump me into the category of "good liars" such as David Geffen, who famously faked a UCLA diploma to get a job at William Morris, instead of being seen as a "bad liar"—on par with David "Rockefeller," the French swindler who passed himself off as a great-grandson of J. D.

But all I had was time, which was luckily on my side. By the next week, the flame-out of my faux pas faded into history as "Chic Happens" gleefully reported that Naomi Campbell was back in rehab.

## THE PUBLICIST'S JOB REQUIREMENTS

• Deliver press hits. They should splatter your name and face all over magazines, newspapers, respected Web sites, and television screens. If they're savvy, they'll be on top of who's editing or producing which segment or section, and be familar with every major writer and their territory to know exactly how to successfully "pitch" you—and your brand—to the media network.

• They'll keep embarrassing details of your life out of the gossip columns, like the amount of money you're getting in a divorce settlement, scandalous affairs, and drunken incidents you'd rather not discuss. If it's impossible for them to completely cover up your flubs, at the very least publicists should be able to "spin" your ordeals in a positive manner. (Perfect examples: "She's not going to jail. She's taking time off to give back to society," and "He's not in rehab. He's resting.")

• Publicists are good fibbers, exaggerators, manipulators, and protectors. They can make you seem more important—and desirable—than you really are. Once you reach the limelight and suddenly can't even go out to dinner with your brother without people talking about the new guy you're sleeping with, publicists will manage damage control (i.e., they'll get you secret entrances to public venues, shoo away the paparazzi, and make journalists print retractions to the news, especially when it leaks that you were once involved in the "adult film industry").

## TABLE MANNERS

# WHO'S THAT GIRL AND WHY IS SHE AT OUR TABLE?

### Karen

*I* didn't want to go to Vegas. No way. No how. I had just returned from a weeklong fast at We Care, a colonic farm and holistic detox spa in Desert Hot Springs, California, and in my newly Zen state of body and mind, the last place I wanted to be was a smoke-filled environment where addictions and silicone were considered assets. But there was a Bruce Springsteen concert and a weekend of celebrity events, sponsored by the Hard Rock Hotel & Casino. I knew that if I went, I'd leave with tons of stories to write about. But I didn't want all the hard work I had just done, cleansing my body, mind, and soul—the wonders of a week's worth of colonics and consuming only juices—to go to pot. I'd surely succumb to French fries at four A.M., donate the little extra cash I had to blackjack dealers, and suffer through sleepless nights.

I kept saying no, but the publicist who was producing the parties pressured me . . . so much so that she bought me a ticket! "Now you have no choice," she sniffed, tucking her cell phone into her Louis Vuitton bag. "Besides, you just had a high-profile birthday party. You need to be seen at these type of events."

The night of the concert, there was a posh dinner party at Nobu, the Japanese restaurant owned by Robert De Niro. A dozen television crews waited to pounce on the celebs—Mark Wahlberg, Leonardo DiCaprio, Cindy Crawford, Lara Flynn Boyle—who showed up for the pre-Bruce bash. I got to dinner early in order to secure a good seat. When I walked in, however, the tables were empty . . . except for one. Christina Applegate, her gorgeous husband Johnathon Schaech, and Robert Downey Jr., whom I've had a crush on since I was fourteen, were schmoozing over edamame beans. I had two choices: sit with them or set up shop at an empty table, like the loser in sixth grade who has no one to eat with at the cafeteria.

I took a deep breath, prepping myself to approach and take a seat. "Do you mind if I sit here?" I asked sheepishly as I

pointed to a chair. Robert extended his hand to introduce himself and Johnathon passed the seared-tuna salad my way. Although I knew that they were normal people, no different from
you and me, I couldn't help but feel intimidated. Just as I was
thinking, *I'm the only nonceleb at a table,* Juliette Lewis and
Rose McGowan joined us. I was dying as they talked about the
movies they were doing and their film-festival circuit. What did I
have to contribute? I stressed. I was in no movie. I had no TV
deal. I was no one! I remained silent. Suddenly my PR hero, who
was planning the party, came to my rescue. "Do you all know

Karen?" she asked. "She is the best writer on the planet." With that, the conversations began to flow.

What do you write? they wanted to know. "Don't worry, not celebrity gossip," I joked. "Good," they said, relieved. Johnathon and I bonded over our blackjack winnings earlier in the day (we both took in $500!). Rose joined in and told me that I reminded her of one of her friends. Christina and I chatted about her amazing red knee-high boots—and a pair of shoes we both coveted for fall. When the temperature in the room dropped and I began to shiver from the chill in the air, Robert got up and in one swift motion removed his brown Hugo Boss trench coat from behind his chair and placed it over my shoulders. (I actually used the bathroom to call a friend to tell her that I was wearing Robert Downey, Jr.'s jacket! She told me to check the pockets for junk. For the record, there was none.) In the rest room, I bumped into someone I went to high school with and she said, "I thought that was you! My God! What are you doing at that table?"

"I have no clue. It's so surreal," I said.

"Well, you look like you belong there," she complimented.

I felt like I was no longer an outsider, at least for a short while. We all traveled to the concert together and sat near one another. We even exchanged friendly hugs. And the paparazzi snapped away, getting close-ups of all of us. I remember specifically posing for one shot with Johnathon, Christina, and Juliette.

The next week, it ran in the pages of *People* and *Us* magazines . . . without a hint of my existence! I didn't even get a "with friend" or "gal pal" credit. I was just plain-old cut! The curls of my hair were airbrushed right out of the shot!

I guess I was an outsider, after all.

# Ask Not What You Can Do for Your Publicist; Ask What Your Publicist Can Do for You

### HERE'S WHAT TO REQUEST

- A press plan, a formal detailed strategy for securing your press coverage.

- A party. A publicist will often double as a party planner. Having a party for yourself is a savvy move, whether it's your sweet sixteen, tenth annual twenty-first birthday, or even an intimate dinner to celebrate the opening of your back porch. Your publicist should be able to canvass corporate sponsorships (from Moët & Chandon to Adidas), create dazzling invitations, and cull the appropriate guest list.

- Introductions to other publicists, celebrities, or pseudo-celebs, who will, in turn, recognize your celebrity and contribute to your growing profile. Consider such intros as your foray into the A-list circle and remember: you're only as good as the least famous person around you.

- Invitations to the most prohibitive, hard-to-get-into parties. One famous film director is notorious for having fired his publicist when she was unable to get her client into the *Vanity Fair* Oscar party in LA.

- Around-the-clock flattery on demand. Your publicist is your head cheerleader. When you're feeling depressed or—even worse—anonymous, one call to your publicist and you'll be reminded just how fabulous and famous you are.

- Media coaching. You should be trained to handle interviews without degenerating into a Farrah Fawcett–like abyss.

She was slaughtered by the media after a painful interview, where she seemed high, out of it, and incoherent on *David Letterman*.

- A surrogate mommy. Your publicist should feel your pain. When you feel sick, she's the one who throws up. She should kiss all of your boo-boos good-bye, carry your umbrella when it rains, and hold a personal grudge against anyone who's ever crossed you.

## TRUE LIES

## FRONT-ROW PERENNIAL

· · · · · · · · · · · *Melissa* · · · · · · · · ·

*T*wice a year, the circus comes town, setting up big white tents, parading beautiful girls in spangled costumes, and executing death-defying acts of courage and bravado. I am talking, of course, about Fashion Week. Seven heady days of air-kissing, champagne-sipping, and goodie-bag-stealing adventures; blindingly fabulous runway shows; boutique launch parties; and a riot of multiple diva acts. It's a time when celebrities as diverse as Tori Spelling, Rudy Giuliani, and Lil' Kim band together in the name of style. But the most important thing to remember about Fashion Week is that it's not who you are; it's where you sit that matters.

Typically, the front row is reserved for those occupying the highest echelon of fashion—New York socialites, Hollywood actresses, the editors-in-chief of *Vogue*, *Harper's Bazaar*, *W*, and *Elle*, powerful buyers from Bloomingdale's, Barney's, and Saks Fifth Avenue. Applying the trickle-down theory, a front-row seat is a sign that one is a true fashion heavyweight; the second row is reserved for those one notch below on magazine mastheads; while junior editors and correspondents from small regional publications occupy the third to fifth rows.

Several years ago, as an aspiring fashion scribbler for a small independent Web site, whatever invitations I received to the fashion shows arrived with the lowest seat assignment possible: "Standing." Which meant, of course, that I didn't even merit a seat of my own. Standing? I was incensed. How could this be? All right, so maybe our subscriber base would never come close to matching the numbers put up by Condé Nast style bibles, but we did count a rabid and devoted following of several thousand fashion freaks. A standing ticket is much like flying standby: there was a chance I would never even be able to get *inside* to see the shows, much less report on them. On the very rare chance that I was actually given a seat, it was usually one in the nosebleed section, reserved for eager, underage FIT students and the designer's relatives from Columbus, Ohio. I might as well have stayed at home and watched the shows on cable!

There is one benefit of a "standing" ticket. A few minutes before the show is about to begin, any empty seats in front or elsewhere are up for grabs. If one is aggressive (and shameless) enough, and blessed with a sharp left hook that can be played off with the polite utterance of "Pardon me," a front-row seat can still be had. This free-for-all is similar to the depraved sight of pigeons fighting over scraps of bread. Only the truly obnoxious survive.

I was a hardened veteran of the Front-Row-Seat Dash, but felt it would look unseemly this time around. I had convinced a reporter from a local paper to write a profile on me as part of her publication's fashion coverage that week. Her assignment was to accompany me to a fashion show so she could observe me, the fashion editor of the "leading independent fashion Web site," in my element. If she saw me waiting on the standing line, seated in the back rows, or indelicately scrambling for a front-row seat, she would undoubtedly ascertain my diminished status, call her editor, and spike the story. But first she would laugh—long and hard. I had to find a way to fake A-list fashionistadom somehow.

Rumor had it that the hottest show of the season was Benjamin Cho's, an up-and-coming Asian designer who made sexy dresses out of crocheted horsehair and counted Jennifer Lopez and Claire Danes among his fans. There was a serious buzz about Benjamin, and it was the show everyone in the fashion set looked forward to all week. I needed to be there, front row and center. I faxed Benjamin's publicist the following hoity-toity statement and crossed my fingers: *Melissa de la Cruz is the senior fashion editor of the leading independent fashion journal on-line. She is being profiled in a very important newspaper during Fashion Week. This is a request for a front-row seat at your show. Please let us know if you will accommodate Ms. de la Cruz.*

After receiving the fax, Benjamin's publicist then called my "publicist" (a.k.a. me). I told her about the lavish two-page spread about "Melissa" that was going to run. After much prevaricating on my part about my own importance, she reluctantly agreed to put me in the front row.

The night of the show, I arrived an hour and a half late. The place was packed. When I checked in at the reception desk and gave them my name, the publicist stood up, placed two quick kisses on my cheek, and said, "Oh, my god! Thank God you're *here*! *Now* we can start!" She escorted me to the very first row, where an empty seat awaited me. It was obvious she had kept my seat vacated at a very steep price—the standing and backroom crowd shot me daggers as I sat down.

Once ensconced, I fully enjoyed the unobstructed view to the runway. I was two seats down from Claire Danes and Chloë Sevigny, and a hairbreath away from Kate Betts, who was the editor-in-chief of *Harper's Bazaar* at the time. I blew kisses to assorted colleagues and fashion editors of my acquaintance who were madly waving and trying to get my attention. Because of the spectacle my entrance had caused, paparazzi came by and snapped my photograph. I had died and gone to fashion heaven. The reporter assigned to write about me was seriously impressed.

The next day I attended another fashion show, fully prepared to journey up the bleachers with the riffraff for my back-row seat. I presented my ticket to the gatekeeper. "Oh! Melissa de la Cruz! Follow me, please." She smiled broadly and escorted me to a front-row perch. Good news travels fast in the fashion world.

# FRIENDS FOR HIRE

## *Karen*

$\mathcal{R}$adu is the ultimate trainer to the stars. He's gotten J.Lo in shape, kicked Cindy Crawford's butt, and tortured many a celebrity. He charges $150 per hour, and there's a year's wait list for the hot time slot between six A.M. to nine A.M. (when all of his power people train). In the name of hip slimming and inner-thigh trimming, I wanted him to whip my bod into shape. But when I contacted his gym, a posh setup on Fifty-seventh Street, I was rebuffed. There was no way Radu could fit me in, and no amount of pleading and explaining my awful predicament (that I had gained a few pounds and my clothes were getting tight) worked. I became obsessed with working out with him. Maybe it was because I couldn't have him, but I began to truly believe that I'd never be thin without Radu's help.

I was desperate.

So I got creative. I asked my friend Nicole, a connected gal-about-town, who knows Radu, to put in a recommendation call. She's the type of girl who's persuasive without being pushy, slick without being creepy, and forthcoming without being demanding. She would be my perfect faux-publicist. A day later she called me and said, "Girl, you owe me big."

Not only did she get Radu to fit me into his schedule—but for free! She told him that I was a rising It girl and he *had* to work me out—that if I looked good, he'd look good. I don't know what else she said (she wouldn't give away her secrets), but whatever it was, it did the trick. When I walked into his gym, I was greeted with the most welcoming of hellos. The receptionist who wouldn't give me the time of day earlier that week was warm and fuzzy, kissing me on both cheeks, giving me free Radu T-shirts and cross-trainers. Then Radu introduced me to everyone who worked at the gym as a VIP. "Give her anything she wants. She's a very special client," he said.

I must have been. I started training with him at a plum eight A.M. slot three days a week. His workouts were a sweat-induced frenzy. He had me climbing up walls, using gymnastics rings, chasing him in circles while we were enclosed in a super-strength and supersized rubber band, at such a frantic pace you'd think I had to change my body completely for some kind of movie role. After the fifth session, my body was in so much pain that in order to wash my arms in the shower, I squirted pump soap on the wall and rubbed my shoulder against it!

Was looking good worth this much agony? I decided it wasn't. But at least I can say I trained with Radu, even if I look nothing like Cindy C.

# YOU, THE PR GURU!

If you can't hire a publicist, here's how to become your own.

• Invent the name of your PR firm and make all of your own calls as if you were the senior rep or principal of the agency. ("Hi, I'm from In-Your-Face PR and I'm calling about the hottest new It girl . . . [your name here]").

• Consider holding your nose to create a nasal, high-pitched voice, or talk with your chin tucked closely to your chest, which will give the effect of a deeper, huskier baritone sound.

• Begin talking about "my publicist" incessantly, even if you're breaking up with your boyfriend or talking to your mom. Try these on for size: "My publicist does not think I should be involved with you, Jimmy. You're not good for my image," and "Mom, I can't talk. My publicist and I have a conference call."

• Investigate the magazine industry and learn the names of all of the editors and the sections they edit. This way you know who to pitch yourself to.

• Use your PR alter ego before you go anywhere in order to inform people of your impending appearance. For instance, before you hit the hottest restaurant in town, call the manager or owner to let him or her know a VIP is coming to dinner. Order yourself a bottle of champagne to be delivered to your table when you arrive. This way people will start to buy into your new persona. It might take three, four, or five visits to the same place before your star status sticks, but in time they'll get the message and treat you like the star you are.

• Order letterhead so you can fax people on official stationery that looks professional. Get a voice mail and, with your nasal voice, leave an outgoing message for your firm.

- Use your PR alter ego to set up meetings for yourself with tastemakers, trendsetters, store owners, gallerinas, gossip columnists, event producers, club promoters, and basically anyone who has the ability to elevate your profile.

- Do not feel self conscious while you're pitching yourself in the third person. The worst that can happen is someone says no. And remember—you didn't get rejected; your publicist did. Eventually, when you put on a new voice, you can go back to the original people who wouldn't meet you and try again as someone else. Be persistent. Don't give up on anyone until they agree to meet you (or rather, your "client").

- Intern at a PR firm near you in order to learn tricks of the trade—and perhaps swipe a Rolodex or two.

Note: If you can't pull this off, ask, beg, or bribe a friend to do the job for you.

*Days 5–8:*

# HOLY ENTOURAGE!

*It really isn't anybody's business how many people we have working for us. What's offensive is that I'm portrayed as this prima donna with these sycophants telling me how great I am all the time. Yes, they do work for me, but we're working together for a higher good.*

—*Demi Moore*

Famous people travel in packs. The more famous, the bigger the herd. J.Lo globe-trots with no less than twenty-five people. *Vanity Fair* revealed it takes the efforts of fifty-seven people to keep Salma Hayek in the spotlight. Halle Berry thanked everyone from her lawyer to her hairstylist during her lengthy acceptance speech at the 2002 Academy Awards ceremony. Mariah Carey goes so far as to make members of her staff sign nondisclosure agreements.

Like twenty-five-karat diamonds, the entourage is the ultimate accessory of the famous—the bodyguard, the stylist, the hairstylist, the makeup artist, the photographer, the chauffeur, the trainer, the nutritionist, the astrologer, the assistant, the assistant's assistant, the assistant's assistant's intern, and so on. How can you be somebody all by your lonesome? It's impossible. Only the anonymous fly solo. But famous people need a flotilla of handlers and hangers-on in order to navigate their way down the red carpet. The phenomenon is out of control. P. Diddy has even brought his peeps into the sauna with him—and stationed another member of his entourage outside the sauna door to answer his cell phone and deliver it when necessary. You might not require a man in an earpiece to direct you to Leeza's microphone during the Golden Globes, but just like the sorority president of Gamma Gamma Gamma, having a gang of thieves at your heels will help convince people you're famous.

This chapter will show you how to pull off the perception of being the most popular kid in town by attracting a posse of individuals who, knowingly or not, contribute to your star power. We will give you the inside scoop on getting an assistant (for free) and show you how to subtly turn your friends into your little helpers. We will walk you through a detailed, comprehensive list of people to consider adding to your personal team and show you how to create a fan base of admirers who will shower you with love, adoration, affection, and compliments. Because, come on, what good are you if nobody's around to remind you?

## IT'S PERSONAL

# INTERNAL MEDICINE

*Karen*

*F*amous people need assistants. It's a fact. And I knew I needed one during the two-week challenge, when my life became unmanageable. By day seven of my celebrity makeover, my multitasking skills had reached their saturation point. I could no longer be everywhere at once. I was overbooking my social calendar, making two to four appointments for every hour of the day, and slowly but surely losing my mind. I needed a Mini Me. And I needed one fast.

I couldn't afford to pay for a full-time employee. So I contacted career counseling centers at local schools like NYU and Columbia. I made the job sound super-appetizing with an ad that read, *Join me for a fabulous life of glamorous red-carpet parties, fun assignments from glossy magazines, and celebrity sightings.* Dozens of résumés came my way. Within a week I had an intern I could call my own. I figured, I might not have money to offer, but what I couldn't provide in green, I could make up for in perks (free beauty products, the best parties in town, contacts, and a foot in the door of a difficult industry).

She sorted my mail, deleted junk e-mails, organized my files, photocopied my writing clips, jockeyed my calls, handled all of my interviews and fact checking, took care of my research, and basically made my life a helluva lot easier than it had been. She sucked up to me, told me I was fabulous, and did whatever tasks I placed in front of her.

"Wow. I'm impressed that Karen has an assistant," coworkers said when they reached my new assistant on the phone. "She must really be doing well."

"Well, she *is* famous," my intern said (as per my request).

The beginning of our relationship was heavenly. Now, let me just say that I had been a lowly intern many times in my life, and I remember how miserable it was to be treated without respect, to be relegated to a closet, folding socks for hours on end and searching endlessly for an extra-large safety pin that fell off a Versace dress. I remember being scolded for saying hello to an editor-in-chief of a magazine (apparently editors-in-chief do not like making chitchat with junior employees, especially the non-paid ones). And I remember being told to "develop thicker skin" when I asked to leave—midday—because I had a fever of 103.

So I decided to make a concerted effort to respect, value, and appreciate my intern. I invited her to every posh event I covered. I let her borrow clothes. I got her a free haircut and facial when she needed them. I treated her to manicures on Fridays. And the more I gave, the more she took. She stopped doing the interviews she was scheduled to take, and instead I caught her on Internet dating sites. She began to show up late without apologizing for it. It started innocently—five minutes here, ten minutes there—but in no time she was clocking in ninety minutes after her expected arrival time.

I felt awful about saying something. I didn't want to hurt her feelings. And I didn't want her to quit, even though she was no longer doing me much good (though she still answered the phone properly, for whatever that was worth). It was like I was trying to make up for all the awful jobs I had had to do while I was paying my dues. So I didn't say anything to her. Until she took things one step too far.

The last straw was when I came home from an appointment and found her in my bathroom, wearing my top, using my makeup, on a long-distance call—on my dime. "Oh, I have a party tonight. I didn't think you'd mind," she said. I lost it. I don't remember exactly what I said, but I know I used the phrase "borderline personality" when I asked her to pack up her stuff and go.

She left in tears. I felt bad for letting things build up in such an unhealthy way. But it taught me a valuable lesson. It's called boundaries. And with my new intern—and my intern's new intern—I have loads of them.

## KAREN, I AM NOT YOUR ASSISTANT

. . . . . . . . . . . *Melissa* . . . . . . . . . .

"*K*aren Robinovitz's office!" This is the standard greeting you would receive if you called my friend and writing partner Karen Robinovitz. Karen never answers her own phone—she has an army of interns to screen her calls. Whenever I called Karen, I would always guffaw whenever I heard her assistant answer the phone in such a manner. I knew Karen was sitting a few feet away, unwashed and in a tank top and the same torn sweatpants she's been wearing since sixth grade. Karen Robinovitz's office, my ass!

Karen can only be described as, well, bossy. (She is an Aries, after all.) But it's an assertiveness that is imbued with a tremendous generosity of spirit. She asks people to do things for her in such a charming way that they are only too happy to do her bidding. I've seen saleswomen, rug merchants, computer technicians, and snooty maître d's at restaurants gladly perform the favors she asks of them. You can't say no to Karen, and few people do.

I certainly didn't. At first it was just small tasks—usually related to our joint projects, which I didn't mind performing. "Mel, will you write down this idea?" "Mel, will you remember to call [our agent, our photographer, our publicist]?" "Mel, will you make a Xerox of [our magazine article, our book proposal, our film treatment]?" After a while, however, I found that not only was I completing these miscellaneous errands, I was also constantly checking Karen's e-mail and reading them to her while she was (a) getting a colonic at the We Care spa in Palm Desert, California, (b) attending the Winter Olympics in Salt Lake City, or (c) watching Sting perform at a private party in Cannes. The chore that broke this camel's back was when she called me from a yacht in St. Bart's and asked me to pick up an important package she was expecting from the post office while I was sitting at home, in below-zero weather in New York City.

"KAREN!" I yelled, "I AM NOT YOUR ASSISTANT!"

There was a hurt silence. "I know," she said in a small voice. "I'm sorry! It's just that I trust you more than anyone else I know." Confronting Karen with her habit has improved our friendship tenfold. She has never asked me to read an e-mail or photocopy an article since. But oops, while I'm writing this, the phone is ringing and Karen has generously lent me her duplex for the weekend while she's away in Palm Beach and my apartment is being renovated.

I pick up the phone and sigh. "Karen Robinovitz's office."

## GETTING PERSONAL: HOW TO TURN ANYONE INTO YOUR ASSISTANT

A personal assistant is the lackey in your life who makes your dinner reservations, gets your dry cleaning, and does every task you haven't a minute for. No time to call back your father? Have your assistant tell him you love him— and his check is late. Need someone to keep up your correspondence, call people back, or sign for your flowers? Call the assistant. Coffee, researching, photocopies, deliveries, RSVPs, answering your phone? That's what assistants are for. That and squeezing in an electrolysis appointment between your astrology session and a yoga class.

• Who can be your assistant? Anyone, even if it's your younger brother's friend, whom you pay $5 to fetch your dry cleaning, or the guy who's hopelessly in love with you, who will come over at any time to fix your computer, hang a photo, and move the sofa.

• Hire an intern. Call a local college and speak to someone at the career center. Make up a bevy of important job descriptions, and before you know it, an educated, eager beaver will be at your disposal—and perhaps even receiving credit for helping you out. Since you're not paying someone, you will have to provide some perks, which can range from an occasional lunch, a manicure, or job contacts the student can rely on after graduation. It's only fair.

• Post a listing for an intern on a Web site that is affiliated with whatever university, grad school, or school of continuing education is in your hometown. Make your ad sound appealing and fun by using phrases like *meet high profile people*, and *attend the best parties*. Just screen carefully. Good help is so hard to find these days.

• Begin to refer to your assistant at all times. "Oh, I'll have my assistant call you to make a plan." It will give you the appearance of being successful, socially desirable, and very, very busy.

• Have your assistant call people that you want to talk to, and when the desired person answers the phone, the assistant should say, "I have Melissa de la Cruz on the line for you. Are you available to talk to her?" Then the assistant should "patch" you in.

• Your assistant should always answer your phone by saying, "[insert your name here]'s office," even if it's your two-hundred-square-foot studio.

• Your assistant must be able to reach you at any time in case of emergencies. When important people need you, your assistant's job is to track you down.

• Instruct your assistant to tell people you're in a meeting when you're unavailable (i.e., in the bathroom) or not in the mood to talk. That way, you'll always seem like you have something important to handle.

• Your assistant should also keep a "call sheet" for you. That is a detailed list of who your calls are from, why someone is trying to reach you, and return phone numbers (even if you already have them, have the assistant get them; it will save you from the hassle of going through your phone book later).

# EXCUSE ME, CAN YOU TAKE MY PHOTO?

· · · · · · · · · · · *Melissa* · · · · · · · ·

During our two weeks of fame, the magazine informed us that we were not going to be assigned professional photographers, and instead we would have to document our experience ourselves. Armed with a host of instant cameras and a video recorder given to us by *Good Morning America* for a possible television clip, I recruited friends, publicists, journalists, and assorted strangers to act as my own personal paparazzi anytime I left my apartment. This was harder than it sounds. Asking strangers to take my picture at film premieres and restaurant openings made me seem more like an awkward tourist than a haughty up-and-comer who deserved to be in the spotlight.

My first day, Michael Musto, the famous gossip columnist for the *Village Voice* and a friend of mine, invited me to the premiere of *The Rookie*, a Disney film starring Dennis Quaid. The Disney people had invited Olympic athletes to the event, and upon spotting Michelle Kwan in an aisle seat, I immediately pounced. The problem was, I couldn't very well ask her seatmate, the actor B. D. Wong, to take our picture. Instead I roped an usher into taking the photo. "Are you really from *Marie Claire*?" Michelle asked as the flash went off. I tried to assure her I was, even though with my cheap Instamatic camera, I looked more like a fawning fan than a real journalist.

I thanked her, assured her it would run in the magazine, and went back to my seat. The movie was about a washed-up gym teacher who realizes his dream to play in the minor leagues—or something of the sort. I can't be certain, as Michael and I bolted after the first twenty minutes of saccharine small-town dialogue (but not before we had helped ourselves to the free popcorn and Diet Cokes!). We made our way to the ESPN Sports Zone restaurant in Times Square, a gargantuan sports-entertainment-and-food complex, where the after-party was held. Hordes of photographers and camera crews were already set up to capture the stars' entrance on the red carpet. I was one of the first people to march down the crimson-colored walkway, typically reserved for the rich and famous, but not a single bulb exploded or microphone was stuck in my face. They were all waiting, reasonably enough, for Dennis.

"Here, I'll take your picture," Michael said gamely, grabbing my Instamatic. I struck a pose in front of the restaurant. Unfortunately, he couldn't figure out how to work the flash and I wound up standing still for five minutes with a frozen grin on my face. A group of real tourists had assembled in front of the restaurant, and they noticed our amateur photo shoot on the red carpet. I heard a suburban mom gush, "Oh, how cute, they're *pretending* she's famous!" The horror!

This was never going to work. If I was going to be famous, I would have to stop traveling solo, *avec* cheap camera. Who could I recruit to pretend to be a professional photographer? When I got home, I noticed my husband had taken it upon himself to paint blackboards on our kitchen wall. *Hmmm.* Mike was a creative architect who dabbled in photography.

By the next week, he was happily munching appetizers at a

restaurant opening with his impressive-looking Nikon strapped to his chest. He dutifully captured my mug next to assorted demi-celebs. It was certainly an improvement. I didn't have to coerce strangers into taking my photo anymore. But I still had a ways to go—*real* paparazzi never help themselves to the hors d'oeuvres!

## ONE IS THE LONELIEST NUMBER

• • • • • • • • • • *Karen* • • • • • • • • •

*If* you ever wondered how famous people do it all—and look so good—it is because they have a team of people who do things for them. I had the skeleton of my squad—a therapist who would listen to me vent, an astrologer who would warn me when Mercury was in retrograde, a yoga instructor who would keep me grounded and in shape, a rolfer who kept my spinal cord in line, and an intern/assistant—but I needed a superficial circle, a group of people who would enhance my persona by coagulating around me whenever possible. Since so much of celebrity is about smoke and mirrors, I decided to round up a (faux) troop for my two weeks of celebritydom.

My first order of business was asking my friend John to follow me around with his digital Sony. Nothing says fame like a TV crew recording your every move. I brought him with me to parties, shopping excursions, and dinners. His wife, Sally, a dear friend who has always wanted to be a photographer, acted as John's lighting expert. She followed him with camera flashes and portable lighting systems while he followed me. When I asked my yoga instructor for advice on my diet, I decided I could call her my nutritionist. I turned to a makeup-artist friend and asked her to do me up for all public appearances. Anytime I left the house, I called it an appearance. ("Sweetie, can you do my makeup today? I have to make a cameo at the pharmacy.")

I asked the guy I was dating, a former wanna-be thespian, who gave me some impressive insider tips on looking good on camera, to temporarily act as my manager, a manager who would hold my bags and screen anyone who wanted to talk to me. He happily accepted the job—and made me pay him back later by giving him many foot rubs. Taking cues from a Madonna interview I had read, I began to casually refer to each member of my new team. When someone gave me an assignment, I'd say, "Oh, you'll have to call my manager." When I got in the backseat of a taxicab, I'd say with a sniff, "Sir, can you slow down? My rolfer will not appreciate what this bumpy ride is doing to my sacrum." Trying on clothes, I might exclaim, "This is the red my makeup artist was talking about!" At dinner I would announce, "Oh, my nutritionist thinks I should avoid complex carbs." (I considered having my assistant call all restaurants before I went out to get some intel on the menu in order to ensure that it met my dietary constraints, but that just seemed a bit much even though many a Hollywood assistant performs such idle tasks every day.)

Then, while I was doing errands, two cute twenty-ish-year-old women named Joey and Tanya approached me to find out if I was Karen Robinovitz. We had a friend in common, and after a bit of chatting, I learned that they were two of Britney Spears's stylists. They were about to launch a new line of clothing, and when I said, "Maybe I could write about it," they offered to dress me for a night on the town. Just like that, I had two stylists on my team.

For our fitting, they rented a suite at the Regent Wall Street Hotel—the very suite Liza Minnelli used before she got married months before. We ate beluga caviar between taking measurements. After I'd slipped in and out of a dozen frocks, my stylists convinced me to go out wearing a tattered leather skirt slit up to there, a matching newsboy cap, and nothing but a bra on top. "Famous people like to be naked," they said.

I didn't feel like I could pull it off. "I don't know. My abs are so not made of steel," I said.

"Girl, just work it like you've got it and you'll pull it off. You look fierce," Joey assured.

I conceded; being naked was a part of my brand name, as per my story, "The Naked Truth," in Step I. Besides, I was sure the outfit would garner me much-deserved attention. So I sucked it up (and in), gulped down a glass of wine, and prepared to make my exit for the night. When we went out, I air kissed the doorman, a burly dude in faux fur, as if we were old pals. He let the rope down for me (must have been the belly button) and people actually started believing my hype. I slinked right past the crowd and made myself cozy at a plum table in the center of the party—along with my troop that included a videographer, a photographer, a trainer, an astrologer, four friends, two stylists, a makeup artist, and a large guy friend who doubled as my very own bodyguard that I nicknamed Big Rob, after Britney's legendary thug. The next day I got a call from a friend of a friend, who said, "I saw you last night, and all of these people were surrounding you. I was trying to make my way over to you, but I couldn't penetrate the crowd. Who do you think you are—Puff Daddy?"

"K. Robby," I said. The next best thing.

# THE FAME MAKEOVER

## *Melissa*

$\mathcal{F}$or a brief time in my life I was employed at a beauty magazine. One of the lasting lessons I learned from working at this publication is that hairstylists are the most amenable people in the world. When I worked there as a beauty writer, I would call the city's most sought-after hairstylists at all hours—asking such questions as: "What do you mean when you say, 'flatten the root'?" and "How exactly are you supposed to towel-dry after conditioning?" and "Did you say boar- or bear-bristle brushes are best?" One of the hairstylists who bore the brunt of my calls was Stephen Knoll, who owns the luxurious Madison Avenue salon where the likes of Elle Macpherson and Kim Cattrall get their locks trimmed. Stephen spent many an hour explaining to me just the right blow-dry techniques. Upon the publication of my piece, Stephen sent me a nice note saying, *If you ever need anything—please just ask.*

Little did he know I would keep him to his word—even if it was two years later. Once I accepted the "get famous" assignment, the first thing I did was look in the mirror. My roots had grown out so much my hair was two-toned. My skin was pale and dry. If I was to become a celebrity, I would have to look like one at all times. I realized I needed "people." I had no people. I did my own hair and applied my own makeup. I called Stephen, reminded him of his promise, and he generously agreed to furnish me with a "fame makeover" and to provide hair and makeup for all my public appearances for two weeks.

On the first day, "Team de la Cruz," as I nicknamed my coterie of stylists—Theresa (color), Kenneth Tepper (cut and blow-dry), and Melissa Silver (makeup)—was thrilled to see me. I made chitchat and lighthearted conversation with each of them. Kenneth gave me a fun, piecey Kirsten Dunst shag; Theresa turned my mousy brown locks into a ravishing red; and Melissa gave me a bronzy J.Lo glow.

Midway through the week, however, I began to feel paranoid every time I stepped into the salon. Melissa and Kenneth were as gracious as ever, but I felt increasingly guilty because none of their hard work had yet to surface in a photograph of me in print! I began to feel like a fraud. I regaled them with stories of the film premieres I had attended and the fashionable parties that were on my schedule, but I detected a faint and understandable skepticism under their enthusiasm. For all they knew, I was pulling the wool over their eyes. It's very hard to have "people," I learned. The weight of their expectations (of my fame) laid heavily on my conscience. I never thought I would ever have to worry about disappointing anyone with my failure to become famous—except for my parents, that is.

At the very least, I made my husband happy. Mike thoroughly enjoyed my metamorphosis from frumpy work-at-home writer to gadabout ingenue, and he expressed his sorrow upon knowing the hair and makeup sessions would soon end. "Will you ever look this way again?" he asked sadly. "I've never seen you look so good!"

Team de la Cruz's morale shot up on the second week, however, when photographs of me and my new look were plastered all over *Gotham*, *Ocean Drive*, *New York* magazine, and the *New York Post*. We exchanged cheerful high-fives, and Stephen personally came by to congratulate me. Later in the week, as Kenneth gave me one last blow-dry and Melissa dusted my nose with powder for the last time, I thanked and tipped them profusely. But I didn't know whether to emerge triumphant or slink out the door. Even if I had delivered on my promise to become famous, I still felt like I had gotten away with something. But maybe that's the secret to fame, after all.

# THE PERSONAL LIFE COACH

· · · · · · · · · · · *Karen* · · · · · · · · · · ·

*D*onna Karan has Deepak Chopra. Oprah has Dr. Phil. Richard Gere has the Dalai Lama. Members of species famous like to have a maharishi, spiritual healer, or some form of personal guru who helps them through that little journey called existence. Meet Stuart Gelles, my life and energy coach. I heard about him through a very fancy socialite I interviewed. "He has changed my life," she oozed over chopped salads at Barney's. She was adamant that I meet him. He was once a bigwig in the Hollywood scene, coaching important directors, actors, and moguls. "He really understands famous people," she said. (I wasn't sure that she was lumping me in the "famous" category, but I nodded knowingly, regardless.)

She went on and on about how she used to be a "doer," someone who just went through the motions of life, and now she's learning how to be a "be-er," someone who really feels and balances it out with her "dreamer," a term that embodies her spiritual and creative side. According to Stuart, there are three types of people: be-ers (the emotional energy that affects relationships, intimacy, self-esteem, and the heart), doers (the results-oriented energy that's all about acting, reacting, organizing, goal setting, project managing, analysis), and dreamers (the spiritual energy, the side of oneself that thinks about creation, life purpose, divinity).

All three must work together equally for one to thrive. But the real challenge, as per Gelles's teachings, is to live from another place, the altitude—which is almost like having an out-of-body experience—where you can see yourself as a be-er, doer, and dreamer, and understand the difference between them and your actions.

I wasn't sure what to make of this so-called miracle man, but I was not in a great place at the time. I was struggling with serious boyfriend issues (the issue being: I wanted to break up with him and kept getting sucked back into his charm). After much contemplation (and an abominable weekend with the guy), I came to the conclusion that I needed professional help. Hey, the first step in solving a problem is admitting you have one. Besides, I have always been a sucker for all self-help modalities, and having a life coach on my team could do nothing but add to my grand entourage of players.

I called Stuart. He had a full, buoyant voice and a chatty personality. "You have to feel your pain and release it," he said, "Pull the doer out of the equation and stop analyzing every detail and flushing out the drama. You can change your life by noticing what's occurring in the three energies and learning to manage it. This is about having a life-management system."

Well, it made sense to me. So I made an appointment immediately. When we sat down at his plush Connecticut office, he drew a picture of three circles—two overlapping adjacently, and one underneath, also overlapping. The top left represented "be-er" energy, the top right was "dreamer" energy, and the bottom was "doer" energy. He shaded in the common areas to explain that there is balance when all three are being used equally. The shaded areas formed the shape of a lotus flower, a known symbol of balance. (Coincidence? I think not.)

When Stuart evaluated my "three circles," we saw where I was unbalanced. I was using more doer and dreamer than be-er, which all made sense. My life was in a state of perpetual motion. I was chronically overloading my schedule, writing dozens of articles, all while trying to be famous. . . . I was doing, doing, doing. I was dreaming, too, using my creative vision to come up with ideas for aquiring celeb status, stories, books, screenplays, and such. And my poor be-er was all left out.

"Life is more than 'how do we feel or what do we do' or 'how do we feel about what we do' and 'what do we do about how we feel.' Integrating the spirit into the be-er and doer, finding a balance between them, is where the power is," he said. Yawn if you want to, but this all resonated with me. It helped me see myself beyond the boyfriend troubles. My doer, generally speaking, was searching for the limelight, preventing my spirit from finding the light from within.

After one session, I broke up with the boyfriend, moved on beautifully, and haven't had any man drama since (well, maybe a little, but who's counting?). Now I call Stuart for pep talks every time my circles are out of whack and he's always there, reminding me of the lessons I need—and what a star he thinks I am!

## WHO'S ON YOUR TEAM?
### TO BE FAMOUS, PUT THESE EXPERTS ON THE PAYROLL

• A hairstylist. No more flitting from salon to salon in search of the holy hair grail. Find an affordable, affable hairstylist (try the local salon-type school or an assistant at the best and most expensive salon near you; assistants at high-priced salons are often surprisingly cheap) and make a commitment to him (or her). Someone who has intimate knowledge of your hair is key—you need to be able to pop into the salon (or invite the stylist over) for

TANYA BRAGANTI

*The Privé Beauty Team*
**From Left: Vanessa Mitchell (hair), Ludovic Audesson (hair color),
Mel, Maureen Wolfe (makeup), Karen, Roman Lilley (hair).
If we don't look good, they don't look good!**

emergency blow-outs without worrying about big-hair missteps. Keep your relations with your stylist friendly, so you can always secure an appointment, even during rush-hour hair traffic. That means tip them well—and send holiday gifts and cards.

• A stylist, whose job it is to dress you for big occasions and help you cultivate a personal style. While celebrities rely on stylists who make well over $100 an hour just to pick the right plunging Gucci top (or in Mariah Carey's case, the wrong one), all you need is a good pair of eyes and the advice of your most fashionable friend. Take her shopping with you and follow her advice. Also become friends with the manager of the hippest store in town, and eventually the two of you will be shopping together at flea markets and chic boutiques all over the city in order to develop your wardrobe. Call that person your stylist.

• Makeup artist. Celebs and even some fashion editors we know pay makeup artists to arrive at six A.M. at their homes to do their "faces" every morning. If you can't afford a makeup artist, scout a beauty-training school or class or someone who's just starting out and can do the job on the cheap.

• Photographer. Before you attract the attention of real paparazzi, you're going to have to travel with your own. Ask your significant other or a good friend to carry a camera and snap your photo at crowded parties. Soon enough, people will be asking, "Who's that girl?" and before you know it, other (real) camera flashbulbs will start blinding your vision, too.

• Trainer of some sort, be it yoga, pilates, weight lifting, boxing. Travel with this person, if possible. Sting never goes anywhere without his two yoga instructors. He has taken them to Italy, France, London, you name it.

• Dermatologist. They're the new therapist, always on call to make you feel better about yourself with microdermabrasion, shots of Botox, and pimple-popping capabilities. This person should be on your speed dial—and make friendly house calls without charging you. So if you don't have a dermo-friend, make one. Fast.

- Plastic surgeon. This is for advanced levels of fame—and those over forty—only. Find someone who's discreet and won't make you look like Melanie Griffith.

- Some kind of spiritual healer, coach, or guru. Celebrity comes with its own share of problems—lack of privacy, pressure to be perfect, a private jet that's always late. You'll need some serious aura cleansing.

- Bodyguard(s). It could be your most buff friend, a trainer at your gym, or someone who makes you feel safe, even if it's an ex-con. Celebrities need to be protected at all times. The latest trend is hiring former government operatives—FBI, CIA, and Israeli army secret service agents.

The bodyguard, Lou. Never leave home without one!

RONNIE ANDREN

- Other forms of security, such as bouncers who surround you to prevent the riff-raff and D-list from getting in your way. In fact, they should be so big and tough that no one should be able to see you when you walk across the street. Warning: This type often causes fights and commotion, which may not be a bad thing when you're seeking attention.

- Your assistant's assistant. For advanced levels of fame only.

# I GIVE IT FIVE STARS!!!

*Melissa*

*L*ike every author who's ever had a novel published, I was anxious about its critical reception. I was worried that the book's light tone, caustic humor, and picaresque plot might not receive as warm an embrace from critics who favored weightier, more serious subject matter—like childhood traumas and the lonely lives of people who lived in remote rural villages. So it was a relief when the reviews came in—and most of them were good. Some were solid raves, and while there were a few (you know who you are!) dissenting voices that crushed my spirit and sent me rollicking down the valley of insecurity and despair, I was thrilled with its acceptance by the publishing and media communities. But I had yet to meet an author's worst nemesis: disgruntled readers on Amazon.com.

Every week, I eagerly looked forward to checking my Amazon ranking to see if anyone had chosen to review my book. In the first weeks of the book's release I garnered ten awesome reviews— all of them had given the book four or five stars! I was on a roll and feeling smug about my success.

Until the day I clicked on the Web site to find that a reader had given me *one* star—the lowest rating available on the Amazon system! The reader called it a "complete waste of paper" and wished that "zero stars were possible."

*Ouch!* That hurt! Who was this wretched reader? Why had he or she bothered to buy my book in the first place, let alone review it? How much spite could a poor, innocent author deserve? There it was, out in public—for anyone to see—someone calling my book absolute trash. It was a kick in the gut, a slap in the face, as if something you had so carefully nurtured with love and care was suddenly stomped on violently. Without further ado, I quickly penned a rebuttal, saying it had a "wicked sense of humor" and had the makings of a "cult hit."

So there! I thought.

A few months later, I received another bad review that threw it "three barely flickering stars" and called my protagonist "positively annoying" and from a "useless margin of humanity."

Three barely flickering stars?? Hello? Useless margin of humanity? Yikes! I guess next to Saddam Hussein, over-the-top fashionistas were the spawn of Satan. I resigned myself to living with it. But a few months later, it started to grate on my nerves that this dismal review was the first one displayed every time I checked my Amazon ranking. Once again, I decided to take matters into my own hands. This time I would impersonate one of my loyal constituents—a flamboyantly gay man. I even gave him a name, "Ignatius Adricula"—he would be Filipino, like me! "Ignatius" thought my novel "wicked," "lovable," and "charming."

Yeah for "Ignatius"!

A few months later I received another lukewarm (three-star) review and a blistering (one-star) one. Apparently, Chinese baby–adoption jokes don't go over well with a certain segment of the book-buying populace. This time, however, I was too exhausted to combat their ill will with my forced cheerleading. I could only call my own book "wicked and hilarious" for so long. I gave it a rest, and I haven't checked my Amazon ranking since. (Not true! At the latest count I clocked in at 6,195.)

# WHO NEEDS A FAN CLUB WHEN YOU HAVE FRIENDS?

* * * * * * * * * * *  *Karen*  * * * * * * * *

*I* had a very important date one breezy winter night in 2001. It was a blind date, and I felt a lot of pressure to impress him. He—we'll call him Alec—was one of the fabulous beautiful people—a DJ, video music producer, and artist—and I wanted him to think I was fabulous, too. I pulled my trump card—my biggest fan, who is also known as my ballsy, go-up-to-anyone-and-say-anything friend Katy.

Before I stepped out in my zebra-print skirt and black knee-high Marc Jacobs boots, Katy and I mapped out a plan. Her mission: to approach me as an admirer who loves my work. The goal: to make me look *goooood*. I wanted to rehearse, but Katy promised she'd be better if she improvised. "It'll seem too forced otherwise," she said. "Trust me." I did—trust her, that is—though I had to admit, I was a little nervous. One false move and I'd wind up looking like the biggest heel in Manhattan!

At Canteen, a chic boîte in Soho, Alec and I fidgeted through idle, get-to-know-you conversations about where we were from and what we did. It was somewhat awkward, as all first meetings are, and as my glass of wine started to take its mellowing effect on my mind, Katy burst on the scene.

"Karen!" she exclaimed, "Karen Robinovitz! Is that you?" My skin got hot. I was sure I was bright red. I probably would have been just as embarrassed if the scenario weren't premeditated. She was yelling! "Oh-my-God. I thought that was you. You look *so* good," she gushed. "God, I haven't seen you since you introduced me to Sarah Jessica Parker." It was true—I did introduce her to Sarah Jessica Parker . . . in a roundabout way. The previous year I helped cast a story for *Marie Claire* where I found three single women to go out with SJP, who spent a night on the town, trying to fix the girls up with eligible men.

"Oh, that's right. But anyway, how are you?" I said, tucking my hair behind my ears, trying to downplay that angle.

"Forget me. It's all about you," she continued. "You're everywhere. I see your articles in every magazine. You're so fabulous. And I love your hair. Did you darken it? It looks beautiful. You are such a rock star."

I smiled and thanked her. But I wanted her to stick a sock in it! I was mortified. It seemed so fake, so forced. (Duh!) "Well, this is Alec," I said, introducing her to my date.

"Alec, I hope you know how lucky you are. Karen is such a keeper," she said. And with that, she gave me a pretentious kiss on both cheeks and said, "I'll have my assistant call your assistant so we can rendezvous."

I never saw Alec again.

# CHEERING SQUAD

Jared Paul Stern, a nightlife columnist for the *New York Post*, a Page Six contributor, and an all-around swell guy, was sympathetic to my "fame" assignment and had offered his help. Jared and I had been friendly acquaintances for years, as we both started out in our careers by writing for the same edgy downtown newspaper, covering the trendy-people beat. After a few days of pestering, he agreed to have dinner with me at Meet, a hot new downtown boîte, and invited me to the Volvo Anniversary Party during Automotive Week—like Fashion Week, but for cars. (New Yorkers will celebrate the opening of a door.)

The party was a blast—right in the middle of Times Square. Jon Stewart worked the crowd and Sugar Ray performed a private concert for the invited few, which drew a large crowd of fans who were able to watch it from beyond the police barricades on the sidewalk. I was enraptured. Mark McGrath is one of my favorite singers and there I was, standing two feet away from him! I even exchanged chitchat with two of my childhood heroes—Suzanne Vega, the arsty folk singer, and the New Wave band Modern English, who also performed a private concert (and their classic prom ditty "Melt with You"). At the end of the evening, after we had received our goody bags filled with crystal candleholders displaying the Volvo logo, we exited through the stage door, where a large group of Sugar Ray fans and assorted tourists were assembled.

"Hold on!" Jared said. "I've got an idea—Mel, you go back inside." I did as told. I waited for a few minutes, then wondered what Jared was up to. Tired of waiting, I exited through the doors once more. Once outside, I was greeted with a tremendous roar. "Omigod!!! There she is!!!! *Oh, my God!!!!!* It's *her!!!!!*" There was cheering, yelling, and crying. Jared had whipped the crowd into a frenzy. He had asked them to affect mass hysteria in my name. I blushed. At first I was shocked, amazed, and slightly embarrassed. But as the cheering escalated, I found myself grinning. I began to wave madly to the crowd, and to blow fake kisses. It was exhilarating to have inspired such pandemonium. So this was what it felt like to be Madonna!

Volvo's publicist came out to see what all the ruckus was

At a private Sugar Ray concert. Mark McGrath is singing to me . . . almost!

MIKE JOHNSTON

about. When he saw me acting like a star, he assumed I was some-body and invited us to a private after-party with Mark McGrath and company at their hotel suite. I was delighted! Jared's plan had worked! But instead of heading for the hotel, I chose to schlep it homeward. I was tired. It was after midnight. I said my good-byes to Jared (who also chose to hoof it home), and hiked three blocks in the rain in my stilettos before I found a cab. A proper star exit, all right.

# MVP,
# YEAH, YOU KNOW ME

· · · · · · · · · · *Karen* · · · · · · · · · ·

*T*he Knicks are New York City's darlings, the underdogs we al-ways root for and adore, even when their defense sucks. Anyone can go to a game, but it's not just anyone who can go front-row style. Floor seats are a $1600-a-pop commodity, reserved for the likes of Spike Lee and Woody Allen. And there are always free front-row seats for VVIPs (very, very important people). Those are typically given to the supermodel of the moment, a major star who's in town (think Jack Nicholson status), or someone high up in life, like the mayor. I had never sat courtside, and un-less I became really, really rich, dated a big-time celeb, or mar-ried a Knick, I never would. Until I made a fan in Miss U.S.A.

After reading about my birthday party in the *Post*, the beauty queen's publicist called me and asked if I'd like to attend a Knicks game, courtside, of course, with the Halle Berry look-alike. "I really want her to meet more people like you, and you'll love her," he said, referring to me as a "star on the rise" and "the one to know." It was my first official fan call from someone who wasn't related to me by blood. How could I say no to such kind words— and a close-up look at Sprewell, charging down center court?

My ticket was awaiting me in an envelope at Madison Square Garden. And two men in suits escorted me to a private suite, where Candace Bergen was dining and model Karolina Kurkova was admiring her new basketball, signed by all the Knicks players. I grabbed some shrimp cocktail and waited for my date.

Miss U.S.A., clad in Cavalli jeans and an off-the-shoulder top, entered the room with her publicist and marched right toward me. "You have to be Karen Robinovitz," she sang. "I could tell. You have such a glow about you." (Her publicist must have trained her well.)

She introduced me to her friend Ananda Lewis, the former MTV VJ and current host of a morning talk show, and the three of us made our way down to the court.

My seat was insane—so on the floor that I could feel the vibration of the bouncing ball and the thump of the size-fifty feet of the players as they bolted by. Paul Simon was sitting to my left. Chris Rock was across the way. Carrie Modine, wife of actor Matthew, was nearby, cheering her face off. It was better than I had imagined. The supermodels were two rows behind me. I sipped my Diet Coke (the courtside area is equipped with waitresses). I gave a nod to my front-row peers, as if we were all members of the same elite club. This was life in the famous lane, all right. After Angela Bassett's publicist introduced me to a handsome New York Giant and an even more handsome actor from that show *CSI*, I realized I could never go back to being just another spectator sandwiched between sweaty, fat face-painters again. Yes, this world suited me just fine.

I didn't know what was more exciting—the fact that we were winning or that I had these famous-people-only seats and I kept catching the camera guy's lens (turns out my face appeared on television; a friend called me the next day and asked if I was at the Knicks game, because she saw me on the tube). At the end of the game, a random person asked if she could take my photo with Miss U.S.A. and Ananda. One moment with two stars—and front-row seats at a Knicks game—and I had already cultivated a fan! "Will you three lovely famous women get together so I can take a picture?" she asked.

She thanked us for our time. And then she asked me what I'd been doing since "that show, *Blossom*."

I didn't have the heart to tell her that I wasn't Mayim Bialik . . . or admit to myself that I had no real fan in my nonexistent club.

# FAN YOURSELF!

### WITHOUT FANS, YOU'RE NOTHING.
### HERE'S HOW YOU CAN CULTIVATE THEM

• Bribe people (even strangers) to be your admirers, who will serve to prove your worthiness to the general public by approaching you with compliments.

• Recruit family members and friends. Remind them that you'd do the same for them if they asked.

• Send yourself flowers when you're stationed in a busy place. Or before you arrive at a restaurant, call and send a bottle of champagne or an overwhelmingly indulgent dessert to yourself. When it arrives, pretend someone famous sent it to you.

• What's wrong with being your own fan? Start your own on-line fan club. Post fan letters, adoring slogans, and glowing reviews. Give this job to your assistant.

• Get glossy photos of yourself (headshots!) and return them—via mail—with a form letter that says, *Thank you for your support and being in touch. Lots of love!* to anyone who contacts you.

• Post photos and posters of yourself on lampposts, tree trunks, walls all over town, along with a slogan about your grandeur. It will make people familiar with your presence on the planet—and you will be recognized before you know it.

*Days 8-10:*

# MANAGING THE PRESS MACHINE

*I*n your quest for fame, the press is your number one ally. Without magazines, ad campaigns, television, and radio, we might never hear about the important things in life, like when rap moguls get arrested for toting guns in nightclubs, Oscar nominees shoplift from major department stores, pretty young starlets come out of the closet, or when a very well-known actor cheats on his fiancée with his latest costar. Think of the press as the ultimate introducer, a way for your brand to meet the world.

The second a magazine or newspaper declares someone "It," everyone wants to know who it is and why. Talent agents pounce. Film deals pour in. And that person becomes "It." Why? It creates a "buzz." It gives you recognition, because being the subject—or a subject—of an article is the biggest affirmation of your rising status, proof that someone thinks you deserve praise. Fame is a media-driven industry, and if you ever want to work in this town again, you have to realize that the press is your conduit to an adoring public.

You're going to have to amass a large scrapbook of press clips, images of you in magazines, printed news reports on what you're doing, who you're doing it with, and how much it cost. The only problem with press is that it can make you so famous that you may want to hide from the media, rather than chase it. Love of the limelight can lead to danger, a life without privacy, a prison of gawkers. You have to learn to control the press so it does not control you. This chapter will give you the inside dirt on courting the press, the science of dissecting magazine mastheads, inside secrets of turning ordinary parties into media extravaganzas, and how to work the camera, get on television, and be in command of your public persona. Fame, after all, is nothing more than image.

## FULL-COURT PRESS

# WHY DON'T YOU THROW FOOD AT THE HILTON SISTERS?

• • • • • • • • • • *Melissa* • • • • • • • • • •

*Y*ou're not anybody in New York unless *Village Voice* scribe Michael Musto has written about you. Michael is the doyenne of downtown, the consummate arbiter of fame, the one who championed RuPaul into stardom and wrote about Madonna before anyone else did. (He even used to be in a band that opened for her.) Prior to the *Marie Claire* assignment, I had met Michael once a year before, when we were both invited to be featured in a panel discussion for a magazine feature on fame. My novel was about to be published, so I was asked by the writer at the last minute to fill in for a teenage socialite (Stella Schnabel, the painter Julien Schnabel's daughter) who had dropped out, crying "homework" as her excuse.

Meeting Michael was a dream come true. As former club kids, my friends and I used to shadow him at nightclubs like the Roxy, the Copacabana, and Amazon. (He and Isaac Mizrahi were our favorite targets in the early nineties.) I told him about my teenage obsession and we hit it off. He even provided a generous blurb for my book. So when *Marie Claire* came calling, he was the first person who came to mind.

Michael is used to obsessive fans and wanna-bes vying for his attention—Courtney Love used to stalk him in her pre–Versace makeover days. "She used to ring my doorbell at odd hours in the morning—this was way before she had ever met Kurt Cobain; she was living in New York, and she wanted to be famous." Fortunately for Michael, I didn't know where he lives, so I resorted to e-mailing him every hour, to remind him of my existence and our burgeoning friendship. He finally agreed to meet me for lunch.

To become famous in two weeks, Michael told me, I needed to do something scandalous—and make sure I was photographed doing it. He told me a famous story of Sylvia Miles, a seventies star and current Manhattan party animal, who made her name by assaulting a theater critic. "She dumped a plate of spaghetti on his head after he gave her a bad review. It was in all the papers—it *made* her. Everyone forgot about her acting. She became a star because of her personality!" We cackled over our crab cakes. "Hey," he said, "why don't you throw a plate of food at one of the Hilton sisters? And make sure Patrick McMullan is there to document it." (The Hilton sisters are the pretty blond Hilton hotel heiresses, barely over twenty, that Page Six has labeled "the hot-blooded hotel heiresses." And Patrick McMullan is New York's most ubiquitous paparazzi machine.) It was a tempting plan, but I didn't know if I wanted to cause that much pain—after all, the teenage siblings might faint at the sight of food!

Michael dispensed some advice on seeking fame. "The public has to connect with you. Journalists like me, we can only hype things up so much—look at Matthew McConaughey; he was supposed to be the biggest star on the planet. Everyone wrote about him. But he never connected with the public. There's a limit to how much influence the press has. We can certainly introduce—but we can't *sway* the public. Ultimately, people make up their own minds." I felt a little deflated. If I was going to be famous in two weeks, there wasn't much time to cultivate an adoring public.

"But that doesn't mean you can't do it," he said. "Why don't we concoct a story about how you're the goddaughter of the Dalai Lama? That'll get you attention!" Michael also told me that the people who are dying for attention in his column never get put in. "I never wrote about Courtney Love," he admitted. I guess I adopted the wrong strategy.

Michael's a staunch ally nonetheless, and during my two weeks, he not only took me to some pretty fabulous parties, but also to the premiere of *The Graduate*, starring Kathleen Turner,

Jason Biggs, and Alicia Silverstone. I had never sat so close to the stage before! The play was atrocious, but we got a great view of Jason's abs and Kathleen in all her naked glory.

I never did make it in his famous "La Dolce Musto" column. But a few months after the fame game ended, I opened an *Ocean Drive* magazine, where Michael also writes a

**NIGHT WATCH**
BY MICHAEL MUSTO

*Ivana, Dennis, and Me!*

## It Girls and Hairy Ladies

The sprawling **ESPN Center** party for *The Rookie* brought out the movie's star **Dennis Quaid**, plus tons of sports figures who looked vaguely familiar, as well as **Melissa de la Cruz**, a writer doing a piece for *Marie Claire* on how to get famous. On my advice, de la Cruz was all set to tell people she's a **Rockefeller** granddaughter, but instead she dropped the guise and became intoxicated by the fame of others, gushing right up to **Michelle Kwan** and nicely enough not asking why the skater was in the B section. That's the wonderful thing about fame—while chasing it, you totally stand in awe of it, even if it's seated in the wrong area.

Then there was an **Ada** dinner for the **Andie MacDowell** movie *Crush*, where I took my own crash lesson in notoriety. The extraordinarily well-known divorcée **Ivana Trump** refused to trash the flick at all, extending the diplomacy of someone well schooled in the fame game. Ivana told me, "The movie has English scenery I recognized, some nice music and some lines I can't repeat." A friend of hers whispered them in my ear, and even I was shocked!

The abundance of **Prada** outfits made things tasteful again at the **Meet** party for *It Girls*, a WE Channel documentary by **Robin Leacock** that explores the world of trust-fund socialites who lunch. (Full disclosure: I am briefly featured in the show, but only as a commentator, not an "It" anything.) As *It Girls* from **Estelle Warren** to **Monica**

*It parade: Estella Warren arrived at the It Girls party.*

*Major league: Dennis Quaid attended The Rookie party at the ESPN Center.*

*Foreign diplomat: Ivana Trump had such a negative word to say about Crush.*

*Star tracker: Writer Melissa de la Cruz at The Rookie party.*

"I wasn't in the car with Lizzie. I don't want to be in the story," Tara Reid insisted.

wanted to be comfortable." Granted, Casey was in a loudly beaded and sequined jacket, but as Sale pointed out, it was antique and worn with jeans. Meanwhile, **Paris** and **Nicky Hilton**, who will

**Daly**, their every move having been chronicled in the tongue-wagging columns, and meanwhile she also distanced herself a bit from **Lizzie Grubman** after it leaked out Tara was with Lizzie earlier that

OCEAN DRIVE MAGAZINE / PATRICK McMULLAN

column. I flipped to his page and yelped! A full-length picture of me from the *Rookie* premiere ran next to one of Ivana Trump! It was awesome! I was the lead item! I called Michael to thank him and realized an important lesson in fame. *Don't ask* and you might receive.

# PRESSING ALL THE RIGHT BUTTONS
### HERE'S WHAT YOU SHOULD DO

• Befriend gossip columnists, a nosy tribe of journalists who get off on scandals, the misfortunes of others, and badly behaved recovering child stars. They are the ones who bestow boldface status upon unknowns. When they write about you, whether they have something good or bad to say, it makes a statement that you are one to watch. Most gossip columnists live by cocktails and cigarettes, so finding out where they hang out and cozying up to them at a bar is a good start. The other way to their hearts is by providing them with gossip-worthy fodder. If you are privy to anything noteworthy, like spotting a married NBA player leaving the apartment of a woman who isn't his wife (Karen used to see a former Knicks MVP come and go at odd hours of the morning and night from her neighbor's apartment in her old building), call or e-mail the columnist immediately.

• Learn who all of the party reporters are for your local paper(s) and publication(s). They can usually be spotted behind the velvet ropes and VIP doors of the best events, talking to hipsters, social mavens, politicos, business moguls. They report who's going to events and what people have to say about them. Read their sections so you know the kinds of quotes they like to get. Craft one and go in for the approach. After being seen repeatedly, you'll eventually work your way into this person's favor.

• Acquaint yourself with fashion and lifestyle editors, the cool hunters whose job it is to spot—and cover—the latest trends and emerging personalities for local newspapers and magazines. They are always looking for the next big thing for their pages, and it's high time you captured their attention. Have your publicist fax them on letterhead to give them story ideas about you. Follow up once a week. Persistence is key. Even send flowers.

Everyone responds well to gifts.

• Contact music, book, film, and theater critics if you have something they can criticize. Send them free tickets to your shows, copies of your manuscripts, and whatever you can to grab their eyes. Of course, you can't predict if you'll get a good review, but, as a wise T-shirt slogan once said, "It's better to be looked over than overlooked."

## MEDIA MANIPULATION

One of our friends used to be a junior features editor at a high-profile fashion magazine. She told us the following story about a certain striver who successfully sought a write-up in their publication.

"I received this press kit for this young woman who had just designed some award-winning video game for girls. She had sent us her bio, as well as a glossy 8-by-10 picture of herself. She was quite attractive—blond, blue-eyed, the whole bit. It was obvious she knew her stuff. It was almost as though she knew my job was to fill in the front-of-the-book feature section, where we write up a hundred or so words on new up-and-comers. She was completely right—I was high enough on the masthead to green-light that kind of piece, but not so low to have no power at all. I have to admit, she was perfect for us, but I felt like she was such a media manipulator and kind of gross. I didn't write her up.

But a few months later, she sent the same kit to a colleague of mine who had the same job I did, and he responded favorably. She ended up in the magazine after all. Later, I heard she was even named 'One of the Fifty Most Beautiful People' by some downtown publication. She was a great self-promoter. I have to hand it to her, I wasn't convinced by her, but there are others out there who were."

## DISSECTING THE MASTHEAD

Before you try your hand at networking, you need to know who to work. Below, we explain what the confusing titles on mastheads of magazines mean. This way, you'll be able to figure out who to contact—and how to contact them.

**Editor-in-Chief:** The head-honcho, the person who makes all of the final decisions. By all means, do *not* (we repeat: do not!) contact this person. He or she is way too busy handling real celebrities, magazine sales, and important people to have time *pour vous*.

**Deputy/Executive Editors:** These people are right under the editor-in-chief in job status (and salary). While they're often unapproachable, getting in with them is a surefire way to make sure your pitch is heard. They are down with all of the internal workings of the publication. They know what theme issues are coming up, where story holes are, and how to get the editor-in-chief to give the go-ahead on a project. Be warned: they rarely answer their own phones and they will probably take a few months to get back to you, if they do at all.

**Features Director:** This person is in charge of pulling together all of the features that will be published in each issue. He or she makes sure the underlings (the senior features editors, features editors, and associate features editors) are doing their jobs, coming up with ideas. This person does not work with fashion or beauty, but rather, the rest of the meat of the magazine. They're overseers, not necessarily the ones to talk to.

**Entertainment Editor:** This person is way too busy, trying to convince Jennifer Aniston to be on the cover of the magazine to deal with you. EEs have cozy relations with the who's-who of Hollywood, and their job is to get the stars in the magazine pages—and sometimes write about the stars. They are often socialites themselves or the offspring of someone famous. Warning: they can be hazardous to your self-esteem.

**Fashion Director/Fashion News Director:** Fashion directors handle what clothes get in the pages of the publication, and they often do some styling. The fashion news director is the one who writes about fashion—up-and-coming designers, new stores, labels, and trends. If you're an aspiring designer, send your samples and photos to these people; if you want to be a socialite or muse, you may be able to work your way into the magazine as a mannequin (they sometimes photograph "real" women instead of paid models).

**Beauty Director:** This girl gets to try out all the new lipsticks, creams, and nail polish colors under the sun. She often gets free massages, haircuts, and spa visits. She covers all of the beauty-related trends and makes sure her underlings are doing the same. If you are an aspiring aesthetician, eyebrow waxer, or dermatologist, this is the department to hit.

**Associate Editors of Any Kind (Beauty, Fashion, Features, Entertainment):** Associate editors work directly with senior editors and directors. They are often pitching the ideas and convincing their superiors of their value. They weed out the mail, pitches, press kits, and ideas for their bosses and decide which ones to push. They are not too big for their britches (yet), so they will have time to hear your pitch. This is your ticket. Send them your material and be kind. The nicer you are to them, the nicer they will be to you. Unfortunately, they don't have any decision-making powers, but keep in touch with them. They are usually on their way up the masthead, and who knows? In three to five years, they may be directors. If you play your cards right, they'll remember you.

**Editorial Assistants:** They hand out mail, fold clothes, file, fax, and get coffee. They answer the phones for the bigwigs, but sadly, they can't do a thing for you. Still, remain polite. Today's editorial assistant is tomorrow's associate editor.

### Who else can't really help you:

**Bookings Editors:** They book models. So don't even bother with them unless you're six feet tall, 110 pounds, and already repped by the Ford Agency.

**Art Directors:** They're in charge of what the magazine looks like—photographers and such.

**Market Editors:** They go into the fashion market to pull clothes for photo shoots. Only bother with them if you're a wanna-be designer.

**Anyone on the Second Masthead Page That Deals with Ads and Promotions:** Skip it. They have no editorial control . . . unless you become a big advertiser in the magazine. Come to think of it . . . that's not a bad idea.

Note: Befriending anyone at a magazine, even the copyeditors (those who check for dangling participles), is always smart. You never know who they're friends with on the inside.

## CELEBRATE YOURSELF!

• • • • • *Melissa* and *Karen* • • • • •

"We are not labeling envelopes," we declared, blanching at the sight of 850 invitations.

It was the first sign that "fame" had finally gone to our heads. Two weeks before the Tattinger champagne, Alizé-cocktail enhanced, *Marie Claire*–sponsored extravaganza, complete with Krispy Kreme doughnuts and cotton candy from a restaurant called Aix, to celebrate this book, we pulled a diva act. "Can't an intern do this?" we begged someone at Full Picture, the PR firm we convinced to produce our affair.

The party's guestlist provided a succinct snapshot of New York nightlife: "Columnist" (Page Six, Rush & Molloy, Intelligencer, *Women's Wear Daily*), "Social" (**Ann Dexter Jones**, **Alexandra Lind**, **Shoshana Lonstein**), "Art Social" (**Damien Loeb**, **Julian Schnabel**, **Ahn Duong**), "Actor" (**Sarah Jessica Parker**, **Parker Posey**, **Liev Schreiber**), "Television" (**George Whipple**, **Roshumba** from *Entertainment Tonight*), and "Model" (**Stephanie Seymour**, **Karen Elson**, and **Kylie Bax**). So we thought ourselves superior to the mundane task of stuffing, labeling, sealing, stamping, and mailing their invitations. Weren't we on their level?

Planning the party began as something of a joke, a hoax, just to see how much we could get away with. No one has a book

MARIE CLAIRE
PRESENTED
THE FAB CELEBRATION FOR THE FORTHCOMING BOOK
## "HOW TO BECOME FAMOUS IN TWO WEEKS OR LESS"
BY: MELISSA de la CRUZ & KAREN ROBINOVITZ
AT LOT 61

**What:** A glittery, exclusive bash feted contributing writers Melissa de la Cruz (author of the novel "Cat's Meow" and the chi-chi "The Fortune Hunters" fiction column of Gotham Magazine) and Karen Robinovitz (author of Clarkson Potter's forthcoming title, "Fete Accompli! The Ultimate Guide to Entertaining in Style," Contributing Editor at Elle, and feature writer for Harper's Bazaar).

The duo just finished their book, **"How to Become Famous in Two Weeks or Less"** (Ballantine, August 2003), a hilarious tale of how they clawed, begged, bribed, emailed, faxed, and air-kissed their way to fame, based on their much-gossiped about story for Marie Claire's August issue.

The girls, outfitted in sable coats from Christian Dior, diamonds from Jacob the Jeweler, and Valentino snakeskin clutches, arrived at Lot 61 with a gaggle of 20 Ford male models, driving Vespas.

80s pop star Laura Branigan performed "Gloria," "Self Control," and two new songs.

14 year-old spin-meister prodigy, Jonathan Shriftman (brother of powerhouse publicist Lara) DJ'd, fresh from his role in Fast & the Furious II.

Boxes of Krispy Crème Donuts, Aix's lavender marshmallows & cotton candy, and Alize's special cocktail Celebrity Passion were consumed.

**Guests:** **Foxy Brown, Janice Combs, Ingrid Seynhaeve, Ann & Annabelle Dexter Jones, Rita Schrager, model Ralph Jacobs, Designers Elissa Jimenez & Richie Rich, Fabien Cousteau, 20 Ford male models on Vespas**

**When:** Monday November 25, 2002
8-11pm

**Where:** Lot 61

**Photos:** Getty Images: www.gettyimagesnews.com
Image Direct: www.imagedirect.com
Patrick McMullan: www.patrickmcmullan.com

**Contact:** Ereka Dunn/Full Picture

*Send out a tip sheet with your party highlights to the press.*

*deal* party, just a book *launch* party. So the entire thing was a bit self-indulgent, which, we rationalized, is just what celebrity is all about. Plus, the fastest way to get press for yourself is through a glittery event. So our goal was to do something as glittery—and obnoxious—as possible. (After all, we wanted to write about it in our book! In this very chapter!)

Could we ride in on a horse, à la **Bianca Jagger**, circa 1978, Studio 54? "**Heidi** (**Klum**) did it last year," yawned Ereka Dunn, our swan-necked point-girl at Full Picture. Apparently horses were passé. "You need a grand entrance that's fresh," Dunn said, suggesting we arrive by Vespa—nay—a *fleet* of Vespas, twenty Vespas—driven by male models! A Vespa motorcade! Eye candy and Italian scooters!

Perfect. But we wanted more. If possible, a famous performer who would add luster to the whole enterprise. But who could we wrangle? As we contemplated, we got a random call from Steven Laitmon, Karen's college friend, a music manager. He wanted Karen to write about **Laura Branigan** of eighties top 40 "Gloria" heyday, because the songstress was trying to make a comeback. "I have the perfect opportunity," Karen yelled. "Our party!" We had just seen her on VH-1's *Behind the Music* tearfully recounting her grand past.

And just like that, Laura was in at no cost, as long as we got her a complimentary hotel room, designer outfit, and hair and makeup. No problem! By dropping Laura's name during calls made to the Regent Wall Street Hotel, **Alvin Valley**, a designer known for the slim-cut pants worn by **Gwyneth** and **Cameron**, and **Warren Tricomi**, she was all set. When we mentioned our idea to Mr. Laitmon to round up the Vespas, he yelled, "My father is the marketing guy behind the brand!"

Now all we needed were the models. Luckily, when we broached the subject to our work associate **Bill Ford** of Ford Models, he was feeling generous. Days later, we received a fax with a list of our future chauffeurs. We fought over who would ride with Travis, as in the Calvin Klein-underwear-model-on-Times-Square Travis, and were devastated to learn it was the *wrong* Travis. Apparently there are six male models named Travis, in Manhattan. Regardless, everything was falling into place and we even locked in celebrity DJ prodigy to spin at the party: fourteen-year-old **Jonathan Shriftman**, fresh from filming *Fast and the Furious II* and brother of PR princess **Lara Shriftman** of Harrison & Shriftman. **Lara** is a friend, and she flew him in from Florida—on a school night.

Buzz was starting. Rush and Molloy gave us a mention, offering NYC proof of our event. (If no one writes about your party, did it even happen? we wondered.)

So there we were in Karen's kitchen, attacking the invitations, papercuts and all. It turned out to be propitious, as there were three hundred more labels than invitations and *serious* reprioritizing was in order. The *Topeka News Herald* had merited one, but **Pia Getty**'s label lacked a home. Clearly, things were awry. We barked names to each other as we decided whether to "peel-and-replace" or "keep-and-seal." "Does **Magnus** deserve an invitation?" "Who's **Charles von Mueffling**?" We banished non–New York press to the trash (they wouldn't be in town anyway), while models whose names we recognized made the cut. **Malgosia**, **Sienna**, and **Karolina** were welcome, but **Ania**, **Kemp**, and **Kansas** were not.

As for our personal friends, who would actually *attend* the party, they got an e-vite, while A-listers like **Molly Sims** received the prized black cardstock in the mail. We begged PR pals to celebrity-wrangle for the event. "Please, can't you make **Courtney Love** come?" we whined to her rep. "No, she's filming

*Macbeth*," she replied. We were crushed to learn **Angie Harmon**'s flack did not return calls and that party perennial **Moby** was out of town. But actress **Dina Meyer** (who had an affair with Brandon on *90210*, to our mutual delight), socialites **Ann** and **Anabelle Jones**, **Fabian Cousteau** (grandson of **Jacques**, and according to *People* magazine, one of the sexiest men alive), somewhat made up for the loss when they RSVPd.

In our social-climbing fervor (**Rob** and **Marisol Thomas**! **Russell** and **Kimora Lee Simmons**!), we completely forgot to send an invitation to our literary agent. And two days before the party, Tanya Braganti, the photographer who was documenting the event for our book asked, "Um, do you think I'll get in? I didn't get an invitation." Worse, Melissa's husband was still sore that the party was scheduled on his birthday.

P-Day: we decided to capitalize on every aspect of the night, even getting ready. So at five P.M., **Edward Tricomi** himself and **Douglas Bielanski**, a **Sue Devitt** makeup artist, arrived at Karen's apartment to doll us up for the night. They brought along a photographer, who posted pictures of our primping on www.beauty.com (God forbid we get ready without a

*Why bother getting ready if the world isn't watching!*

fleet of cameras!). Edward, who is something of a celebrity himself (clients pay upwards of $300 to have him personally do their hair, and he's flown via private jet to tend to the stars' Oscar preparations), made quick decisions. "We'll do waves and a flip," he said, fluffing Melissa's hair. "And for you," he told Karen, "we'll do big and wild! Dynasty!" When Edward was done with us, we placed ourselves in front of Douglas, who promised smoky eyes, elegance, major drama, and the juiciest lips!

At eight-forty-five P.M., forty-five minutes after the party started, we met our model posse at the corner of Tenth Avenue and Twentieth Street. It was straight out of *Zoolander*: twenty poster boys on bubble gum–hued Vespas, lined up in a row, madly honking their horns and trying to pop wheelies (and failing). We hopped on the back of our designated scooters, posed for the camera crew who was tipped off (by us!) about the happening, and then made our way to the club . . . driving west on an east-bound street. (Nothing gets attention like going the wrong way down a one-way street!) It was the rush of a lifetime. Especially when we zoomed inside the center of the club, as our fourteen-year-old DJ blared Sheila E's "Glamorous Life" (he had to download it from the Internet the night before). Not bad for a girl who never had a date in high school (Melissa), or for one whom the boys nicknamed "Meatball" (Karen).

Flashbulbs exploded. Papparazzi yelled at us as if we were **Lizzie Grubman**, the uptown PR girl who pleaded guilty to mowing down sixteen people at a Southampton nightclub, making the first post-jail appearance. We were blinded from all angles. It was exhilarating to command so much attention. If this was life in the celebrity lane, we were never getting off! People treated us as if we were truly famous. Publicists propped us next to their famous clients for the cameras. *Victoria's Secret* ingenue **Ingrid Seynhaeve** put her spaghetti-thin arms around us. Impossibly blond **Janice Combs** (mother of **Puffy**) held court at our corner banquette (her publicist drove all the way to New Jersey to fetch her, and we bribed her with a free **Elisa Jimenez** couture gown to get her there!). Halfway through the evening, we were ushered to the front of the club in order to welcome **Foxy Brown**, who agreed to make a cameo. (We begged her publicist, a friend of Karen's, to drag her and it worked.) Our friends wanted to hug us, but they were unable to penetrate the paparazzi barrier.

Looking back, the entire night was a blur. We were pulled in a hundred different directions and we can honestly say that we don't recall one conversation or sitting still for a moment. So much for the free alcohol—we hardly had a sip. We didn't even get to eat one doughnut, though we posed holding a glazed number for a picture with Gap model **Ralph Jacobs**, who was eating one!

The biggest thrill of all was **Laura Branigan**, even though she had a diva moment or two before she performed (there was a fuss about how we had to hand her the microphone, as if we were going to hurl it at her). The woman hasn't been in the spotlight since the early '80s, but man, could she kick it! Everyone was dancing and singing along ("Gloria, Gloria. I think they got your numbah, Glo-ri-ah!"). She even pulled us on stage to sing "Happy Birthday" to Mike (Mel made up for having the party on the eve of his twenty-ninth year by surprising him with a cake and sparklers).

We were the belles of the ball. Until celebrity photographer

Traveling in style!

We couldn't wear helmets—
we'd ruin our hair.

"Zoolander," watch out! Our male-model motorcade. (We each thought, Why did she get a cuter model?)

Partying with Laura Branigan and Foxy Brown.

Celebrity shutterbug Patrick McMullan. We hope he remembers us next time!

With our fourteen-year-old DJ, who got more press than we did!

With model Ingrid Seynhaeve.
Could we _be_ any shorter?

"Gloria! Gloria!
I think they got your number, Gloria!"

Laura sang "Happy
Birthday" to Mike
(and Mel's forgiven).

ALL PHOTOS BY TANYA BRAGANTI

*We have arrived!*

TANYA BRAGANTI

**Patrick McMullan** dashed in and snapped shots of designers/ media darlings **Richie Rich** and **Elisa Jimenez**—and completely ignored us. He had no idea who we were, even though we've both met him dozens of times!

Our B-list status was confirmed the next day when www.people.com ran a photo of **Foxy Brown** on a Vespa outside our party . . . without even a hint of our faces, let alone our names. Page Six ran the same photo of **Foxy** (they at least put our names in bold, although we were secretly bummed that there was no photo). *TimeOut New York* wrote about our Vespa entrance, but once again, without a photo. The *New York Post* party section also printed a blurb about us, with no photo in sight. And in the piece, our DJ merited an entire paragraph. We were trumped by a fourteen-year-old from out of town!

Still. We pulled it off. The party received rave reviews. We should have been over the moon. We weren't. We couldn't shake the empty pits in our stomachs.

# POST-PARTY DEPRESSION

· · · · · · · · · · *Karen* · · · · · · · · · · · ·

*I* had a great time at the party and loved every second of it, especially the cutie who drove my Vespa. But during my cab ride home, alone, I was sad. Really, really sad. I wanted to have someone to share it with—and I didn't. All of the glitz and excitement is an amazing thing that I have been lucky to have, but the truth is, when you don't get to relax and have soulful downtime with someone you care about, it means nothing. Sure my best friends were there, but I hardly talked to them—or even saw them—I was so busy flitting about. During the party, everything was so superficial and "for show" that I didn't get to experience genuine connections with anyone.

At the end of the night, when things were calm, I went to look for some friends to catch up with them. They were gone. And I hardly had a moment to even say hello. I stayed in bed late the next day. It was as if I had a really bad hangover (and I didn't have a sip of anything harder than water). I couldn't work. I couldn't eat. And I couldn't believe what I was feeling:

lonely. It took me two days to shake the emotions, the crash after the high, which was so intense that I didn't even care when I had to return my (sinfully unworn) Dior threads.

When I called Mel for some sympathy (she was feeling similarly, minus the lonely thing, as she has a fabulous husband who loves her—and lets her shine), we talked about having a low-key book launch party in September 2003, after we hit the shelves at Barnes & Noble. Then we thought better of it: naaah! What's glamour without a little tragedy? Seconds later, we were thinking about wearing Versace and wondering which pop star we could get to entertain us!

. . . . . . . . . . . *Melissa* . . . . . . . . . .

*It* was all a little too much to deal with—and I was so relieved it was over. During the party preparations, I felt terrible about forgetting my husband's birthday. While I was excited for all the hoopla, I also wished we were spending the day together and celebrating his birthday properly. The best part of the evening for me was when Laura asked us up on stage to sing "Happy Birthday" to Mike. He had no idea that was going to happen and I was so glad to have pulled off the surprise.

All the attention is gratifying, but if you live by the scene, you die by the scene. While we were able to generate all this hype for one night, with a wave of a wand (or a flash of a camera), it was all gone by morning. Like modern-day Cinderellas, our diamonds and couture gowns disappeared in a poof, courtesy of messengers who came to claim the borrowed wares the next day. I wonder if I would be able to keep my head on straight if everything was happening for real, and not just as the hoax that we pulled off. The party was a fabulous dream—but like everybody else, I have to wake up and take the subway in the morning.

## marie claire

presents

One Fabulously Glamorous Night
(so put on your bling-bling and get ready for your close-up)
To celebrate the forthcoming book

'How to Become Famous in Two Weeks or Less'
by
Melissa de la Cruz & Karen Robinovitz

November 25, 2002
Lot 61
550 West 21st St.
8-11 pm

Special performance by Laura 'Gloria' Branigan
Music by Spin-meister Prodigy Jonathan Shriftman

RSVP: Full Picture 212.627.0001 ext. 109

Special thanks to: Ballantine Books, Ford Models, Jacob & Co. (a.k.a. Jacob the Jeweler) and Vespa

*Our invitation for the party.*

# HOW TO PRODUCE
# PRESS-WORTHY EVENTS

• Turn your birthday party into an extravaganza. Be over the top. When it comes to parties, less is never more. Make a grand entrance on a horse, just like Bianca Jagger did at her Studio 54 bash.

• Invite every media person you can think of, whether you know them or not. Have your "publicist" follow up with them to make sure they come—and pitch them a story about your party. Just make sure you have an angle for a story about your party, a newsworthy hook. Do something different at your party that no one else is doing in order to make the angle appealing (i.e., have a silent party, where no one can talk and communication occurs via note passing).

• Send out a tip sheet, a one-page memo to editors everywhere that details the highlights of your party: performances, noteworthy guests, what you'll be wearing.

• Don't spare a single expense while celebrating yourself. Charter a yacht. Fly friends to a destination on a private jet if you can arrange it.

• Get ambulances to shepherd guests home (Pamela Anderson did this for Tommy Lee's birthday).

• Roll out a red carpet. Install velvet ropes. Produce a laser light show outside. It draws a crowd.

• Hire dancers, naked waiters, celebrity look-alikes. Then leak all the juicy details to gossip columnists and press people. Have your publicist call newsmagazine shows and pitch the idea of extravagant birthdays of the fabulous.

• Piggyback with a charity. Make a baby shower a fundraiser for poor orphans in some third-world country. You'll be able to have a good time while doing good. If possible, hook up with an organization that has star power, like amfAR and DIFFA. Maybe you'll be able to swing a celebrity cohost and you can both tell people, "I just want to give back."

• Get a corporate sponsor, which is when a company backs the party (financially) and gets kudos on the invitation. They may even help find a charity to partner with and make a donation in a celebrity name, thus ensuring the celebrity will appear at your party. This will elevate your event to a new level of glory.

• Hire a company that specializes in getting celebrities and well-known figures to events. These are called talent booking agencies. They do wonders, but they charge a pretty penny.

• Stage a guerrilla renegade party, where your soiree takes place at the same time and location as a highly hyped and anticipated event. You'll upstage it and everyone will talk.

• Throw your party at a space before it opens. People always like to go to the latest hot spot before anyone else. The press will be all over it.

• Be a culture vulture. Organize readings, plays, performances, and art openings. The arts are a great way to get involved and in print, as journalists always cover such happenings.

# SUNDAY
# NEW YORK POST

## Page Six .com
### Richard Johnson
With Paula Froelich
and Chris Wilson

## Snaps
## The late show
By JEFFREY SLONIM

At Lot 61, Marie Claire magazine feted a book deal that came about from one of their articles: "How to Become Famous in Two Weeks or Less" by Melissa de la Cruz and Karen Robinovitz. To spin, The Post's Karen Robinovitz. To spin, 14-year-old deejay Jonathan Shriftman (p.r. princess Lara's brother) flew in from Florida, where he still attends high school.

*Matthew Peyton/Getty Images*

**‹PREVIOUS I NE**

**FEELING FOXY:**
Singer Foxy Brow
arrives at the boo
party release for
To Become Fam
Two Weeks Or Less" in
New York City on a
foxy red Vespa.
(Matthew Peyton/Getty
Images)

**Foxy Brown** revs her engines at the book launch at Lot 61 for "How to Become Famous in Two Weeks or Less" by **Melissa de la Cruz** and **Karen Robinovitz**.

*This picture from our party also ran on people.com!*

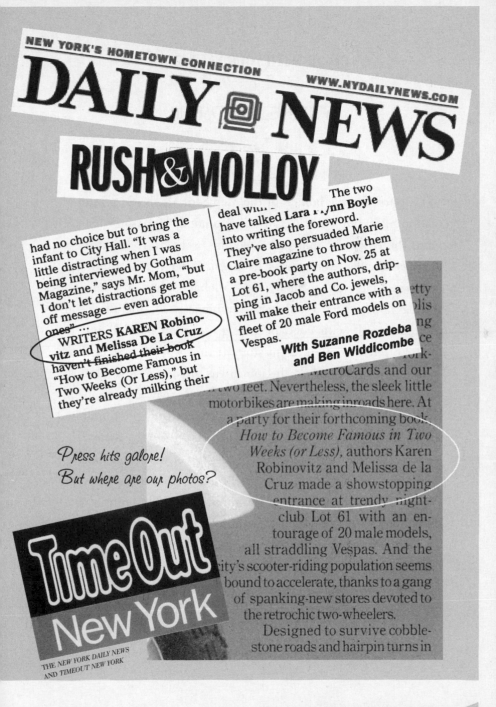

**NEW YORK'S HOMETOWN CONNECTION**

# DAILY ◉ NEWS

WWW.NYDAILYNEWS.COM

## RUSH & MOLLOY

had no choice but to bring the infant to City Hall. "It was a little distracting when I was being interviewed by Gotham Magazine," says Mr. Mom, "but I don't let distractions get me off message — even adorable ones" ...

WRITERS **KAREN** Robino-vitz and Melissa De La Cruz haven't finished their book "How to Become Famous in Two Weeks (Or Less)," but they're already milking their

deal with ... The two have talked **Lara Flynn Boyle** into writing the foreword. They've also persuaded Marie Claire magazine to throw them a pre-book party on Nov. 25 at Lot 61, where the authors, dripping in Jacob and Co. jewels, will make their entrance with a fleet of 20 male Ford models on Vespas.

**With Suzanne Rozdeba and Ben Widdicombe**

... MetroCards and our ...two feet. Nevertheless, the sleek little motorbikes are making inroads here. At a party for their forthcoming book, *How to Become Famous in Two Weeks (or Less),* authors Karen Robinovitz and Melissa de la Cruz made a showstopping entrance at trendy night-club Lot 61 with an en-tourage of 20 male models, all straddling Vespas. And the city's scooter-riding population seems bound to accelerate, thanks to a gang of spanking-new stores devoted to the retrochic two-wheelers.

Designed to survive cobble-stone roads and hairpin turns in

*Press hits galore!*
*But where are our photos?*

# Time Out
## New York

THE NEW YORK DAILY NEWS
AND TIMEOUT NEW YORK

# STRIKE A POSEUR

* * * * * * * * * * * *Karen* * * * * * * * * * * *

At a party for the launch of the Mercedes Maybach, a limited-edition $250,000 vehicle, Lara Shriftman of Harrison & Shriftman, the company that produced the event, introduced me to Michael Michele, the actress from *ER*. After a few minutes of chitchat, I cut right to the chase: "Michael, what's the secret to getting famous?" I asked her. Her biggest tips included: surround yourself with good people; go to good parties; and get photographed as often as possible. If that was all it took, I felt confident that I could do the job. I was already at a good party, surrounded by good people. I just had to be seen and immortalized on film with some of them. Sadly, I wasn't photographed with Michael because the paparazzi mafia pulled her away from me and asked her to stand alone at the top of the spiral staircase for some pictures. Damn them! As I took notes on her posture, in awe of her poise, grace, and Carolina Herrera ensemb, a commotion began: Jay-Z was in the house!

Camera flashes flickered so wildly at him, you would have thought we were at a Pink Floyd, "The Wall," show. I forged ahead by elbowing a few innocent bystanders out of the way and managed to stand right next to Jay-Z. He put his arm around me, as if we had been friends for years, and the cameras kept on snapping. After our intimate interlude, I told him my name.

Within seconds we were canoodling. (Okay, we just shook hands, but at least it was skin-on-skin contact, which has catapulted many others to the top.) I surveyed the room in search of more paparazzi moments to crash. I spotted Kimora Lee Simmons, the model wife of music mogul Russell and a favorite subject of camera crews. She was talking to someone I knew, so I went in for the kill. Before I could say, "Hi, I'm Karen," the photographers caught wind of the situation and attacked. I did the same with Eleanor Lambert, the doyenne of fashion publicity, and once again, a lensman noticed and hit the almighty red button of his camera. I successfully pounced in on four other Kodak moments and gave my name and card to the photographers, so they'd know exactly who I was in the future.

The climax of the evening was slated for ten P.M., when the Mercedes-clan unveiled the actual car, which was to be dramatically revealed by airlifting a velvet tapestry from the specimen's frame. At precisely nine-forty-five, I smooth-talked a VP of Mercedes, informed him of my plight for fame, and begged him to let me see the car before anyone else. I thought that if someone witnessed the fact that I was getting a special sneak peak, then they'd think I was *someone*. It worked. As he escorted me to a roped-off back area, where the car was on display, a herd of camera wielders followed. Dozens of photos were taken of the Mercedes bigwig and me shaking hands in front of the car, which I saw before anyone! By the time I exited the party thirty minutes later, I heard a paparazzi guy yell, "Karen, over here. Karen!" as if I were the main event. I turned around to flash a smile, thinking, *They bought it! I'm on my way!* Then I realized he was holding my wallet, which had fallen out of my bag.

# CHINK IN THE ARMOR

· · · · · · · · · · · *Melissa* · · · · · · · ·

*I* know I'm Asian. But I'm also Filipino, which means I'm a mutt—one-sixteenth Spanish, a quarter Chinese, and who knows what else. Some people can't even gauge my ethnicity correctly. They ask if I'm "mixed," which to a Filipino is always a compliment. Ah, we do like our mestizos. A lingering colonial mentality has made this so. Generally, I approve of my looks. I don't attempt faux insecurity about them. The problem is my eyes. They tend to slant when I smile. Not just slightly upward, no. They turn into tiny folded slits, pushed up by my cheeks, making my face resemble that of a chortling Buddha.

When I first received the proofs of the photographs taken during my two weeks of fame, I was appalled. I looked ghastly in each of them. There I was laughing over a glass of wine at a restaurant, or else mugging for the camera while flanked by two models, or greeting guests at my dinner party, and in all of them I flashed the Buddha smile. When I have a lot of fun, I show it. I don't stop and "pose" for pictures. Instead, I carry on just as usual, laughing, smiling, my eyes steadily getting smaller and smaller in each successive shot.

Why do famous people always look good in pictures? Because they have learned to restrain their impulses—to present an artificial, more attractive version of their face to the camera. No one naturally smiles with big eyes, flashing teeth, and their chin thrust down and forward in a flattering angle. Maybe those who are blessed with photogenica do. But most of us, when happy, let down our guard. We smile naturally, eyes crinkling, chin wobbling, letting the cameras click away without paying attention to what we look like. And that's where the unattractive photographs come in.

As you can imagine, it's not much fun trying to look like you're having fun while you're really trying to remember to open your eyes wide, keep your chin down, and shut your mouth so you don't flash your crooked teeth. For two weeks I concentrated on being alert at all times, so I could present the "face of fame" to the camera.

Sometimes, though, I couldn't do the game face. I decided that I didn't really care all that much. As narcissistic as I can be, at the end, I didn't want to sacrifice a good night out at the altar of vanity. Even if I knew that when the pictures were published, I'd complain, "I look terrible! My eyes are slits!" at least I'll look at them and know that I was having a blast. Even if I looked constipated.

# PHOTO SHOP

**EVERYTHING YOU NEED TO KNOW ABOUT SMILING FOR THE CAMERA**

- There is no such thing as being ugly—only badly lit, as Barbra Streisand will attest. (The diva brings her own lighting and camera crew to everything—even the Oscars—to make sure she is dewy-looking at all times.)

- Consider carrying low-wattage lightbulbs wherever you go and pull the ol' switcheroo on the sly. Dimmer lights are more flattering than bright fluorescent ones.

- Clench your teeth together for all photos. It enhances your jawline and makes it appear more pronounced.

- Use Visine before posing. It will make your eyes look whiter.

- Stand at an angle with one leg slightly in front of the other in order to narrow your silhouette.

- Stand on the left of any photo opportunity. In magazines, when they print pictures, they always name names from left to right. If you can, force your way next to the person whom the picture is *really* about. That way, your name will have top billing.

- Cozy up to paparazzi photographers who cover the best parties. As they get to know you, they will start to take your photo.

- Look your best. Don't leave home without full hair, makeup and the latest coup of your shopping excursions. Studios yell at actresses who show up at premieres with sloppy suits and bad hair. Do not let that happen to you.

# TV OR NOT TV, THAT IS THE QUESTION

## NO DOUGHNUTS IN THE GREENROOM?

· · · · · · · · · · · · *Melissa* · · · · · · · · · · · ·

*A*s I mentioned earlier, I had crashed my fiancé's bachelor party dressed as a man for an article in *Marie Claire*. This nefarious activity transformed Mike and me into must-have guests on the daytime television talk-show circuit. Producers from programs of such caliber as *The Ananda Lewis Show* and *The Other Half* begged us to appear on the air. With great reluctance, we agreed. (Actually . . . we weren't that reluctant. We couldn't wait to see ourselves on TV!) We called everyone we knew, telling them about our imminent appearances, only to be met with puzzled glances. "Who's Amanda Lewis?" "The other *what?*" Nobody I knew had ever heard of these shows. "What happened to *Good Morning America?*" my mother would ask in an indignant tone. (We had been scheduled to appear, only to be bumped at the last minute, and my parents were still sore because they had spread the word to all of their friends and coworkers, only to be shown up as liars when the segment got cut. They have yet to live down the shame.)

For some reason, I was under the delusion that as honored guests of Ananda Lewis, we would be treated with first-class service all the way. In the beginning it boded well—Mike and I were thrilled when the black Town Car appeared at our door. We eagerly flipped through the free magazines tucked into the backseat. *People! Vanity Fair!* This was the life! When we arrived at the studio, housed in a bunkerlike warehouse building with *CBS* engraved on the front doors, a gloved doorman opened the car door, and a headset-wearing production assistant escorted us to the Ananda floor. Each guest was "assigned" his own PA (production assistant), as we were not allowed to wander around freely on our own.

Our first inkling that appearing on *Ananda* was not going to be as glamorous as we'd hoped was the contents of our greenroom. Where were the bouquets of flowers I'd heard *Today* show guests always received? The platters of appetizers, hors d'oeuvres and doughnuts Oprah's stars chomped on? In my imagination, greenroom doughnuts of the celeb talk-show circuit had assumed mythical status. But it was not meant to be. Instead, we had to make do with two dry turkey sandwiches, a few wan grapes, and a minuscule chocolate square. Plus, we had to buy our own Cokes from the soda machine down the hall!

After we were suitably coiffed and pancaked at the hair-and-makeup stand, we were called to the set, where we spent another hour watching the "preshow" from backstage. A dancing midget—apparently a "professional audience member" who is *paid* to attend daytime talk shows and clap herself silly—performed a lip-synch version of Britney Spears's "Oops! I Did It Again" to warm up the audience. Mike and I turned to each other in horror.

We had been there for four hours and had yet to meet Ananda. Five minutes before the show started, she swooped through and gave all her invited guests a brief hello, without even stopping to shake our hands. She looked fantastic—creamy mocha skin, perfect hair, and vertiginous heels—every inch the aloof star.

Mike and I were the first segment, and after a brief introduction ("What really happens during the groom's bachelor party? Woo hoo!"), we entered the shabby set. I am still amazed at the power of television. Everything looked so much better on the monitor. In real life the set is small and dirty. The carpet looked like it had never been vacuumed. In fact, the only thing that doesn't look good on TV is real people. Mike and I looked chunky and pasty on the monitor. Ananda looked like a goddess. No wonder she was famous.

"So, Melissa . . . tell us about what you saw at the *strip club*!" she said, widening her eyes. The audience made a scandalized *"Ooooh"* sound. I stared back at her in absolute terror, my mind blank, stammering my answers. I was stricken with stage fright, my eyes wide as saucers. My answers were curt and incoherent. I mumbled something about being "too numb to understand what was going on" and I failed to follow the one directive we were given by the producers ("Never stop talking . . . dead air kills"). Mercifully, it was over in a few minutes.

We were escorted out of the building by our production assistant, who cheerfully deposited us on the sidewalk. The Town Car was nowhere to be seen. We didn't even get a free ride home. So much for being "invited guests."

A month later, when we appeared on *The Other Half*, we prided ourselves on our lowered expectations. But sadly, we did not lower them enough! The greenrooms were again lacking in doughnuts, let alone soggy turkey sandwiches. For refreshment purposes backstage, there was a half-eaten bag of pretzels and bottled generic-label water. I had also been told that the show would provide hair and makeup for us, but when we arrived in the dressing room, the two beauticians scolded us for not showing up camera-ready. They chewed their gum and boasted that they had been nominated for an Emmy Award for their work on the show. We congratulated them and wished they wouldn't smoke in our faces while they blow-dried.

Mike and I were also a little uncomfortable with the tenor of the program. The producer of the show had sold it as a fun morning show, but backstage was populated by a roster of freaks, including particularly unattractive young couples who were on the segment on "the disadvantages of reproduction." I guess we should count ourselves lucky.

When we were brought onstage, we noticed that the studio audience held fifteen people—and five of them were my relatives! (I had assuaged my parents by getting them free tickets.) On the bright side, Mario Lopez (formerly "Slater" from *Saved By the Bell*) and Danny Bonaduce were a lot warmer and friendlier than Ananda, and Mike and I, clocking in our third television appearance, were chatty and glib like two old pros. Mike even made a joke that got the whole audience laughing. At the end of the segment, we were rushed out of the studio—but not before my aunt tracked down Dick Clark for an autograph.

# YOU CAN'T SAY THAT
# ON TELEVISION!

## Karen

Gail Parenteau, a PR guru and talent agent who represents model/*Entertainment Tonight* correspondent Roshumba, approached me one day to find out if I was media trained, which is industry-speak for "skilled in front of the camera." Being media trained, to some extent, is natural for some, but being proficient about technicalities, such as working with an earpiece in a studio while talking to newscasters via satellite, requires education and practice. "You'd be great on TV. I just know it," she said. She went on to tell me about satellite media tours, a new wave of television whereby someone hosts a segment by way of satellite, which is then broadcast to dozens of shows. It is really a marketing gig, albeit one that can pay up to $20,000 for a few hours of work. Besides, this was my chance to get on about twenty morning news shows in one day. If that's not fame, what is?

This is how it works. A company, like a toothpaste brand, will pay a satellite media firm to find an appropriate "talent" to talk about the product in a flattering way. The firm, in turn, contacts television stations across the country and pitches them a segment idea that revolves around the toothpaste (maybe it's what brand celebs are using or how to get a Janet Jackson smile on the cheap—insider Hollywood tips). These pieces are filmed live, and while they require only four to five minutes of being on camera, the challenge for the talent is to say the right thing, making the few specified points in a subtle and poignant manner, in a very short period of time . . . without coming across as being too PR-y.

Gail informed me that I'd have to "start low—four thousand dollars or so—because you're new, but I'd love to get you going with this," she said. Four grand! Just enough for the Dior leather jacket I coveted! If that was starting low, I was game— even if Gail would get the requisite 15-percent agent fee. I had made two television cameos (refer to pp. 31–32) in the past, but I figured I had learned my lessons and would never make a stupid mistake on camera again. "I'm not media trained," I confessed, "but I've definitely done my share of television work."

After an interview with the satellite media company, I was hired to talk about "getting the celebrity beauty secrets on the cheap." The day before the tour began, I was introduced to the three products I'd be plugging and the three to five points to make about each. It sounded simple in theory. We began to rehearse. Everything seemed to run smoothly. The hair product smelled great because of the grapeseed oil; the skin care regimen was quick and easy: the cleanser removed dirt and makeup, and the cream was packed with SPF 30 and vitamins E, C, and D; and the toothbrush, a $10 battery-operated number, was equipped with fixed and oscillating bristles and was just as good as the $100 electric version—just brush three minutes every morning and three minutes every night and you'll be smiling like Courteney Cox in no time.

I thought I'd have no problem at five o'clock the next morning when the real shows began. But when you have only forty-five seconds to discuss the individual products—in front of a blank wall because you're in a studio, removed from the station that's broadcasting you—and you're working with an earpiece and bouncing off of a faint voice through a wire, I quickly discovered how difficult doing media tours could be.

I had to do my few-minute bit repeatedly for five straight hours, one after the other after the other. And because the segments were live, they had to be perfect. If I had the hiccups or an uncontrollable yawn, the entire viewing audience was going to be a part of that magic. The pressure was on. My first time was . . . well . . . average. I got a little nervous . . . okay, very nervous. In fact, the words got so mumbled as they emerged from my mouth that I actually screeched (loudly!), "Aaaaah," to center myself and continue. I could tell that the team who monitored everything from behind the two-way mirror was not happy with my performance. I felt like an Olympic-gold-bound gymnast who nails her routines perfectly during practice and falls smack on her head on the beam when competition begins.

By round three, however, I was getting the hang of it. As time passed, it got easier. Until round twelve in Salt Lake City. I was feeling so loose and natural that my real personality came out. I stopped acting in a staged way and began to talk to the camera as if it were my friend. "Who the hell wants to use three types of products to cleanse in the morning instead of one?" I asked. I even threw in the perfect catchphrase they all wanted me to say: "Turn into a drugstore cowgirl and you'll be red-carpet ready—without breaking the bank—in no time!" I smiled in triumph.

On the break, the producer emerged from his box behind the two-way mirror. He was red in the face and screaming, "You can't say 'hell' in Salt Lake City! What were you thinking?"

"Did I say that?" I asked.

"You did. Come see this tape," he barked. I watched in horror at my mistake. The H-word was so pronounced, it was as if it were the only thing I uttered. H-E-L-L! It echoed in my brain. "It must have slipped," I said, "I'm sorry."

I felt like such a failure for the rest of the day. Being the perfectionist that I am, I tortured myself over my faux pas. But when I got a copy of my reel, there was a bit from CNN that rocked. I killed! In one three-minute chunk of time, I nailed all of the points the media-tour client wanted me to make, and I added in a few celebrity Botox jokes, to boot. I looked natural on camera. I was bubbly without being annoying. My red sweater looked fantastic on air. My hair and makeup looked ideal. I was so confident through my segment that I even did "the lean" with my right elbow on the display table. As I signed off, the CNN reporter said with a laugh, "Easy for her to say all that—she looks like she's twenty-four." There it was—words of approval for all the world to hear. My mother called me, screaming, "My famous daughter, my famous daughter! You were gorgeous on air. You even wore the right bra!"

I have such an amazing segment on film from CNN that a producer from MTV saw it and called to talk about putting me on the air. And another producer wants to set up a meeting to possibly develop my own show! So who the hell cares if I made a few mistakes along the way?

# TELEVISION APPEARANCES

It's not enough to smile and have good posture in order to look great on TV. There's an entire science to how to stand, where to stare, and how to carry yourself so you don't look like a novice—or a fool. Here's how to get with the program.

• Wear solid colors. They show up better on camera than prints. Try not to go all-black, as it may wash you out on camera. And avoid white at all costs. It looks ghastly on TV.

• Don't trust mirrors. Take a Polaroid before you go on air to make sure you look okay.

• Record your voice with a tape recorder and listen to it. Watch out for pronunciation mishaps and perfect them before you go live. Also, on camera you should never talk too quickly. Pace yourself at a rate of roughly ten seconds for every fifteen words.

• Don't look directly into the camera. Instead, talk to the host or whomever speaks to you. And if you're being filmed in a studio, sans interviewer, act as if someone is standing to the right of the camera, pick a spot on the wall, and talk to it.

• Make a concerted effort to restrain from fidgeting and indulging in nervous habits like hair twirling, cuticle picking, scratching, and touching the part of your body that is close to the microphone clip (that hinders the sound).

• Be expressive. Use your hands. You have to be "on."

• When crossing your legs while sitting, point them at an angle, preferably toward the host (it makes for inviting body language). If your legs directly face the camera, they will look fat.

• If all else fails, seek media training. There are companies that will school you on everything you need to learn from A to Z, though it might cost $1,500.

## IT'S ALL ABOUT IMAGE

# WHAT'S IN A NAME?

• • • • • • • • • *Karen* • • • • • • • •

*B*y night four of our two-week challenge, I was so down with the program that it became natural for me to breeze right past the velvet ropes as if I were born to be inside. When I walked with such confidence (and a very short skirt), no one stopped me. On my journey of nights out, I wound up in the VIP room of a club called Suite Sixteen, a plush den with red banquettes that often double as the dance floor for hard-partying players. I chatted up the club's owners, Noah and Jason, two well-connected, twenty-something club promoters/marketeers who have an impressive Rolodex bigger than the waiting list for a Balenciaga handbag. The guys mentioned something about the birthday party I recently had—and the fact that it was covered in the *New York Post*.

"We want to know if you'd host our year-anniversary party," they asked. Hosting that kind of event really means nothing more than, "Can we put your name on the invitation?" And the fact that they asked to use my name in order to kick the party appeal up a notch confirmed that there was K.Ro hype and it was spreading. For the sake of continuing to put myself out there, I said yes (it was an honor to just be nominated). We celebrated with a bottle of Cristal. After two glasses, I pulled a high-maintenance act and asked for some things I, the host, wanted: a table in the middle of the VIP area, enough free champagne to satisfy my entourage of ten, and car service to and from the event. They agreed to my terms (if you count "take a taxi" as providing car service). And we shook hands to seal the deal.

The following week, over two thousand sleek blue-and-white invitations were mailed to the city's coolest hipsters, models, socialites, and celebs, including Mark Wahlberg, Alicia Silverstone, and Ralph Fiennes. The party would certainly be covered in all of the gossip sections, and there would be no way they could dutifully write about it without mentioning that I was hosting. Soon everyone would know me. My answering machine was flooded with phone messages from people who got the invitation and couldn't believe that I, the girl who always leaves the party first, was hosting such a wild (and late) night. Even my parents, who live in Florida, heard the news and called me. "Our famous daughter is hosting a party and we weren't invited!" (The son of a family friend told his parents, who spread the rumor to mine!)

I was ecstatic.

Then I took a close look at the invitation. My name was misspelled! Instead of Robinovitz, I was Rabinovitz. I was sick to

Noah Tepperberg and Jason Strauss
cordially invite you to celebrate the
One Year Anniversary of

## Suite 16
127 Eighth Avenue at 16th Street

## Thursday April 4th 2002

Music by Jus Ske / RSVP or Reservations 212.420.9420
Festivities Begin at 10pm / Hosted by Karen Rabinovitz

*Such a faux pas!*

my stomach, recalling something Madonna once said: "It doesn't matter if you get good press or bad press . . . as long as they spell your name right." Oops.

# LANDING ON SKID ROW

•  •  •  •  •  •  •  •  •  •  *Melissa*  •  •  •  •  •  •  •  •  •  •

$\mathcal{I}$t was the first time I was going to be on TV. The publicist for my novel had booked me and Kim DeMarco, my friend and the illustrator of the book, on a local talk show called, and I kid you not, *Jersey's Talking!* We were psyched! We'd never been on television before. Who cared if it was a local channel in the wilds of New Jersey, accessible only to those within a ten-mile radius of exit 11. At least it wasn't cable access! We were on a bona fide news program. My publisher sent a limousine to pick us up. Three hours later we were lost on the Jersey Turnpike. I kept calling the show's producer to get directions. When we finally arrived at the studio, Kim and I were surprised at how laid-back everyone was. They didn't even seem to care that we were late! They waved us over to the taping as if we had just strolled in for a chat.

The studio consisted of a panel, a backdrop, and two chairs. The host was a genial gray-haired gentleman. We were going to be on right after a lady NASCAR driver, who was droning on about her life "on the track." Kim and I watched the lady NASCAR driver on the monitors. She was wearing a bright yellow suit jacket, full makeup, and big hair. Sounds frightening, right? But she looked *incredible* on television. It was my first inkling that maybe, just maybe, I should have left my Skid Row T-shirt at home.

My novel was about a kooky fashionista—someone who'd wear thigh-high boots, ostritch feathers, and a hooded sweatshirt to the supermarket, and I wanted to embody the spirit of the character—the cheeky irony and offhand cool of mixing several different "influences" in one outfit. Which is why I was wearing a rhinestone-studded Skid Row concert T-shirt and a choker of chunky Chanel pearls for my first television appearance. It was ironic chic! High-low! Low-fi! Fi fi! I thought I looked the bomb.

The Nascar lady was done, and Kim and I were invited up to the panel. Two assistants "miked" us. They clipped tiny microphones to our shirt collars, the wires snaking down our backs underneath to receivers we stuffed down our pants. The host greeted us amiably. Kim and I sat down and got comfortable. They asked us to speak into our mikes to test them. Suddenly a voice from the control room sounded: "It's not going to work."

The host shook his head. "You"—he motioned—"you've got to take off the pearls; they're clanking against the microphone."

Take off the pearls? Excuse me? If I took off the pearls, my whole high-low, low-fi, ironic chic fashion statement was nil. Boof. Nada. If I took off the pearls, I would be making my first television appearance . . . in a Skid Row T-shirt! Without the pearls, I would cease to be a fashionista and just look like . . . *a metalhead!*

Which is exactly how I made my first television appearance. In a stupid Skid Row T-shirt. I looked like an overweight teen who still had a fixation for Sebastian Bach. My entire glamorous and fun persona was stripped away with my pearls, which were not TV-appropriate and microphone-friendly. Next time I'm on TV, I'll be wearing big hair, full makeup, and a bright yellow suit jacket.

## IMAGE CONTROL!
### HOW TO MANAGE YOUR PERSONA AND BECOME AN ICON

• Overexposure is a no-no. When you're in the media too much, you will be known as a press whore. And no one will take you seriously. Backlash is not pretty.

• As you acquire fame, pick and choose your events carefully. You never want to wind up with the adjective *ubiquitous* before your name.

• As you reach full-blown fame, associate with people who will enhance your reputation, even if you can't stand them. Stick to parties where the guest list is at your level—or above.

• Only date up. You don't want to canoodle with anyone who's beneath you in the totem pole (horizontal canoodling, however, is acceptable).

• If you don't have something nice to say, say it in private. You will be slammed for slamming others publicly.

• Learn the art of announcing, "No comment," with grace.

• Hold your liquor. You don't want a reputation as a hard-partying drunk.

• Make sure people spell your name right. (See Karen's anecdote pp. 171–172.)

- Always have a good lawyer on your side.

- If you do something stupid—and get negative attention for it—hire a publicist who specializes in controlling your media image.

- If none of these things is working well for you, screw up your image (release an X-rated tape of you and your boyfriend, peddle it on-line, and then make a public statement about how someone must have broken into your home, stolen it, and violated you). Once you have the attention of your peers, you can strategically change your image and become everyone's sweetheart.

*Days 10–12:*

# THE SCHMOOZE FACTOR

The schmooze is part flattery, part small talk, and 100 percent charm. If you're a wallflower, shake off that caterpillar shell and make a 180-degree turn to social butterfly. Only people who are incredibly famous can afford to become hermits, like JD Salinger, who is so famous for being a recluse that he has made his daughter, his son, and his estranged former eighteen-year-old mistress famous, too. Unless you're planning to become a notoriously moody literary phenomenon, a critically praised legend who writes novels that are studied in high school English classes, you're going to need some help. In this world of ego and ambition, staking your claim on fame is about having a larger-than-life personality—one that sucks the oxygen out of any room and guarantees all eyes will always be on you. You'll need to learn how to chat it up, so practice your exuberant "Hello, so lovely to meet yous" in front of the mirror before you take it public. Put on a happy face, perfect interesting—but inoffensive—opinions, and manufacture a likable, extroverted, captivating persona that will not only enable you to meet tons of people, but—better yet—make tons of people want to meet you.

This chapter will serve as your instruction sheet to schmoozing, the time-honored techniques that will serve you well in your pursuit of stardom. You'll learn whom to schmooze from the bottom to the top rung of any social ladder. Today's assistant editor is tomorrow's executive producer, so don't forget to keep close and friendly ties with those who have potential to make it, even if they're interns when you first encounter them.

These pages will also teach you to take note of your social environment. Are you hanging out with friends who can possibly help you on your way to iconization? Fame is a phenomenon that is often bestowed on groups at a time—Jack Kerouac, Allen Ginsberg, and William S. Burroughs were deadbeat Ivy Leaguers who used to hang out in cold-water tenements, shoot heroin, and write poetry, but they all became famous together once one of them hit the spotlight. When John Goodman, Dana Delany, and Bruce Willis were struggling actors, they hung out together at a bar on the Upper West Side, singing piano tunes until the wee hours of the morning. Naturally, when one was "discovered," it was just a matter of time before Hollywood found the other two (after all, they were standing right next to each other).

Once you have the schmooze down pat, we will teach you to use your new talent to build a network of helpful contacts. While schmoozing successfully will make you likable, your contacts will make you famous. But you have to be careful not to go overboard and fall into the trap of overschmoozing, which can quickly backfire and brand you a grasping social climber, a reputation you can definitely live without. But don't worry; we will explain all of the things you need to avoid doing so you never come off as an insincere, sycophantic player who's only out for herself.

Time to get started. You're only a handshake, a hilarious anecdote, and a few strategically placed compliments away from being the next big thing!

## TALK OF THE TOWN

# PHONE(Y)!

### *Karen*

When I began my writing career, the best piece of advice I ever received was from a famous writer I had the pleasure of meeting on the subway. He told me, "This business is about who you know. So start schmoozing." I was always the kind of kid who played well with others. I have a bold personality. I strike up a conversation with anybody—the man who bags my groceries, the intimidating boss, even the hot guy at the bar. If "making it" was a result of social skills, I was golden. So I picked up the phone and began cold-calling magazine editors to schmooze my way into getting an assignment. At first I didn't have much luck. I left very upbeat, chatty messages on various voice mails, always making sure to compliment the person I contacted. ("Hi, this is Karen Robinovitz. I'm a freelance writer. I have a ton of ideas that I think would be perfect for you. And I just love your section. It would be a privilege to contribute. I look forward to talking to you soon and possibly working together. Thank you.") Almost nobody returned my calls. It was discouraging. But I refused to let it get me down.

One afternoon, after yet another editorial rejection, I caught *The Secret of My Success* on Lifetime, television for women. It's that Michael J. Fox movie about a small-town kid who schmoozes his way to the top in the big city. I was inspired. I turned off my TV and vowed that persistence would be my savior. So I kept calling and calling and calling what I hoped would become my future contacts. I was diligent about following up with people once a week. I began to leave hints of my ideas on answering machines to try to entice them. I faxed. I sent e-mails. I messengered detailed letters. And eventually people returned my calls— and gave me work.

At the onset, my assignments were small—how to handle hair on the nipples, a one-hundred-word piece on the legalization of garbage disposals in New York City, and a breakdown of the multisyllabic words used by Pamela Anderson and Tommy Lee in their much-hyped sex tape. I had to prove myself and build my reputation. In time, little pieces led to large features and, within months, I was getting published on a regular basis. The more articles I wrote, the more editors called me back. I landed a column at *Marie Claire*, and when my editor left the magazine to work for another, we had built such a chummy, schmoozy relationship that she put me on contract to pen monthly features for her. I made sure to keep my relationships friendly and positive. The magazine business is not a strict and conservative one. Staffers wear jeans and talk about orgasms in office meetings. Many of my appointments with editors and other writers revolved around long chats about the latest restaurant opening, dating traumas, and the minutiae of our daily lives. What can I say . . . I have a gift for gab. Before I knew it, I was writing full-time, breaking into all of the magazines I had always dreamed of working for.

Except for one, which I'll call *Magazine X*. For some reason, I could not penetrate my one and only contact at that publication (we'll call her J). I met J at a dinner party and mentioned, casually, that I'd love to write for her. "Call me with ideas," she said. "We're always looking." While this might be a sort of polite, off-the-cuff thing to say—no different from "Stay in touch"—I took her words as a sign of encouragement. I combed through the pages of the magazine each month to get a genuine understanding for their niche. Then I began to call her weekly with a bright new idea.

It took her three months to return my calls. By the time we finally spoke, she hadn't looked at the ideas I sent her—and most of them were "dated." I didn't take it personally. I just kept reapproaching with more ideas. Again, she didn't call me back or reply to my e-mails. I decided to stop leaving messages. But I didn't stop calling. I would just hang up when her machine answered. She seemed never to be at her desk. Sometimes I'd ring her five, six, ten times in a day, just waiting for her to pick up, which happened about once every ten days. (I went so far as to dial *66 in order to block my number from showing up on caller ID, just in case her office had caller ID.) She rejected each and every idea. I was beginning to feel very frustrated. *Magazine X* had become my kryptonite, the one thing that made me feel weak.

"Is there something specific you're looking for?" I asked her when I got her on the phone. I was trying to get some guidance.

"Yes," she said. "Stop calling me."

Ouch! There is a fine line between persistence and stalking, and I guess I had crossed it. I was crushed—and petrified she had warned her staff about me. I didn't know how to mend it. A few weeks later I sent her an e-mail to try to smooth things over and let her know that I would love the chance to work with her in the future. The message bounced back to me! I surmised that she had put me on her "blocked" list. I was blackballed!

But it turned out that the reason the e-mail was returned was because she no longer worked at the magazine and a new editor was in her place. It was a new opportunity to get my foot in the door! So I picked up the phone and made a new attempt at the schmooze. "Hi, this is Karen Robinovitz," I said. "I'm a writer and I used to talk to J all the time. I was actually waiting to hear back from her on a few great ideas, but now that she's gone, I hope to follow up with you and work together." Technically, I did talk to J all the time. I just didn't mention that our conversations were basically one-sided. I wasn't really lying. I was turning a bad communication into a good one. I was schmoozing.

"Great," she said. "Why don't you come in for lunch and we'll discuss?"

I started writing for her immediately.

# THE POPULARITY CONTEST

*Melissa*

*There's* nothing I hate more than meeting new people. Growing up, I was the classic shrinking violet—I shirked from my peers, nodded dumbly at my teachers, and brought home report cards that exhorted me to *Speak up in class! We don't know what Melissa's voice sounds like!* (Friends who now know me as the loudmouth who gets shushed in restaurants are doubled up in hysterics.) High school was the same geeky story. I was the kid who spent lunch at the computer lab or at the library, reading tomorrow's history homework. When I arrived at college, I was determined to leave my shy and withdrawn nature behind forever. I decided to reinvent myself and adopt the personality of the most popular girl in high school—dropping hints about my boyfriend (fictional), my crazy prom night (ditto), and my gang of good-looking friends, whose pictures I displayed prominently in my dorm room (stolen). I crafted a peppy, exuberant, and fearless disposition. For the first time in my life, I didn't flinch when I met someone new—I smiled and chatted. It worked. I was even elected class president.

With my "popular girl" persona in place, I learned to exaggerate, beguile, and mimic the kind of intimacy that turns strangers into insta-friends. I tailored my anecdotes to a few standard ones that showcased my irresistibly "zany" character. But even if I've come a long way from the girl who spent every Friday night watching *Quantum Leap*, schmoozing still does not come naturally to me. A few years ago I was employed at a famous glossy magazine. I had gotten this job through a friend's recommendation. For six years I had been trying to break into the magazine with no luck, sending story ideas and résumés every time they had an opening. But with one phone call from an insider, I was immediately accepted. It probably didn't hurt that I was an alumni of the same ritzy high school that the human resources director's daughters attended (even if I was a scholarship student), and that the editor-in-chief adored the expensive new designer trousers I wore to the interview. Still, I was slightly taken aback at how easily it all happened.

Once I arrived at its frosted glass doors, instead of charming everyone with my winning popular-girl personality, I reverted to my geeky high school persona. I kept to myself at lunch, closing my office door, diligently typing away on my assignments instead of chatting with fellow editors about the latest trendy restaurants and the cuteness of the fashion director's shoes. I exchanged only a few short words with my immediate supervisors in the morning, and curt nods with the junior staff over the tofu platter at the cafeteria. I was paralyzed with shyness. It had always been a dream of mine to work at the magazine, but instead of relishing my triumph, I was wrecked with insecurity and terribly intimidated. I was worried my colleagues would see through my fake "popular" persona and ascertain the real loser underneath, so I didn't even try.

Blind to office politics, I thought I could count on my writing skills to speak for themselves. In retrospect, I should have joined all those hour-long *Simpsons* discussions at the water cooler instead of spending every moment locked up in my office. I was shown the door only a few weeks later. "Everything was great," the managing editor who hired me said ruefully. "The whole package was perfect," he said, waving a hand at my outfit. (I had clocked a lot of compliments on my clothes during my stint—a very important plus, but somehow I hadn't been able to translate it into anything more substantial.) "But somehow it doesn't fit," he said, puzzled. Perhaps it was the story on hair care that I handed in which I compared curls to Chia Pet growth that sealed my fate, but he didn't mention it. I took four shopping bags filled with beauty products, and hightailed it out of there.

I had drinks with a colleague at a rival publication a few weeks later, who said, "You know, to get ahead, it's not about how interesting your work is, but how interesting you are. If you don't contribute a fun personality, there's almost no point. Which is why I'm surprised. What happened? Didn't you schmooze anyone?"

Sadly, I didn't.

## THE BIG ART OF SMALL TALK
### THE SECRETS TO SUCCESSFULLY SCHMOOZING IN STYLE

• Don't go out if you're in a nasty mood. Proper schmoozing requires that you turn your personality "on" all the time. Nobody likes a grump.

• Give a warmhearted hello to all, whether you know them or not. Celebrities who work the media junket, often meeting fifty or more journalists a day, say "Hi! How nice to see you!" to everyone, instead of "meet you," just in case it's not the first meeting.

• Know who you're schmoozing and act appropriately. If

you're not fully aware of what the schmoozee does, who he or she works with and is connected to, and what his or her political beliefs are, stick to neutral topics. "This is the best cheese I've ever had! You must try it!"

• Read. Know the gist of the events of the day (not just the gossip columns) so you can glibly fake your way through conversations about breaking news stories. While you're at it, pick up a copy of "smart" magazines like *The Economist*, *The New Yorker*, *Harper's* (not *Bazaar*, although you will need *Bazaar* for fashion knowledge), or a general-interest publication like *Newsweek* or *Time*. Make offhand references to riveting articles. "So apparently the new American home has a spa, a gourmet kitchen, and an airport lounge!"

• Keep a host of witty or fascinating anecdotes up your sleeve. If you have nothing in your repertoire, get creative. Try building something around a friend in the CIA, an African safari (so what if it was at Animal Kingdom), and your near-death experience. "Oh, my God, it was such a trip to see my body on the operating table!"

• Brush up on things that other famous people are interested in and engage them in a soulful conversation on the topic. Current hot-convo stimulants in Hollywood include: the difference between ashtanga, vinyasa, and anusara yoga, the advantages of taking digestive enzymes (don't ask!), and, when all else fails, Scientology.

• Be helpful to your peers. If you can do anything to support another person in attaining a goal, do so. Give unto others—and ye shall receive. If you generously share and the recipient never returns the love, make a mental note so the next time they seek your help, you can find a way to gracefully decline.

• During conversation, make direct eye contact, and every

now and then softly touch someone's shoulder as you talk. It will make the person you're with think he or she is the most fascinating person in the room.

- Ask many personal questions. People love to talk about themselves. It makes them feel important.

- Use people's names in sentences as you chat. (i.e., "What do you think of that, Calista?")

- Play down your talents. There is an old saying: "Show, don't tell." If you have to remind someone that you're good at something, they will not only be turned off, but they may not believe you. Modesty, my friend, is a virtue. While it's good to be confident, it's bad to be aggressive.

- Excuse yourself from conversations at the right moment. You always want to leave them wanting a little more of you. Just make sure your exit is poised. Some surefire excuses: "Pardon me, I need to refill my glass," "I'm sorry, Donald is waving me over. I must say hello. I'll be right back," and "Will you excuse me? I have to find the rest room."

- Know how much talk time people will allocate you before they start looking bored. When Jennifer Tilly started out in Hollywood, she knew that she was a "thirty-second" girl—that she could converse with big power players for only that long. As she became more famous, she was promoted to a minute and a half of people's time, and at the present she says she clocks in at a solid three minutes of face time.

- When asking people for favors, do not be beneath begging. In fact, you can make begging come off as cute if you smile right.

- End all conversations with, "I'm so glad we got a chance to catch up; looking forward to seeing (or talking to) you again soon."

# FIRST CLASS ALL THE WAY

• • • • • *Melissa* and *Karen* • • • • •

We were flying from New York to Los Angeles to meet with our movie agents—inscrutable men in mirrored sunglasses who called us "babe" and wanted to turn any idea we had into a Christmas movie, where Tom Hanks, Jim Carrey, or any other big-name box-office material starred as Santa. Even if we were confused (Santa?), we were also thrilled—it was our first "Hollywood" experience and we meant to enjoy every minute. Since we had yet to make our agents any money, we had to pay our own way, and we could only afford to fly in the veal pen confines of economy class (the shame). Even more unfortunate, the flight was packed, and we were assigned middle seats (and not in those cushy exit rows either). We were staring at six straight hours of unmitigated hell.

"I heard they sometimes bump models and high-profile people up to first class," Karen said as we bemoaned our tickets. "Should we try it?"

I shrugged. "What could we lose?" We sauntered up to the ticket counter. We struck quite a figure—the two of us were dressed more appropriately for a night on the town rather than a mundane transatlantic commute. Karen was wearing Mongolian lamb, while I had ostrich feathers on (we thought this was very "Hollywood" of us), and we both had sunglasses perched on our heads.

"Hiiiii," we said breathily to the slim, handsome man at the counter. We immediately pegged him as a Friend of Dorothy. He sized us up and grinned. "Let me guess, two one-way tickets to Vegas?" We laughed as if it were the funniest thing we had ever heard in our lives. "Seriously, though," I said, "we're going to Los Angeles to meet with our agents and we have some serious studio meetings set up." (The second was a lie, but I thought I would exaggerate to make it sound more exciting.) He looked suitably impressed. "Are you girls actresses?" We tittered. "No! We're writers! We're writing a book about becoming famous!"

"Any tips for me?" he asked.

"Sure!" we said, as we handed him our IDs. But we soon cut to the chase: "Do you know, we've been given middle seats! Is there any way we can get them changed? We'll do anything! We need to be fresh for our meeting!" His brow furrowed as he tapped on his keyboard. "Let me see. . . ."

While he searched the plane for more suitable seats, we gushed and fawned over him. "How cute is that shirt! Is it Dolce? Do people tell you that you look just like Rupert Everett? What is that cologne you're wearing? It's heaven. Ticket reps are usually so rude! You're such an angel! Whatever you can do is fine by us!"

He frowned. "Well, there are no more aisle or window seats left in economy." We pouted. "And business is full too . . . but wait . . . I do have seats in first class. Do you have any frequent-flyer miles you can upgrade with?" Miles! We didn't want to spare our miles for a lousy upgrade! We'd rather save them for a free ticket! But we didn't want to tell him that. "No, no miles. We don't usually fly on this airline." We made puppy-dog faces. Karen made the mmm-mmm-mmm whine, Bijon-style. "All right, if you were in jeans and sweatshirts I'd never do it, but you girls belong in first class."

Hooray! We air-kissed him, wished him luck on his acting career, and promised to send him a copy of our book when it came out.

As we reclined, fully horizontal, swathed in cashmere blankets, eating warm nuts from a gleaming white china bowl and daintily wiping our foreheads with hot towels, while the latest Hollywood movie played on our personal video screens, we high-fived each other. We had parlayed our cheap tickets into luxurious amenities, thanks to the power of our personalities. Mama was right all along: the surest way to get into people's hearts is through their egos.

*Epilogue:* A few weeks later, we were invited to a party for the launch of a new private jet service at the home of its founder, Steve Green. At a time when flying private was the only way to travel (a celebrity publicist we know got accosted by security people who thought her Celine bullet belt was dangerous) and the ultimate status symbol for a single man under fifty was not his Rolls, but his G-5, Green Air boasted the cutting edge of private jet service, with beautiful Citation and Hawker planes—veritable Aston Martins in the sky. Green Air pilots wore uniforms designed by Prada!

We were introduced to Steve as "the two most famous writers in New York" by a mutual friend, a publicist who spoke only in hyperbole. "You don't say," he said. In turn, we complimented him on his new airline, telling him we'd heard terrific buzz. We were fresh from our Hollywood high, and regaled him with stories from our two weeks of fame-related misadventures. He smiled and said, "Well, you know, you can't be a real celebrity without a private plane! It's a vital accessory!"

We groaned and agreed, thinking a well-placed hint might work in our favor. "Next month we're flying to Miami for the opening of a swanky new club. But God knows we'll probably be stuck in economy again, unless we meet another nice ticket-counter employee who'll upgrade us for free to first class."

He harrumphed. "First class is nothing! You girls deserve your own plane," he said.

"Exactly what I've been saying all along. Mel, I like this guy. He's a keeper," Karen said, flipping her hair, flashing a wide smile, and tapping his shoulder.

Sure enough, on our next flight together, we were reclined, fully horizontal, on tan leather Barcaloungers, with a bottle of Cristal on ice by our sides. We munched on sushi in Bento boxes from Nobu, while a cute copilot in his Prada uniform asked us if we wanted anything else. We turned to each other in disbelief—how did we get here?

To the Green Air mogul, one flight for two up-and-comers is a drop in the bucket, like taking a gallon of water out of the Atlantic Ocean. He probably saw it as an investment. He figured, if we had a good experience, we'd tell people about it and help promote his brand . . . just as he helped us promote ours.

The schmooze had gotten out of control. It was like the Jedi mind trick. By convincing people we were celebrities, we were automatically treated like celebrities. "Do you think we can get him to *give* us our own plane?" Karen asked between bites of toro scallion maki. We laughed it off at the time, but we are sort of wondering: Can we?

# FLATTER THEM

## SOME PEOPLE CALL IT KISSING ASS; WE CALL IT GETTING AHEAD

• Hand out compliments as freely as a Jew for Jesus passes out pamphlets. People love to hear that you love what they are wearing or admire their work. Tell a girlfriend that she looks thin. Ask a guy if he's been working out. People can never hear "You look good" enough. There's nothing wrong with being slightly sycophantic as long as you're sincere. Be warned: Like a bad Gucci knock-off, people can spot a disingenuous comment a mile away. And while you're at it, don't fawn over known enemies. They'll only dislike you more. As a famous person, it's important to come to grips with the fact that not everyone will like you, no matter what you do.

• Congratulate others on recent accomplishments—a job promotion, quitting smoking, throwing a fab party, buying the season's most coveted boots, paying off their credit card bills, getting their preschooler into the right kindergarten. God is in the details—take notice of the little things.

• If someone has worked hard on a project—cooking a meal, finally breaking up with an icky boyfriend, decorating a room—acknowledge it.

• Call people "inspirational." It makes them feel admired, cherished, and appreciated. (During our *minor* squabbles over the writing of this book, we each called another "inspirational" at one point or another to mend the rift. Worked every time!)

• Take important people to lunch. Because there's no such thing as a free meal, they will have to find some way to thank you in the future.

# CONFESSIONS OF A WINDOW DRESSER'S FAN

*Melissa*

𝔍imon Doonan is the acerbic fashion columnist for the *New York Observer*, the quick-witted and arch-tongued Englishman who is also responsible for the outrageous, fantastic, and often controversial window displays of Barneys New York, my favorite store. I have been obsessed with Simon ever since I read (and could not put down) his autobiography, *Confessions of a Window Dresser*, which documented his madcap English childhood,

Simon, my hero!

his days in Hollywood, and his final triumph as the man who put Hello Kitty in Jesus's cradle in the Barney's windows at Christmas. "Kitty Nativity" generated tons of publicity for the store, put Simon on the map as the king of cheek, and turned him into a hero for disgruntled art students everywhere. He is the most famous window dresser in history.

During my stint as an editor at Hintmag.com, one of our regular features involved taking a famous fashion personality out to lunch. Lunch was usually subsidized by the restaurant in exchange for publicity on our Web site, and the famous fashion personality often agreed to meet with us after we had begged them repeatedly for months. Simon was one of our first "Lunch Voxes." I was thrilled to meet him and even more charmed when I discovered he was not only funny and sharp, but warm, friendly, and genuine. A total mensch. When my editor asked him a few months later for some kind words to help promote my first novel, he provided the following much-quoted blurb: *Melissa de la Cruz is the Jackie Collins of the Moomba generation. She's on a collision course with pulp stardom!* I screamed in joy, sent him a rapturous note, and thanked him with a doll from the Barbie Wizard of Oz collection.

But I wanted more of Simon. I wanted to get to know him better, and go beyond the usual cocktail chitchat at random fashion events. Like the starstruck teenagers on MTV's *Fanatic*, who believe that rock stars really "know" what they are going through, I wanted Simon and I to be *close*. Like my earlier obsession with Boy George, I was utterly convinced we would become best buddies if only we had the chance to hang out regularly.

For my two-weeks-of-fame assignment, Simon was one of the first people who came to mind. Here was my chance to see him again! I e-mailed him and asked if we could have lunch. I didn't hear from him, so I took matters into my own hands. I visited his partner Jonathan Adler's home accessories store in Soho, thinking I could "casually" bump into him there. It worked. That very day I spotted Simon in the back next to the geometric pillows I craved. (I'm also slightly obsessed with Jonathan, but that's another story.) Simon was as warm as ever, and agreed to meet me the next day for lunch at DB Bistro Moderne—five-star chef Daniel Boulud's newest restaurant and the home of the very famous $50 hamburger.

I clued him into my mission for fame. "Real celebrities are a pain in the ass," he said. "You should take your cues from Tonya and Joey." (Harding and Buttafuoco.) He told me how he orchestrated his own attention-grabbing stunt for the opening of the latest Barneys store by dressing up as the queen of England and hiring celebrity look-alikes to "vacuum" the red carpet. "We had Michael Jackson, Liza Minnelli, Sylvester Stallone. It was hilarious! And impersonating royalty is always good," he said with a sly wink.

Lunch left me high on Simon. I adored the man. I wanted us to bond in the Hamptons, giggle together at fashion shows, have late-night phone conversations about the latest celebrity incarceration. I wanted him to adopt me!

But in the end, I left him alone. Schmoozing is one thing; stalking is another. I didn't want him to think I was a weird freak. I decided to be content with our current friendly acquaintance. After all, it's more than I ever had with Boy George.

# THE CASE OF
# MISTAKEN IDENTITY

### *Karen*

$O$ne winter, when I was covering the Sundance Film Festival, a friend introduced me to her longtime family friend and colleague whom I'll call Jon. Jon is very powerful film mogul. In the business he is revered and feared, as he can make or break a career. For years I have been hearing my friend talk about him—how brilliant he is, how connected he is, how he's the brains behind some of the biggest names and movies in Hollywood. So I was a bit intimidated by his commanding presence when we met. And because he spent most of his off time with my friend and travel work partner, I, too, spent ample hours with him (and his entourage), snowboarding, people-watching, and taking in indie pictures. I couldn't believe how "real" he was. He had no assistants surrounding him, no pressing office calls. He was just a guy's guy—and a cute one at that. He even bought me a lift ticket. This was the same shark who's known for taking no prisoners and always getting the job done—his way?

I never brought up anything about what he does, who he is, and the kind of power he wields. I was sure that everyone he ever met must suck up to him and ask him for favors and I didn't want to be "one of them." It's like meeting famous actors, who are used to being hounded—it's better to treat them like normal people and not divine creatures, holier-than-thou. I wanted to get his card, however, and possibly call him in the future. From my experience, it's okay to develop a friendly relationship with someone and, at the right time, you can cash in the bond into a beneficial working connection. But you can't broach the business thing too soon or it will seem like you're using the person for your own personal gain.

I sent Jon an *It was so nice spending time with you—even with the bruises on my legs from a horrific day down the mountain* note to his office in the hopes of closing the deal as far as "getting in" with him was concerned. While I had no plans for Hollywood at the time, I thought, *You never know.* A year later I was working on a project (i.e., this book!), and I thought that Jon would be the perfect person to approach regarding a small aspect of it (i.e., helping me convince a celeb to write the foreword). I had no doubt he'd remember me. I was just hoping he would return my call—and want to support my fame-seeking cause. I wasn't asking him to foot a bill for a movie or for anything that would put him out in any way. In fact, my measly assignment would take up ten minutes of his time—max. It was a harmless request. A cry for help, if you will.

I left a heartwarming message for him, where I reminisced about our Sundance moments. His assistant put me on his "call sheet" (mogul-speak for "list of people I need to call back"). Two weeks later there was no reply. I tried again and asked his assistant to make sure that next to my name on his call sheet, she included details of when and how I met him. ("I did that the first time you called," she said, which I thought was rather passive-aggressive.) Still no return call. I waited three weeks and gave it another shot. Not surprisingly, I never heard Jon's voice over the telephone.

Our onetime romance was over, I realized. I meant nothing to him.

A month later I was at a dinner party and everyone was gossiping about Jon. He was supposed to be there. I thought, *Now's my chance . . . just dazzle him with some charm.* I waited for his arrival. When he emerged, I was shocked.

"That's not Jon," I whispered to the person next to me.

"Yes, it is," she said.

*Oh, my God!* I was harassing the *wrong* Jon. Actually, I was calling the right Jon, but I actually met and hung out with the wrong Jon. My Sundance pal was no mogul. In fact, he was just another film buff whom my friend knew. In retrospect, I don't even recall her telling me his last name. I just assumed it was *the* Jon. Maybe out of some sick delusional fantasy, I wanted it to be *the* Jon. And poor *the* Jon! He was probably thinking, *Who is this crazy girl who's calling me about snowboarding in Sundance?* Like he has time to snowboard in Sundance. I considered schmoozing up to him—and telling him about the whole mixup. I imagined that we'd have a big laugh and work and play together happily ever after.

Instead, I took a sip of my wine, politely told the hostess I had to leave, and made a dash for home, where I planned to remain indefinitely!

# WHO TO SCHMOOZE?

- Whoever is in charge of things: the hostess of the restaurant, the co-op board, your apartment's super, the president of your company, a teacher in school, the manager of your favorite store, who will put things on layaway for you when it's really against the establishment's policy.

- Don't forget the little people. Anyone who can do something for you, even if it's the person who works at the smoothie bar (he or she will sneakily let you cut the line when there is a long wait for an energy elixir—or let you in when the store is actually closed), the stewardess on the plane (could lead to extra pillows), the receptionist at your salon (she'll get you in when your stylist is "booked").

- Club promoters, publicists, event planners, producers, restaurateurs, and anyone who has a higher profile than you do. If these people like you, they will invite you to their fancy events and parties, which will help elevate your status.

- The assistants of these club promoters, publicists, event planners, producers, restaurateurs. They'll put in a good word for you.

- A mentor, someone who can help and champion your career. If you don't have one, get one. Rent *All About Eve* to learn the ropes.

## WORKING IT

# THE INTERNATIONAL
# LANGUAGE OF YES!

• • • • • • • • • *Karen* • • • • • • • •

$\mathcal{S}$ometimes you have to schmooze contacts who speak with very strong accents that are impossible to understand. So it is important for all professional networkers to have a knack for faking their way through conversations while still seeming genuine. It's not an easy task, but once mastered, it can bring you plenty of ripe opportunity. I honed this particular skill after meeting an event-planning big shot who hails from the West Indies. Ever since we crossed paths in an elevator ascending to the penthouse for a fashion party, I have never been capable of deciphering anything he says.

It's as if, no matter what he utters, I hear a cacophony of noises that sounds something like, "Oonda a you jileltthrohelun-tush and dat model lether LA for n'bouchet party tonight." He could be telling me that he's taking a model to a party or that he has a kinky fetish for leather, for all I know. When we chat, I spend most of my energy asking him to repeat himself. I wind up saying "Excuse me" and "Pardon me" so frequently that I actually feel bad when I talk to him. There are only so many times a person can say, "What?" So I decided that my best approach in communicating with him would be nodding, smiling, and yesing him to death between saying things like, "You're so smart" and "You're so cute."

Once, he asked me if I was still working out with my trainer. Of course, I had no idea what he was saying. So I said yes. But I actually hadn't worked out with my trainer for ten months! Then he wanted to know how it was going. Again, no clue what he had asked. So I said, "Oh, it's great, never better; you have to join me sometime," hoping that would float. It did. Until he asked me for my trainer's number. I was able to make out the fact that he wanted a number, so I said, "What number?"

I had to ask him to repeat himself three times before I got that he wanted my trainer's number. "Oh, I don't have it. I haven't seen him in ten months," I said.

I felt pretty dumb when he informed me that I had just told him my trainer and I had never been better. I was able to get away with it by throwing in, "Oh, I'm so sorry. I must have misunderstood you. I thought you asked me about my *editor*. I couldn't hear you. I must stop cleaning my ears with Q-tips all the time. It's ruining my auditory canal!"

From that point on, I made a concentrated effort to limit our conversations to e-mails. When he calls, I often say, "I'm running out. Just send me an e-mail and I'll call you later." Then I write him back long, detailed e-mails, so he never gets the impression that I'm trying to blow him off. While I still struggle through most of our conversations at restaurants and face-to-face appointments, the Internet has brought us to great new depths of our connection. And I never have to say, "What?" He even played a part in helping Mel and me produce our big book deal party (see The Main Event, Step IV, for details). Unfortunately, I didn't understand him when he asked if it was a costume party. So I said, "naturally!" He showed up as the Naked Cowboy (see p. 56 in Step I) and was rejected at the door by the bouncers!

## SOLD! TO THE HIGHEST BIDDER?

### *Melissa*

$\mathcal{T}$he year before *Marie Claire* asked me to become famous, I was on the planning committee for the annual amfAR charity ball in New York, Boathouse Rocks. Boathouse Rocks routinely kicks off the summer social season with a glittery bash at the Central Park Boathouse, where luminaries such as Angie Harmon, Macaulay Culkin, Sharon Stone, and Sarah Jessica Parker raise money for amfAR. I was asked to join by my friend Tom Dolby, who was one of the chairs of the event. I was eager to broaden my social horizons and befriend the publicists, fashion executives, and magazine editors who comprised the rest of the committee. The meetings were held once a month, and although my attendance was sporadic, my enthusiasm for actually being on a charity social committee—I was a socialite! Just like Jackie O—remained fervent. During my tenure, I contributed several items for the auction and impressed friends by securing them exclusive invitations to the event.

During my two weeks of fame, Boathouse was in the midst of planning its annual party. I coyly suggested to Tom that since I was too busy to actually help plan the event this year, perhaps I could be part of it instead. The Boathouse signature is to sell

"Celebrity Kisses" for thousands of dollars—MAC lipstick imprints from the likes of Oprah Winfrey, Susan Sarandon, Toms Hanks and Cruise, Nicole Kidman, and the rest. While I knew I was not at the status of "Celebrity Kisses," I thought there might still be a way to capitalize on this. The yearly auction also offered "Nights Out With" packages wherein partygoers could bid on an evening with their favorite New York–based model, TV anchorman, or gossip reporter. Why not a night out with "novelist" Melissa de la Cruz? If people saw that I was being auctioned off like a true star, they would think I really was a celebrity!

I begged Tom to convince the auction committee that it was a good idea. Since I had been so helpful the year before, it was an easy enough task. "Oh, you're the famous writer!" the auction chair said when I gave her a copy of my book. "It would be such an honor to be part of the auction," I told her, laying it on thick. "It's the best party of the season!"

The night of the benefit, wedged next to the dozens of celebrity smudges, was the following display: *Win a night out with* Cat's Meow *author Melissa de la Cruz! Dinner for four at the trendiest restaurant in town! Attend the glitziest private parties for a real New York City experience!* My 8-by-10 author photo was displayed prominently, as was a "personally autographed" copy of my book. But like Sharon Stone, who "hosts" the event every year without actually being present, I was nowhere near Central Park the night of the party. For one thing, I didn't even merit a free ticket! And as a struggling freelancer, there was no way I could swing the $250 entrance fee. Much worse, the woman who handled the press list never called me back.

No matter, Mike and I were invited to spend that weekend at

a swanky hotel out of town (I didn't merit a free dinner at the benefit ball but I was good enough to send on a $5000 junket? Such are the contradictions of "fame"). When I returned, there were dozens of messages on my machine from friends and colleagues who had attended the bash. "Wow! You're such a star! Your display looked great at Boathouse!" "I wish I could have bid, but the starting price was so high!" "Can I hang out with you for free instead of paying five hundred dollars?" "You really are famous!"

I took a perverse thrill in being auctioned off for an evening. Page Six reported that a night out with Candace Bushnell had been sold for $3000. I was in good company. I was all set to bask in the admiration of the fan who had stepped up to the plate for the privilege of spending an evening with me. Plus I was doing a good thing for charity! I was virtuous and fabulous all at once— a heady combination.

It's been six months since the Boathouse benefit, but no one has yet to claim the prize. A night out with Melissa de la Cruz is still available for the low starting price of $500. Tom consoled me by saying, "Don't worry. A lot of our 'night out' things never get followed up on. People do buy them, but they're too shy to call the person to take them out for a night. They probably just took the copy of your book."

To whoever won—$500 is way too much to spend on a $13 paperback! Call me! I'll take you out for the night! I know a great restaurant. . . .

# CONNECT THE DOTS

• Networking 101: Develop a group of contacts who can help you get what you want.

• Attend every social event (even personal parties) as if they were conventions, and dole out your card to everyone you meet.

• Go out even when you don't want to. Sometimes you make the best, most unexpected contacts during these off nights.

• Establish a reputation as the person with the plan, the right reservation, and the party invitations. In time, people will flock to you.

• Don't "work" too hard or you will seem obnoxious. Networking is a delicate art, and the key is to reciprocate and be there for people who need you. People always want to associate with those who are good to them.

• Hang out with famous people. Being involved with them, as a friend, hanger-on, or "extra," will enable you to build a name for yourself as an individual over time. Lil' Kim got started as just another girl in the late Notorious B.I.G.'s crew.

• Get a gig as an assistant to a superfamous personality. It will give you the opportunity to get to know that person's contacts, friends, and colleagues and might bring you close enough to the limelight to eventually claim it for yourself. Trust us, after paying your dues for a year or two, you'll be movin' on up. Look at Anna Wintour's old assistant, who parlayed her stint at *Vogue* into a six-figure book and movie deal.

• Be bold. Don't be afraid to ask someone you just met an itsy bitsy favor that "only he or she can help you with."

• If you make casual social plans with acquaintances, always follow through; don't be one of those people who always promises social engagements but then cancels later. You never want to be known as a flake.

• Always get credit for whatever you do, so you can call in favors later. If you hook your girlfriend up with something, anything (a job interview, a free drink at the bar, a discount at her favorite boutique, an introduction to her new boyfriend), sweetly and subtly remind her that you're responsible for her sudden good fortune.

• Send "it was so lovely to meet you" notes, handwritten on your letterhead or monogrammed correspondence cards, to people who are influential, powerful, and above you on the totem pole.

• Throw an intimate party and always invite a few "reach" guests, three people you want badly to be part of your network—even if you don't know them well. This will familiarize them with your brand, name, and profile.

• Always keep in contact with people you meet. You never know where people will wind up and what the future will hold.

• Donate a significant amount to a popular charity. Open-checkbook socializing gets your foot in the door and lets people know you're a serious player. If you want to get close to Meryl Streep, for instance, get on the Apple Safety bandwagon!

• Congregate at powerhubs—for instance, in New York City, lunch at Michael's is the surest way to indicate you're moving in the media world, Da Silvano is where the Hollywood establishment likes to dine, and art-world power players hobnob at Bottino.

# ATTACK OF THE KILLER DENTIST

· · · · · *Karen* and *Melissa* · · · · ·

*O*n a warm spring Thursday night, we attended a book-launch bash for a plastic surgeon at a groovy club in New York. The amber lighting was sultry (the better to hide your wrinkles, my dear). The vodka was flowing. And a gaggle of publicists were squeezing the doctor in the middle of paparazzi moments with models, B-list actors, and Chloé-clad socialites who put the doctor's night of honor on their party-hopping schedule. We were on our way to the bar for a refreshment—and a much-needed break from the frenzy of the breast-implant mob who schmoozed the doctor in the hopes of a discount—when we were stopped by an attractive brunette who had a budding dental practice uptown.

"Oh, my God, you two are writers. Melissa and Karen, right?" she said, leaning forward (cleavage and all) to introduce herself with a friendly hug.

At first we were flattered. "Yes, yes! We are," we excitedly said, thrilled that someone recognized us for our work.

She went on to tell us that she liked our articles. She even listed a few of them, including our piece about becoming famous for *Marie Claire*. After complimenting us, she wanted to show us how fabulous *she* was. In fifteen minutes we learned that she was wearing a "conservative Gucci" ensemble even though she would rather dress in a sexier manner but can't because of her job; was "best friends" with a well-known fashion designer; eligible for discounts at Manolo Blahnik; invited to the next Chanel sample sale, vacationing to St. Bart's next week; hiring the interior designer who did Anna Wintour's home; a client of ritzy celebrity hairstylist Frederic Fekkai; and the brains behind the smiles of three heiresses who were fixtures of the society pages in *Vogue* and *W.* She went from charming and sweet to painfully annoying name-dropper in sixty seconds flat.

During her monologue, we didn't get a word in. She invaded our personal space by displaying unwarranted physical affection. (When she told us about her invitation to the Chanel sample sale, she hugged us again and said, "I'll try to bring you.") She even told us our smiles needed work! We spent the entire conversation clutching each other's hands, nodding, and faux smiling, even when she informed us that we needed to get our teeth bleached. All we wanted to do was lose her!

We knew she was trying to schmooze us because she wanted some press. That, of course, was confirmed when she flat-out said at the end of the conversation, "I would love you guys to write about me."

We graciously took her card and claimed we didn't have ours on us. We later tossed her card in the trash—but now we're wondering if we should have kept the contact. Our teeth *are* kind of yellow.

# SCHMOOZE, DON'T OOZE!
## ONE FALSE MOVE AND YOU'RE HEADED STRAIGHT FOR THE D-LIST

• Don't act too chummy with someone who's "higher up" than you by calling them "honey," "darling," or "love" during your first meeting. Keep a respectful, professional distance at all times unless the person decides to bring your friendship to the next level in a platonic way.

• Don't overstay your welcome. Exit conversations in the middle of something good, so people will crave a bigger dose of you later.

• When you see people nodding at you, flashing a fake smile and raised eyebrows as you talk, it's time to excuse yourself immediately.

• Never do the neck crane to see if someone more important is in the wings. It's the telltale sign of the social climber.

• Don't promise things you can't deliver on—if your check to that charity ball bounces or if you guarantee press for the bracelet some designer gave you and you don't get press, you will suddenly become infamous . . . and possibly a jewelry thief!

• Don't bring up work at a social event unless the person you're talking to mentions it first. It's best to spend your time building a friendly rapport first—and making a time to have a meeting to discuss business at a later date.

• Don't be disloyal. If you are, be prepared to feel the wrath of the karmic boomerang.

• Don't drop your friends when you're on the road to fame and fortune. Bring the trusted few up with you for the ride and work toward the higher purpose of fabulousness in unison. If you stick together, you will be able to help one another in the long run.

- Stop name-dropping. You never want to hear yourself say, "When we were at a meeting with Sting's yoga instructor and his publicist, who was watching Heidi Klum's dog, we wound up talking to Chloë Sevigny's brother, who's a very big DJ, like Mark Ronson, who dates Rashida Jones, who's on that David E. Kelley show and is the daughter of Quincy, who's doing a deal with a friend I introduced him to."(Unless it's true!)

- Don't burn bridges. Keep your friends close but your enemies closer.

*Days 12–14:*

# INSIDE THE VELVET ROPES

*N*o one ever became famous by sitting at home watching the latest chick show on the WB (and repeats of it at eleven P.M.) in flannel pajamas with a pile of dirty dishes in the sink. No, you, my friend, are going to have to go out. And going out doesn't mean to the take-out Chinese restaurant around the corner. Cozy neighborhood, no-name establishments are not on the agenda anymore. You are going to have to be part of the scene where people like to be seen. Of course, the best parties are often private, invitation-only events with the kind of guest list that reads, *Aristocrat, Fashion, Media, Socialite (Sr.), Socialite (Jr.), Art (Social)*, and *Entertainment* on a PR agent's Rolodex. If you are none of the above, don't worry—you can still make your way inside. We know. We've been there.

See, it has always been a dream of ours to become the kind of people who are allowed past the velvet ropes of snooty nightclubs. It's a small, petty, and laughable ambition, we must confess, and one that *definitely* doesn't reflect well on our goals. We can assure you that we also love babies, home-cooked meals, and shopping at Target, but the point is moot. As girls who started out life as the chunky kids in junior high, the type the boys didn't ask out, being able to waltz past the velvet ropes is a rush. A thrill. A high. A sign of acceptance. It's the world saying, *You belong inside with the fabulous people!* It's a mark of approval and a stamp of recognition . . . or a highly effective ego stroke designed by nightclub owners to make people believe a $10 cosmopolitan is worth something.

But we prefer to see it as the first baby step to fame.

The fame game is all about climbing the ladder. Getting inside a nightclub might not mean much at first, but becoming famous is about building on these steps toward the big picture, i.e., the Photo Shoot in the Sky—otherwise known as two pages in *Vanity Fair*. But before Richard Avedon takes your close-up, you're going to have to conquer the nightlife. How can you become famous if you can't even get past the doorman of a nightclub? We rest our case.

Step one is getting past the doorman. Step two is getting into the VIP room. And step three is hosting a party at the club itself—being in charge of the list rather than being just another name on it. This chapter will teach you the tricks that, if used properly, will grant you access to the inside hangouts of the glitterati. We will cover how to befriend the velvet-rope Nazis, the gatekeepers who pick and choose who can come into the club and who has to go home, feeling rejected. We'll show you how to sniff out the best parties, become the ultimate host, and—for those who are having trouble mastering all aforementioned activities—

we will teach you the devilish art of crashing parties, a skill that, once mastered, will enable you to go anywhere, anytime. So . . . here's to many late nights and more glasses of champagne than you can drink!

## GETTING IN

# MY FIRST NIGHT AS A CLUB CRAWLER

· · · · · · · · · · *Melissa* · · · · · · · · · ·

*I*n 1989, the hottest club in New York City was called MARS. It was located in the far West Twenties, on a desolate stretch of abandoned lots and industrial buildings, and was favored by a host of transsexual prostitutes. The first week I arrived in New York I wanted to go to MARS. Unfortunately, I had nothing to wear.

I arrived in New York City with twelve oversize seventy-five-pound cardboard boxes. I packed so many things for my first year in college that my mother asked me if I ever intended to come back home. Inside these boxes were print dresses from Contempo Casuals, Outback Red button-down camp shirts, and quite a selection of slouchy leather boots from Payless. Even if I had yet to step out of the bunker of the college campus, I knew that nothing I currently owned would ever pass muster with the snobby door mistress of MARS, who famously said, "We won't let you in if you're not wearing the right shoes." I would have to find something else to wear other than a Gap turtleneck.

Fortunately, I did have one thing. It was an outfit I never dared to wear in South San Francisco, California. It was a pleated black Lycra miniskirt with matching biker shorts sewn underneath, a combination of skirt and shorts, but by no means a "skort." It was, in fact, an outfit I had noticed Debbie Gibson wearing in a music video, and one that Christian Lacroix had popularized on the runways of Paris. I bought it at the mall for $25. I wore it with a black tank top, oversize black matte hoop earrings, and a pair of Doc Martens. I left my dorm room.

"Cool outfit," a friend said. "Where are you going?"

"Clubbing," I answered smoothly. Already I was saying good-bye to the preppy suburbanite in the fluorescent T-shirt and Fergie clip-on bows.

"Wow. Have fun," she said. She was wearing pajamas. It was almost midnight.

We arrived at MARS, where a huge crowd had already gathered in front of the velvet ropes. Inside the sanctuary, an Asian woman wearing a baseball cap sat on a high stool, surveying the crowd with pursed lips. "You," she said, motioning to me.

I had the presence of mind not to balk. Instead I sauntered forward, my plastic earrings trembling.

"How many?" she asked.

"Three," I said smoothly, pointing to my two friends, who had affected a manly slouch. She nodded her head to the gorilla in the velvet suit. He unhooked the velvet rope.

We walked through, our heads high and our hearts beating.

When we were finally inside the club, we hugged each other and giggled. "We got in!" we said to each other. "We! Got! In!" we had done it! We were cool! We were hot! We were beautiful, good-looking, and supreme New Yorkers! We laughed. We paid the twenty-dollar admission fee.

Then we looked around.

The nightclub was empty.

## THE PASSWORD, PLEASE . . .

*Karen*

There was a lot of talk about a new bar on the Lower East Side. The word on the street was, it was the new hot spot. The problem: there was no listing in the yellow pages, no sign on the door, and no phone. The only way in was to have the password—or know the owner. Access was reserved for the fabulous set of actors, emerging musicians, important artists, chic designers, partying socialites, and progeny of any of the above. That did not include me. However, I was determined to enter that glamorous world. (In fact, one of my editors gave me the highest compliment I've ever received: "You built an entire career on being fabulous." In my eyes, he was far from the truth. But I promised myself to believe him if I was able to gain access to this mysterious bar.)

I spent weeks calling editors, stylist friends, agents, publicists. No one had the dirt, or admitted to knowing it. I closely inspected every street in the neighborhood, combing Allen Street, Essex, Clinton, Ludlow, Stanton, and Rivington in search of this so-called gem. There were articles in newspapers about it, and in each one the address and any information leading to entrée was carefully obscured. That was the only way the owner would even grant an interview with the press.

I felt tortured that I was left out in the cold, clearly not cool enough to know the inside story. So I researched like crazy. But the more I dug, the less I found. And the less I found, the more I heard about this place. It was open whenever the owner felt like having it open. And they served caviar and pancakes after two A.M. It sounded absurd and pretentious. Everything I dreamed of . . . and more.

It was the talk of the town, but no one I knew had ever gotten in. There was supposedly a waiver that all patrons had to sign, agreeing that they would not tell anyone about the place "unless you trust this person enough to have keys to your apartment." There were rules and regulations posted that forbade men from approaching women they did not know (only a bartender could introduce you; this was the owner's method of keeping his place private and not a typical meat market of pickup lines).

One fateful afternoon, three frustrating weeks later, I was having lunch downtown and two arty looking men, both wearing fedoras, were in a deep discussion about this place. I have excellent hearing and adept eavesdropping skills, which I instantly put to use. I found out the name of the street (which I am not able to disclose, though I can say it begins with an E and ends with an E) and the owner's name (again, something I am not at liberty to share, but it's one of those names that sounds modely and glam if you're a girl and pompous if you're a guy, like Sasha). So the next night I put on my best boots and denim skirt and made my way down to the desired location. On a gritty block, where I stepped over two vagrants sleeping with empty bottles of gin, I came across a black door. There was no number. There was no window. There was no sign that this was the place, making it quite obvious that I was there.

I rang the buzzer. I waited. I rang again. And waited some more. I considered leaving, but suddenly a thin man with a sharp nose, a thick mop of brown locks, and a brown fedora, who was one of the guys I had spotted at the restaurant earlier that week, appeared and asked me if I was waiting to get into [the name of the place]. I was, I said. "I know [the name of the owner.]"

"Really," he asked, "how?"

"From around. You know," I said.

"That's funny," he replied, "because I don't know you."

I turned beet red. "God, I'm an ass," I said.

"You are," he confirmed. He unlocked the door, walked into his bar, and left me standing in the cold. As I turned away in defeat, the door opened.

"I thought about it," he said, handing me the infamous waiver. "You're in."

# BEFRIENDING THE GATEKEEPERS

You, too, can buddy up to doorpeople at clubs, event planners, and OPP (other people's publicists) in order to get access into the hottest restaurants, parties, and clubs.

• Go clubbing on an "off night," and befriend the doorkeepers (the bouncers and clipboard carriers who decide who gets inside). Do this regularly for weeks. After a while, you will be one of their favorite faces—and you'll never have to wait on line again.

• Have your "publicist" contact the club's owner or publicist in order to get your name on the list—and forewarn them of your imminent appearance. It will not only get you in, but assure you stellar treatment.

• People who don't have to wait on line and are always on the list usually toil in the fashion, media, entertainment, and beauty industries. Get yourself a card (make sure the paper stock is good in order to make it believable) to prove you're "in the biz" and flash it at the door as you make your way in.

• Research the club and start dropping names. "I know Rudolph. He's expecting me." If that doesn't work, try, "Is Kenny Kenny around?" (There's always someone important who goes by the same first name—twice.)

• Dress up. No one likes letting in the slobs. It's a shallow life, but someone's got to live it.

• Leave your boyfriend at home. Doorpeople like to let in single women (especially good-looking single women), not single men. So bring your most attractive friends for the ride.

• Flirt. A friend of ours flashed her breasts to a doorman in order to avoid waiting on line and possibly getting rejected at the door. He looked at her, dumbfounded, and said, "Go in." It must have been her triple-Ds. Don't try this unless you can back it up with something as eye-popping.

- If you're a man, consider showing up in drag. You'll be an instant hit and the club will appreciate your "flava." But only if you're shorter than five-eight and a perfect size six.

- Be polite. Bitchiness won't get you anywhere. In fact, it will inspire the doorperson to make you suffer just for fun.

- Slip them a Benjamin. Grease the palm. It's a lot to invest— but you're investing in your future at the club. They'll never forget you.

## SCOPING OUT THE PARTY CIRCUIT

# DIAL R FOR REDIAL

*Karen*

*A* famous drum-'n'-bass DJ-ing duo from London was coming to town to throw some chichi, superexclusive costume party. There was a big buzz about the event, especially in modish downtown circles populated by high-profile artists, writers, musicians, filmmakers, and the ilk. It was even written about in the *New York Times*, but no details of the wheres and whens were disclosed. Ironically, the only prerequisite required for getting in called for just one thing—showing up. The problem: it was virtually impossible to score the coordinates.

Instead of invitations, the hosts sent a card with a telephone number on it. When you called the number, you were told to leave your number on the answering machine. The day of the party you'd be contacted with the details . . . and not a moment before. The shindig could have been in Guam, for all anyone knew. I wanted that phone number! I don't even think I cared so much about the party, even though Dmitri, the famous DJ from Paris, was spinning. I merely wanted the satisfaction of knowing I had the option of going. But I had no clue as to how to make this happen.

That week I wound up on a photo shoot for work and I overheard one of the models talking about the soiree. She said that she had received the coveted card with the special phone number and had just called to report her information. "I can't remember the number, but it's on my cell phone," she told her friend in her charming British accent. "I'll give it to you so we can both go."

She slinked off to wardrobe to change into some Alexander McQueen frock. Her cell phone was nearby, resting atop her Chanel bag. Here was my opportunity to do some PI work. And I took it. Remaining calm, cool, and very *Alias*, I scrolled through the call log and found the ten numbers she had recently called. *No one has to know and no one gets hurt*, I told myself in attempt to ease my conscience. I slyly redialed each, hoping that one would lead to the party line. By my sixth attempt, I was golden. Drum-'n'-bass purred through the phone. A British voice congratulated me for having the secret number. I left my information after the beep. And—lo and behold—I was contacted the day of the party with all of the information I needed to reach the ten-thousand-square-foot loft—complete with indoor pool—near the West Side Highway.

But the night of the party, I got food poisoning and couldn't go! Talk about karmic boomerang! But at least I can always say I was one of the elite few hundred, lucky enough to receive the coveted info.

## HOW TO FIND OUT ABOUT EVENTS AND UNLEASH YOUR INNER SPY

The first step of going to a party is finding out who's throwing it, when it's happening, and where it's being held. Time to do your research. Check out:

• *The Fashion Calendar.* If you want to know about store openings, runway shows, and glitzy fashion parties, the $400 subscription pays itself off in free champagne and caviar. It lists every fashion happening from New York to Paris.

• When all else fails, bribing PR agents is not unheard of. It's common knowledge that those with money but no access—say, investment bankers with the hankering to hang out with models at glitzy media events—routinely pay a monthly fee to be added to PR guest lists.

• Newspaper listings. The Arts and Lifestyle sections of your newspaper are good sources for exclusive events. Once you spot the event you'd like to attend, put your "publicist" to work to find out who's planning the event in order to get you an invitation.

• Start your own Web site. The last time we checked,

www.redcarpet.com was still an available domain name. Register and begin to hit the scene as a "reporter" who "covers" events. Get a business card to make it official and hand them out like crazy. Post photos from the soiree on-line. If you build it, they will log on and tell you when their parties are.

• Trail someone who's going to an event you'd like to attend— and follow them inside the velvet ropes by pretending to be part of their entourage.

• Pose as a photographer, although running around a party with a camera around your neck is not a very fabulous position to be in.

• Put your name on every mailing list for galleries, stores, and restaurants, because when they have events, they are likely to inform you.

• Become a museum or opera member. Art museums, the opera, and the ballet hold lavish affairs that anyone can attend . . . for a price. But most of these galas offer "dessert and dancing" tickets for a fraction of the typical $1,000-a-plate fee.

# MUSIC . . .
# MAKES THE PEOPLE . . .
# COME TOGETHER

· · · · · · *Melissa* and *Karen* · · · · ·

*The* "celebrity DJ" is a nascent trend on the New York party scene and while Hollywood connections are still the easiest way to parlay a talent at the turntables into publicity and easy cash, à la Mark (stepson of Foreigner frontman Mick Jones) Ronson and Paul (brother of Chlöe) Sevigny, and any member of the family Arquette, lately everyone is getting in the game. Fashion designers, magazine editors, boutique owners, and other demi-quasi-semi-celebrities have been taking a turn at spinning at a club for an evening. After receiving yet another invitation asking us to attend a "celebrity DJ night" featuring some veritable no-bodies ("He's spinning? What the hell does the editor of *Outside* magazine know about music?"), we figured it was time we hit the DJ booth.

We convinced publicist Deborah Hughes, who organizes the DJ events at Glass, a new and trendy club in the far west of Chelsea, that we were perfect for their celebrity DJ program, as we were writing a book about celebrity and fame. To bring in a crowd, we convinced Kremly vodka to provide an open bar featuring a "Fame Cocktail," a refreshing and tart concoction that tasted suspiciously like a cosmopolitan. Deborah e-mailed the following invitation to five hundred contacts on her publicity list:

Come hear
K.Ro and Mel-DLC
(Karen Robinovitz and Melissa de la Cruz)
authors of the forthcoming book
*How to Become Famous in Two Weeks*
spin
greatest hits and all-time faves
at Glass
"Fame Cocktails" (they really go to your head!)
from Kremly vodka
10–11 P.M.
RSVP: Deborah Hughes, PR, 555-5555

Soon, colleagues and friends were calling us about our DJ night. "Are you really going to spin?"

"Sure," we answered, even though we had our doubts as to whether we could actually handle the turntables. Neither of us had used a record player since we were fifteen. Because we like to go home early, at first we asked if we could spin from the early hour of seven to nine P.M. "Um, the club doesn't really start going until ten," Deborah warned. "You might be spinning for nobody." We settled on ten to eleven P.M.

We arrived at Glass decked out in DJ gear. Karen wore a black split-sleeved, rhinestone-dusted blouse (recently seen on Britney Spears) with jeans folded to the calf, knee-high patent-leather stiletto boots, and a beret, while Mel opted for a trompe l'oeil sweater with a painted-on necktie, a short denim miniskirt, slouchy suede boots, and a newsboy cap. We were pleased with our getups. But when we arrived, we were a little disheartened to find the club almost completely empty, save for one lone table of smokers at nine-thirty P.M. (We arrived early to practice and prayed for lessons.)

"Hi," we said to the bartender, "we're the celebrity DJs!" He looked at us blankly. No one seemed to know why we were there. Plus, neither of us had thought to bring CDs or vinyl. What exactly would we be DJ-ing with? Luckily, the "real" DJ, an affable guy named Lithium, showed us the ropes. He even lent us his personal collection of disco and house music. We spun greatest hits, all right—all of Donna Summer's! We played everything on her album from "Bad Girls" to "MacArthur Park." At first only a few-odd people were sitting at the bar, but at the end of the evening we had a decent crowd, boozing up with Fame Cocktails and rocking out to our Donna Summer compilation. We were a hit! Instead of DJ-ing for the fifteen-minute time period we had intended to occupy, we lasted a whole hour.

Kickin' it, old school! Word!

We were fading in and out of two songs at once. We even scratched. (Okay, that happened by accident, but it still happened.) "You girls rule," a patron at the bar told us. Perhaps it was only the Fame Cocktail speaking, but we took him at his word. (Actually, Karen took him at his word because—ahem—Mel had taken it upon herself to abandon K.Ro in the DJ booth in order to socialize!)

The next month we fielded requests from several clubs to spin for their guest-DJ programs! Word on the street was: We were down. From now on, no turntable is safe from K.Ro and Mel-DLC. Although we're not quitting our day jobs.

K.Ro and Mel-DLC:
The Vinyl Countdown.

TANYA BRAGANTI

# THROW YOUR OWN VIP PARTY

In order to get invited to great parties, it's a good idea to throw invitation-only events yourself, and to invite those who are known for their A-list parties. If you invite them, they'll eventually have to invite you! It's called manners.

- DJ (See previous anecdote) at a hip place that everyone likes to frequent.

- Lie about your guest list. "Milla Jovovich is coming!" This is guaranteed to rope in the star-seekers. When they ask where the highly anticipated guest is, always say, "She's on her way" or "She just left."

- Have a friend call your expected guests to confirm their attendance at your party. It will make the event seem bigger than it is, and hence more impressive.

- Send out an invitation with an RSVP number—set up a voice-mail service that takes messages.

- Set up a red carpet and a velvet rope at the entrance. Recruit someone to be the doorman with the clipboard—your brother's largest friend. It's called creating an image.

- The guest list is God. If they're not on the list—they don't get in. Puff Daddy is famous for sending invitations that say, *Don't bring an entourage.* And even when a fellow rapper friend comes with uninvited guests, they are turned away at the door.

- Don't let everybody in. For every eight people you grant access, instruct your doorman to send away one, even if it's your mom and she's on the list. "We're at full capacity." Sorry, Mom!

- Rope off a VIP section at your VIP party. This will create even more sensation, as people will be craning their necks to see who's in the VIP section, and worrying about their non-VIP status. Nothing like creating a little social anxiety to make you seem more important!

## CRASH AND BURN

# WILL WORK FOR ENTRANCE

· · · · · · · · · · ·◦ *Melissa* ◦· · · · · · · · · · ·

*I*n the fall of 1993, Yves Saint Laurent launched Champagne, his first new fragrance in a decade. Preparations for this party were inconceivably expensive, as he had a reputation to live up to—for Opium he had thrown a party in Hong Kong complete with authentic Chinese junks. The party was to be held on Liberty Island, under the shadow of the Statue of Liberty. Guests would be ferried over to partake of a lavish spread and to enjoy a fireworks show on the harbor. I was twenty-two, had just graduated from college, and was working a day job as a computer programmer. There was no way I would ever find myself at this party. Except . . .

Except that I did.

A friend of mine who worked at a graphic-arts firm knew someone who knew someone who knew someone who was—get this—the landscape artist for the Yves Saint Laurent party! And better yet, this landscape artist was looking for young, attractive people to help him set up. "Look, if we help set up, we can go to the party! It's an *island*. What are they going to do, throw us out?" my friend Lauren said, enthusiasm bubbling in her voice. It was agreed. Lauren and I would show up to help with the "landscaping" and then do a quick-change into our evening gowns in the bathrooms so we could stay for the party.

The day of the event, the landscape artist—whom I'll call Madison, since that was his name—greeted us cheerfully at the piers. He explained his "vision" for the event and we nodded wisely. When we arrived at Liberty Island, our "work" to realize his "vision" consisted of placing votive candles on the footpaths. That was it. I marveled that someone would actually pay for such an obvious idea, but at least it spared us heavy lifting. Madison thanked us and presumed to send us on our way.

Instead we ducked through the back and hid ourselves in the bathrooms. A few minutes later we emerged freshly made-up and wearing our most expensive outfits. The first ferries were just arriving to unload party guests. Lauren and I blended in, and we were soon giggling at our own white-linen table, champagne in hand, a plate full of smoked salmon, caviar, and oysters in front of us. We ogled the guests, who included celebrities like Cindy Crawford and Ivana Trump. I was particularly enthralled by my first sighting of old guard socialites Nan Kempner and Loulou de la Falaise.

Japanese photographers asked to take our picture. They assumed we were somebody because of our mere attendance at such an A-list event. Feeling brazen, we even made our way to Yves, whose hand we shook. On the ferry back to New York, we heard the boat captain murmur as the guests disembarked, "So beautiful, everyone so beautiful and thin . . . so beautiful . . ." It was such a magical night. At the end of it, I had even managed to forget I hadn't been invited.

"See you at the next party," called a dashing gentleman whose friendship we had made on the ride back.

"Yes, of course," we called back, delighted. Then we turned

to each other. What next party? How would we find out what this "next party" was? There were more of these fabulous extravaganzas? It was my first taste of New York glitterati and I promised myself it would not be the last.


# THEY'RE CRASHING
# OUR PARTY?

• • • • • *Melissa* and *Karen* • • • • •

Shawn Purdy, *Marie Claire*'s publicist who was helping us throw our book deal party extravaganza, called us with some great news two weeks before the blessed event. "You won't believe this," she said, "but people are already RSVP-ing to your party!"

She started fielding tons of calls, since our event became a highly touted one when George Rush, *Daily News* gossip columnist extraordinaire who dishes dirt in his column, "Rush & Molloy," printed a tidbit about our party that read:

> Writers **Karen Robinovitz** and **Melissa de la Cruz** haven't finished their book, *How to Become Famous in Two Weeks (Or Less)*, but they're already milking their deal with Ballantine. They've persuaded *Marie Claire* magazine to throw them a pre–book party on Nov. 25 at Lot 61, where the authors, dripping in Jacob and Co. jewels, will make their entrance with a fleet of twenty male Ford models on Vespas.

"They're totally trying to crash your party," Shawn cooed. We had such a laugh. And, of course, she informed them that it was impossible to RSVP, as invitations had yet to be mailed!

We were actually flattered. It was just the kind of stunt *we* would do!

## THE CRASH COURSE

There is a breed of people, unconnected nobodies, who always seem to get into all the right parties, despite the fact that they know no one and are not socially distinctive in any way. We very much advise that you do not become one of these people. But sometimes (i.e., before you "make it"), you can't help it. If you must crash a party, these are the tricks:

- Slip in with the caterers, barbacks, and delivery people. Wait in the bathroom until the party gets going and then make your presence known.

- Get a job at the location—or with someone who is working at the party.

- RSVP to the phone number on the invitation, even if you didn't receive an invitation yourself.

- Learn to read upside down. Point to the person on the list and say, "Look, that's me." If that person's name has been crossed off, say you're that person's "plus one."

- Pretend to be a journalist, one who isn't famous enough to have face recognition—no one knows what the editor of the Styles section of the New York *Times* looks like, but they'll always let him in. Another trick is to find out who's been invited but isn't going. Show up and pretend you're that person.

• Find out what the party is for and concoct an appropriate identity that will facilitate an entrance. If it's a film party, say you're a producer who works with De Niro, or an agent with CAA.

• Arrive at the party with a town celebrity (i.e., a dog that resembles a famous dog that stars in the latest movie—say it's the celeb pooch!)—a person who would have been invited or would never be rejected.

• Say you're the entertainment. If you act like a seductress and talk with a sultry bedroom voice, they might actually believe you're a burlesque dancer.

• Find a back door or window. Knock. Pretend you just stepped outside for a cigarette and got locked out.

• Plead to use the bathroom. Leave collateral, something you don't care about, and promise you'll be back. Don't return until the end of the night.

• Bring different-colored pens and smudge your hand to approximate the stamp. When you approach the doorpeople, say you've already been stamped, and are just returning.

• Create a diversion. Bring a friend who doesn't want to get in and have her pretend to foam at the mouth (Alka-Seltzer will come in handy). While she's writhing on the floor and all the doormen are freaking out, you can sneak by without a hitch.

• If all else fails, make a scene, storm out, offend someone. If you don't get in, you can at least ruin everyone else's night.

*Day 14—Forever, If You're Lucky:*

# SWAG-A-LICIOUS, BABY!

*John Cusack enjoys the perks of movie stardom. The affable actor is particularly fond of "celebrity looting." During an interview with* Black Book *magazine, Cusack pointed out a Roots clothing store and said, "We did celebrity looting there. . . . They asked me to come over, patronize the store, pick up some stuff. So I took all my friends over, and we went straight for the $8,000 rack of leather coats and took a bunch. The managers, they get all nervous and twitchy. They freak. But you just look at 'em really hard and walk out. That's celebrity looting."*

—*New York Post*, Page Six, Sunday, October 13, 2002

Civilians (i.e., we who are not famous) want what the famous have—beauty products, hotel rooms, spa treatments, lingerie, watches, handbags, shoes, clothes, pens, meals, hairstylists, furnishings, cell phones, sunglasses, even a dinky little votive candle, for God's sake. So it's no coincidence that the first question reporters ask red-carpet-walking gods and goddesses is, "What are you wearing?" We, as a culture, want to know what celebrities don, decorate their homes with, eat for dinner, keep in the fridge, and put on to moisturize. The theory behind the phenomenon is simple: if they have it, it must be good . . . and so we should have it, too.

*"Life on the 'free' way."*
*Swag at its finest.*

The most popular section of magazines is usually the part where they tell you which celeb owns what. It often inspires shopping sprees. For manufacturers, store owners, publicists, and designers, celebrity approval means dollar signs. Their hope is that if *she* (or *he*) is seen wearing/eating/buying *it*, the consumer will run out and buy it, too. (Case in point: Once, Karen was trying on a pair of boots that she felt iffy about, but when she heard that there were only two pairs in stock and Claudia Schiffer purchased the other one, she instantly forked over her AmEx. Sad, but true!)

The irony is that celebrities don't always do their shopping themselves! Often, when you read that so-and-so owns a certain handbag/pair of earrings/lamp/tampon case, it is because the designer sent the item to the celeb as a *gift*—then the publicist reports the "news" to a reporter, who prints it, tempting unknowing readers to run out and buy the same thing, even if the celeb had almost nothing to do with it.

This is *swag*.

Swag is what insiders call "free stuff." It's the *loot*, the ultimate perk of stardom, and a surefire sign that you've made it, after all. And in the land of fame and fabulousness, there's plenty of swag to be had. Daily, stars, socialites, models, and people who possess a commanding brand name are blessed with boxes upon boxes of luxury gifts. They are invited to stores to pilfer whatever they choose. When they show up to parties, present awards on television, or get settled in their trailers on film sets, they are thanked with the most lavish gift bags imaginable— up to $20,000 worth of merch.

# PRESENTERS AT THE 2002 OSCARS
# HAD A GOOD REASON
# TO THANK THE ACADEMY
## THIS WAS IN THEIR GIFT BAGS

- Tempur-Pedic mattress, any size. Value up to $1,700
- La-Z-Boy recliners, choice of four. $539 to $1,199
- Three-night stay at Esperanza, a luxury resort in Cabo San Lucas, Mexico. $3,000
- Allsteel #19 office chair. $1,195 to $1,495
- Hewlett-Packard PhotoSmart 715 camera. $499.99
- Sama sunglasses designed for the Oscars, for women only. $300
- Stainless-steel Ebel watch. $1,600 for the women with a mother-of-pearl dial, $1,450 for the men with a white roman dial.
- Flying Fig scarf. $300 to $1,100
- 90-minute Godiva chocolate body wrap at Ajune, a New York spa. $175
- Jenni Originals VegeSoy candle, handmade from an exclusive blend of soybean and vegetable waxes. $12.95
- Lancôme gift certificates. $200
- Gift certificate for Sonya Dakar, a problem-skin specialist. $500
- Complimentary teeth whitening at BriteSmile. $600
- Birkenstock gift certificate. $300

Receiving swag not only confirms your high-profile status and makes you feel special, but it also catapults your image. Why? Because it affords you glamour, grandeur, glory, and the right to boast, "They gave this to me for free." It's a fact of life that once you attain Julia Roberts status, you'll never have to pay for anything ever again. Cartier watches, Christian Dior wardrobes, Louis Vuitton luggage *per gratis* are part of the lifestyle. A documentary estimated that Madonna has received *$10 million* worth of free designer clothes in her career. But it took her a long time to reach that position in life. Our advice to you is this: be patient. Rome wasn't built in a day. Neither was your star on Hollywood Boulevard, baby. It may take ten, fifteen, even fifty attempts to secure your placement in some kind of hall of fame, but fret not, because once you do, the swag will be yours for the taking.

This chapter offers detailed instructions and tips for obtaining swag, including: how to secure a goody bag at the end of a party (this means, of course, getting invited to the kind of party where there are goody bags to be had—and we covered the party circuit in great length in Step VI), getting your little mitts on free clothes, turning all favors into material rewards, how much free stuff costs (there's always a catch), and what not to do if you're trying to avoid the blacklist. Read it—and start making space in your closet. Trust us, you'll need it!

## GOODY BAGS, THE BEST PART OF ANY PARTY

# THE SIDEWALK IS NO PLACE FOR A LADY

• • • • • • • • • *Melissa* • • • • • • • • •

There I was, a respectable fashion journalist at the star-studded opening of a new designer boutique. Except, instead of being inside the party and living it up with the rest of Manhattan's party faithful—the usual crew of models, socialites, publicists, magazine editors, artists, DJs, and trendoids who populated the scene—I was nursing a bruise from being shoved out the door by a particularly overzealous security guard.

My crime? I was caught stealing nineteen gift bags.

Okay. So nineteen gift bags sounds like a lot—like grand theft burglary, in fact. But I had a good excuse. Everyone else was doing it!

In New York, gift-bag culture dictates that the party aficionado affect uninterest in the contents of the goody bag handed out to guests at the end of the evening. It's considered déclassé to root in your bag in front of fellow hipsters while you're still at the event. The appropriate attitude is: I'm so above all this, I don't even care about the free loot. Too cool for school. But at heart, everyone loves a gift bag. Even if its contents include only cheap-smelling lotion, a magazine you've already read, and a CD of a band that you've never heard of, leaving a party without a gift bag is a form of social defeat. I

*The holy grail . . . otherwise known as the gift-bag table!*

once arrived at a shopping party at an upscale department store too late to obtain the hundreds of dollars of free gift certificates that were handed out early in the evening. It is still the biggest regret of my life!

The night I tried to steal nineteen gift bags, a well-known boutique on Fifth Avenue was celebrating its launch by producing a line of limited-edition designer shirts that would be available only through the gift bag. There was an electricity in the air as the crowd tingled with anticipation at receiving the coveted loot. As I kiss-kissed people I knew and partook of the hearty hors d'oeuvres, I eyed the gift-bag station like a hawk, just to make sure they would not run out of bags before I left. Near the end of the evening, it appeared that the boutique staff was having trouble keeping up with the demand as everyone began to leave. Boxed shirts littered the shelves, the table, and the floors. When the woman in charge of parceling out the gift bags left to bring more, a kind of mania exploded as the crowd pounced on the unmanned table.

Guests began to take up to four, five, ten gift bags each. Greed quickly took over as we all indulged in this unexpected liberty! It was gift-bag nirvana. *We could take as many gift-bags as we wanted!* I was out of breath and furiously cramming shirts into my oversize Prada tote bag as fast as I could manage (although I was still checking to make sure they were all the right sizes). At one point I was on my hands and knees, with six shirt boxes crumpled beneath each arm, frantically exhorting my boyfriend (now husband) Mike to "get down here and help me, for godssakes!" We could get more! One for my sister, one for my friend, one for my editor, one for my mom, et cetera.

Suddenly I felt a tap on my arm.

"Ma'am! Ma'am!"

"What?" I asked, my arms bulging with boxes of the coveted shirts.

*"Only one per person"* the bouncer roared.

"But—look, everyone's taking so many!" I pointed desperately to the guests who were merrily walking away with a dozen shirts each.

*"Put the shirts down!"*

I stared at him defiantly. These gift bags were mine!

*"All right, that's it! You're out of here!"* he said, forcibly removing the shirt boxes from my arms and marshaling me out the door.

The next thing I knew, I was standing outside the boutique, bereft of all but one gift bag. Through the glass doors I saw Mike, who was still inside, give me a puzzled what-are-you-doing-out-there look. He sauntered out of the party, and I told him my woeful tale. He grinned. "Look," he said, opening his coat. Inside were seven shirt boxes. We ended up eleven short of my original goal, but at least I left with more than one!

# GIMME, GIMME, GIMME!

* * * * * * * * * *  *Karen*  * * * * * * * * *

"*A*re you going to the Chanel party?" I asked my friend.

"Totally. I hear the goody bags rule," she said back.

There are some parties you go to just to get the goody bag, a parting gift that usually involves a gaggle of good swag. I've left events with fleece sweatshirts, Nike down jackets, iPods, Puma sneakers (anytime an invitation asks me to RSVP with my shoe size, I sure do RSVP, and add proudly, 6 ½ or 37 ½ European), gift certificates for chemical peels, cashmere wraps, kitten-heel Swarovski crystal-studded shoes. At a Mercedes launch for the new coupe one year, I was given a little red car for a free week-end in the Hamptons. When I sank comfortably into my leather bucket seats, there was a welcome (leather tote) bag, overflow-ing with CDs, driving gloves, a Mercedes beach towel, flip-flops for the beach, SPF 15 lotion, an Inca bikini and sarong, Hugo Boss sunglasses, a leather journal, beach-themed stationery, packets of Altoids, and snacks. Over the course of the weekend, each morning my car was cleaned and filled with gas and there was also a new gift bag, each better than the next. I must have taken home $3,000 worth of stuff—a Betsey Johnson denim jacket, Juicy Couture T-shirts, Kiehl's products, tickets to the polo match, Michael Kors perfume.

So it's easy to understand why a girl can get caught up in the party circuit and leave home just for the goody bags. And one brisk fall evening, I was no different. There were about a dozen fashion-world happenings that night, and I made it my duty to make it to each and every one, just to collect some swag. I left Bendel's, my first stop, with four shopping bags of products (it was a take-whatever-you-want beauty party). I exited the Chanel store opening with a groovy, chunky floral ring that people com-pliment all the time. (I love saying, "It was in a gift bag.") I walked out of a dinner party for a designer with a gift certificate for a suite at the hotel where the party was held, as well as a bottle of bubbly. I was so loaded with gifts that I had to ask friends to help carry my things. I closed the night at artist Damian Loeb's loft, where he was hosting an intimate cocktail party. After downing three plastic cups of red wine and making a few social rounds of schmoozing, I was eager to get home and admire my loot.

As I walked out the door, I saw it—a table covered with gleaming silver tubes. "What great goody-bag packaging," I yelled with delight, pocketing the goods. (Gift bags are usually placed on tables near the exit door.)

I was thinking that I couldn't wait to see what was inside when Damian suddenly jumped off a sofa and pounced. "Those are my paints!" he shrieked, grabbing the shiny silver item from my hand. "They're a hundred dollars a tube! They're not gift bags!"

"Oh, my God!" I yelled. I apologized profusely. I was so embarrassed. I was so used to getting a little token at the end of a party that I had automatically mistaken his personal property for the coveted booty.

It was that night that I learned a very valuable lesson: there are no goody bags in the art world.

## WE ARE, TOO, ON THE LIST!

• • • • • *Karen* and *Melissa* • • • • •

We were having a drink at the chichi Chambers Hotel on West Fifty-sixth Street. And we couldn't help but get distracted by the hullabaloo nearby. At the bottom of an architecturally designed staircase, a wealth of bags, overflowing with what appeared to be some very good stuff, resided on a table. "Karen, it's a goody-bag table," Mel said under her breath, jerking her head to the side to subtly point me in the direction of the aforementioned plunder. It was as if she were an undercover cop, narrowing in on a drug dealer. "Let's go in," I said. She nodded. Our goal: to get into the party and leave with loot in hand. Before approaching the two blond gatekeepers at the entrance, we did a spot of research . . . we followed a woman who was holding a goody bag into the bathroom and found out what the party was for. We figured, if we seemed like we knew exactly what was up, we'd be able to get in. Once we had the logistics, we marched toward the staircase, affecting a VIP posture (shoulder blades melting down the back; head high; navel in; chest out). We smiled, said hello, and walked right upstairs. "Excuse me," one of the blonds said, just as we hit the third step, "it's a private party."

"Yes," we said, spewing out as many details as we could remember. "We're on the list," Mel said.

"Under Cohen," I added, as we continued to ascend to our rightful destination. They didn't stop us. We indulged in a few free drinks and pastry puffs, did a lap, surveyed the scene, and left soon after.

"Not really in the mood to be out," we said to the blonds when we walked back down to the lobby.

"I understand," one said, handing us each a gift bag. Mission accomplished.

# OUR VERY OWN GIFT BAGS

## *Karen* and *Melissa*

*If* a party isn't a party without a gift bag, there was no way Mel and I were having a bash without offering a token something at the door. And because we've become gift-bag snobs, ungrateful receivers who have often left unwanted items in taxicabs, we were going to make it a damn good one. We got on the phone to our network of publicists, who helped us round up the following (for free, of course, as gift bags in the right hands is just a way of getting certain products brand exposure. It's called grass roots marketing):

- The latest issue of *Marie Claire*
- A 15 percent discount card to Language, a hip downtown store that sells Chloe, Marc Jacobs, Stella McCartney, and Pucci
- Baume Levres lip balm. A favorite of Liv Tyler's
- Ouidad hair products for curly hair from Ouidad's swanky uptown salon
- Shampoo from Korres, a hot new line of products from Greece
- Gift certificates for a blow-out or a manicure at the posh Warren Tricomi salon
- Star-shaped candy from Dylan's Candy Bar, a candy wonderland owned by Ralph Lauren's daughter Dylan

Note: Karen didn't get a gift bag at the end of the night. Melissa, of course, did. She made sure to secure hers early in the evening, while Karen plain-old forgot until it was too late and there were none left. The day after, our book editor, Allison, called us because she didn't get one either! "I should have brushed up on those gift-bag tips from the book." She laughed.

## PARTY FAVORS
### BE A VULTURE WITHOUT SEEMING LIKE ONE

- Leave parties early. Goody bags are often first come, first serve. So it's best to beat the crowd and stake your claim before anyone else does the same.

- "Fake leave" a party. Walk out to receive a goody bag and return for the fun soon after.

- Try to snag the bag on your way into the party—if you're lucky, you may just get another one on your way out.

- If you notice that other people have gift bags and you don't, say politely to the person in charge, "I'm sorry. But I can't seem to find my goody bag." This person should remedy the situation.

- If you're given a particularly good goody bag and you want another, tell the person who's manning the gift-bag station that you would like to get one for your friend who came to the party but forgot to take hers, or for a VIP, like "my editor" or "my friend Lucy Liu."

- Keep an eye out for the gift-bag table, and as soon as it's set up, make your move.

- If the bags are unmanned and simply scattered on the shelves or on the floor, help yourself. Nothing's fair in love and gift bags. (If someone stops you, just apologize and act like you had no idea that what you were doing was inappropriate.)

- If, by some awful twist of fate, you did not get the goody bag, call the person who threw the party (or the person's publicist) and sweetly ask for one. "Thank you for organizing such a wonderful party. I was having so much fun, I left without the gift bag!" Subtle hints will ensure that a goody bag will be messengered to your door the next day.

## CLOTHES WHORES

# ONE-NIGHT STAND

### *Karen*

*T*wenty-four hours before my thirtieth birthday, in the midst of all the hoopla about my gala, I was stressing out over what coat to wear. I didn't own the kind of dramatically elegant evening coat that makes a statement and screams, *"I'm here!"* when you enter a room. I was a wreck, I tell you! A wreck! I tore through department stores, boutiques, and sales racks to find something special. No luck. As the hours ticked away, I became more and more frustrated. How could I go out without the right coat? I needed something fierce. Otherwise, my micromini pink tiger-print dress would be ruined—and everyone would realize it was all a fraud. A famous person always has the right coat. I was convinced I'd have no grand entrance without one.

Then my phone rang. I was so depressed, I screened the call. "Hi, Karen. This is Ann Dee Goldin," a voice said. "A little birdie told me it was your birthday and I wanted to invite you to borrow . . ."

Ann! Dee! Goldin! My heart skipped a beat. She is one of the most chichi furriers, who has worked with designers like Narciso Rodriguez and Karl Lagerfeld, as well as all of the socialites. Now, I never thought of myself as the kind of girl who wears fur. Not just because of animal rights and my fear of red-paint-throwing activists, but because it always seemed so "rich bitch." But since fur has been in every magazine, on the slim shoulders of everyone from P. Diddy and Cher to Naomi Campbell (years after she posed for PETA ad campaigns, spewing, "I'd rather go naked than wear fur"), Foxy Brown, and all the junior socialites of the city, the once-politically-incorrect material has become more than a fashion statement, even—dare I say—socially acceptable. Fur—politics aside—symbolizes instant glamour, which is just what I craved for my big night.

I first met Ann Dee Goldin the year before, when I wrote about one of her pieces for the Styles section of the *New York Times*. The last time we spoke, she told me I could call her if I ever needed something. I didn't think "free fur" would be an appropriate thing to ask for, so I never called. But now she was calling me! I knew this was going to be a good conversation, so I immediately picked up my phone. "Yes, this is Karen," I said, acting as cool as possible. To make a long story short, her publicist told her about my party, and she wanted to know if I'd wear one of her coats for the night.

Here's the thing about celebrity style. We see them waltz

down the red carpet wearing the most glamorous of threads, a different ensemble each and every time we see them. It is often because they are wearing something on loan. It's called "clothes for a night," otherwise known as "one-night stands." Sometimes a whole bunch of one-night stands are better than making a commitment to one frock that you'll likely get sick of or wear only once anyway (this in no way reflects my dating ethics). People like Iman, the Lauder sisters (as in Estée), and Jennifer Lopez have all borrowed furs for their nights out, and I wanted to, too, dammit! In Tinseltown, it's all about borrowed glamour. Why do you think everyone is always in Versace? And suddenly Ann Dee was letting me in on the A-list action.

I hopped in a taxi and made my way to her showroom, where I draped myself in sheared minks, chubby fox furs, long sables, and fluffy shawls. It was heaven. Each piece was softer, more luxurious, and more expensive than the last. Then Ann Dee brought me to her vault, where she archived her special pieces. I instantly fell for a $20,000 chinchilla. I named her "Chin-Chin Rodriguez" and declared her mine.

She would work perfectly with my slutty pink dress! It was an Ivana Trump moment. Even if I had to sign a release form that said I would pay for it if it wasn't returned by noon on Friday.

I returned the coat, along with a thank-you note and a photo. And she was so touched by my gratitude that she sent me a present—the savage-looking partially sheared fox-fur chubby I was flipping out over in her showroom. Free fur! I think the only free fur J.Lo's gotten was a Dolce & Gabbana jacket from Ben. I heard she named hers Chi-Chi! Great minds think alike.

# GIFTS FROM THE DESIGNER

## *Melissa*

$\mathcal{I}$ was all set to do my two weeks of fame on the strength of my own wardrobe. I was, after all, a shopaholic and a fashionista, so how hard could it be? But being famous meant going out every night and making sure I was photographed in a new and different and up-to-the-minute outfit that no normal person, no matter how deep their closets, could possibly put together on their own.

As a fashion journo, I was familiar with one of the industry's standard practices, "pulling for a shoot," otherwise known as borrowing clothes from designer showrooms for magazine editorials. I made an appointment with a showroom that represented the likes of avant-garde designers Alice Roi and Ulla Johnson. They typically provide clothes only for fashion photo shoots, but I convinced them that it was *practically* the same thing, since I would be photographed wearing them at several "high-profile" events that would run in several media outlets. "We'll get credit?" the showroom manager asked skeptically. "Of course!" I promised, keeping my fingers crossed behind my back. He finally agreed, and I was allowed to leave with a week's worth of outfits. I was so loaded down with my two heavy shopping bags that I tripped on a step as I exited the showroom. "I'm all right!" I assured them from the doorway. It was not one of my most dignified moments. In fact, I must have looked like a thief making a bungled getaway.

Still, it was a start. And the next day, fresh from last night's success, I brazenly called Celine, the Michael Kors–designed couture line, to borrow a knockout dress for several premieres I would be attending. I heard that they were particularly generous loaners for celebrities. I spun my tale and promised "high-profile" publicity. "Sure," the manager said. She just had one question: "What size are you?"

"Um, a ten," I replied. There was an ominous silence.

"Our samples are sixes. Very, very small sixes. And unfortunately, Angelica Huston has all our tens for the Academy Awards," she informed me.

I felt defeated upon learning I had the same body size as a fifty-something woman! Even if it was Angelica Huston.

Undaunted, I cold-called the Alvin Valley studio. After reading in the *New York Times* (um, in an article that Karen wrote!) about the Cuban designer's sexy, leather-waisted trousers that turn any girl into a leggy Cameron Diaz (who's a customer), I decided I must have a pair. Jennifer Pearson, Alvin's PR rep, was more than happy to accommodate me when I fed her my line about "multiple photo ops." They fitted me for several pairs of pants, and Alvin personally selected a Julia Roberts–like cutout black jersey top for me to wear. There's even a self-esteem bonus—in Alvin's sizing, I'm a svelte eight!

I twirled and admired myself in the mirror. "These make my butt look great," I said as the seamstress cuffed the hems. They planned to messenger them to me in the A.M. Then Jennifer asked, "Should we charge this to *Marie Claire*'s account?" Since they were customizing the pant length, it would have to count as a "sale" and not a "pull."

"Um, no. The magazine isn't paying for that kind of thing,"

I stammered sheepishly. And there was no way I could pay for them. The pants were $400 each! And they had fitted me for three pairs! "Hmmm," she said. "I'll talk to Alvin."

The next day, the pants were sent to my apartment, beautifully hemmed, with a note from Jennifer: *Alvin would like you to keep the pants as a gift.* I hugged myself in relief. I wore those Alvin Valley pants everywhere. I became known as "the Alvin Valley girl." When our "Two Weeks of Fame" article came out, Alvin sent me a box full of three new pairs. I felt so honored.

But it didn't stop there. During the next week, as photographs of me in my borrowed garb appeared in magazines from *Ocean Drive* to *New York* magazine, a strange thing began to happen . . . I began to receive packages from other designers sending me their wares. Rock & Republic, a new Los Angeles–based designer worn by Sheryl Crow and Courteney Cox, sent me three pairs of their herringbone, suede-trimmed, low-rise jeans because the designer was a fan of my novel and had loved my "famous" piece in *Marie Claire*.

"Oh, my God!" a fashionable friend said upon seeing my new jeans. "Those are so next season! You can't even buy them yet!" For my wedding, jewelry designers Slane and Slane, who craft elegant and one-of-a-kind pavé diamond and pearl necklaces, gifted me with an exquisite set of matching diamond earrings, ring, and necklace. They even threw in a gorgeous sterling-silver cuff link and shirt-stud set for my husband. If this keeps up, I may never have to shop again!

# BLING! BLING!

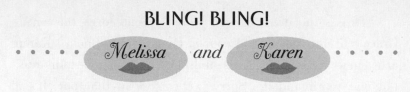

*Melissa* and *Karen*

As the details of our book deal party came together, we had only one thing left to stress about: what to wear! For the two of us, picking the right ensemble is a science, something that often requires trying on everything we own, shedding some tears when things don't look quite as good as we had hoped, and complaining that we have no clothes, when our closets wholeheartedly disagree. We needed to shine at our party and nothing in our wardrobes would do.

Enter celebrity dressing. The red-carpet parade is a walking advertisement for designers, so it's no surprise that luxury design houses staff entire departments solely for "celebrity dressing." Their goal: to get stars in their designer threads. They fly out to the Oscars and film premieres with trunks full of gowns and accessories, hoping and praying to wardrobe the brightest stars.

What designer represents celebrity like none other? The answer: John Galliano. We had a contact at Christian Dior who put us in touch with Grace Cha, who handles celebrity dressing. We faxed a request and three days later, we were on the thirty-seventh floor of the plush LVMH offices, rifling through racks of leather pants with mirrored embellishments, silk knit and tulle gowns, racy dresses that laced up the front—and the back. There were leather jackets, kangaroo fur coats, dazzling T-shirts with fishnet sleeves. It was a dream come true, even if most of the things were too long for K and too small for M.

"This is the dress Kirsten wore." "Sofia loves this one," Grace told us. (Meaning of course, Dunst and Coppola.) Karen ached to wear a stunning silver-and-black Grecian-style minidress, but was reprimanded, "Sorry, we can't loan that out. It's a Spring. No celebrity has been photographed wearing it yet." So she chose a leather miniskirt and T-shirt (but later hemorrhaged her month's rent for a chartreuse Gucci frock because she wanted something more like the dress she fell in love with but was not allowed to wear). Melissa was relieved to find something she could squeeze into: a bright red *stretch* wool strapless dress, embellished with sequins and beads. It was very "fiesta."

As we air-kissed our way out, Dior garment bags in hand, we bumped into Gina Gershon, who began sorting through the racks for another party that week. We snickered that she would have to make do with our "rejects" . . . until we realized that the covetable spring collection probably wasn't off-limits to the likes of her.

From there it was on to a fur showroom (Ann Dee Goldin again!), where Ann Dee gave us the pick of the litter—a buffet full of chinchillas, mink, silver fox, animal-print numbers, and over the top coats—for our party. We frantically tried on dozens, grabbing hanger after hanger of plush pelts. Do we wear the floor sweeping sable, the chubby squirrel, the hot pink shearling? Oh, such decisions! After twenty minutes of living out our Audrey Hepburn fantasies, we were ready to leave with $20,000 of merchandise. Sadly, however, we had to sign a release form of responsibility—if something were to happen to the coats, we had to pay. Unable to deal with such accountability, we passed on the fur and went back to Dior for swing wool coats with fur collars and buttons—sans release form.

*Raiding the fur vault at Goldin Feldman. Can we keep them all?*

TANYA BRAGANTI

TANYA BRAGANTI

*Twelve karats of diamonds each!*
*The studs J. Lo wore on the cover of Vanity Fair!*

We were in the middle of a fashion fairy tale and our day was far from over. We had handbags and jewelry to find. After our party invitations went out, a grateful recipient invited us to his Upper East Side "socialite" boutique called Vivaldi. David Trugerman, the store's owner, greeted us at the door—and led us to the back room, where an oversized velvet poof cushion covered with Valentino bags awaited us. "Pick any one you want," he said. "Consider it a gift from us for the two stars."

"We couldn't," we said. "That's too much." But who were we kidding? We could! And we did! Should we take the deco clutch or the suede pouch with the gold V buckle? Celebrity looting at its finest! (We could get used to this!) We both wanted the leather floral bag that would have cost us over a grand if we actually bought it, but because there was only one, we decided it wasn't worth the fight. So we opted for matching snakeskin clutches with a small rhinestone V emblazoned on the front. Very chic. Very mod. Very celeb. Very us! We said our farewells calmly and coolly, as if this sort of thing happens to us all the time. But once we hit the street, we jumped up and down, giddy with laughter. Admiring our new coup, we screamed with delight, "This is crazy! It's not normal!"

We stopped for a chamomile tea in order to calm down and get our bearings before our next appointment: As per an invitation from a publicist, who wanted to help dress us for the party, we were planning to pay a visit to Jacob & Co., the jeweler of choice in the hip hop and music communities. P. Diddy, Michael Jackson, Britney Spears, and Justin Timberlake wear his outthere diamonds—giant microphone pendants, huge ID necklaces, enormous crosses.

*Picking Valentino bags at Vivaldi.*
*Thank God they're free!*

We tried on rock after rock, trying to figure out if we should go for rare and outrageously precious pink diamonds, or a necklace with a diamond-encrusted revolver the size of a small football? In the name of classic elegance, we each chose twelve-karat diamond earrings, the exact same ashtray-size studs that J. Lo wore on a cover of the music issue of *Vanity Fair* in November 2002. They were bigger than our lobes—just what the doctor ordered.

We couldn't wait to flash our new wares. When all was said and done, we would each be worth a mere $178,000 for our debutante ball, but we felt like a million bucks.

# CLOTHES CALL

## PUMP UP YOUR WARDROBE WITHOUT BREAKING THE BANK

- Write a fan letter. Our friend wrote one to Balenciaga designer Nicholas Ghesquiere, and he was so flattered, he sent her a lace top, a veritable gift from God.

- Tell PR gals at designer showrooms your pictures are scheduled to run in the papers. They will loan you clothes gladly if you're able to get them press mentions. If you land a good "hit" they might even let you keep the swag!

- Become friends with talented designers before they make it. Don't know any? Try hanging out near fashion schools, like FIT and Parson's in New York or St Martins in London.

- Befriend the owners of a store you adore. If you're a good customer, they may not be opposed to loaning you something for a night.

- "Call in" (meaning: request) clothes from designer show-

TANYA BRAGANTI

*Dying over Harry Winston diamonds. I'd like to thank the Academy. . . .*

rooms for glossy magazine photo shoots. (Don't have one? Just make it up.) Take the items for a road test and return them—as promised—in good condition (the showroom will often make you sign a consent form that says you are responsible for any damages). They'll never know your "shoot" was merely a job interview/first date/birthday party.

• No luck scoring swag on your own? Move to LA and get a job as the personal assistant to a major celebrity. If you play your cards right, some of their loot may be yours (there's only so many free Gallianos one person can have).

• As you become more famous, free threads are a given. People will want you to wear their clothes, because if you look good, they look good. You may even become the designer's model—and get paid for wearing his or her creations. Look at Penelope Cruz and Ralph Lauren.

## SYMBIOSIS: SWAG IS A TWO-WAY STREET

# PARTY GIRL

• • • • • *Karen* and *Melissa* • • • • •

*Melissa* wasn't planning to have a bachelorette party. But I was not letting her transcend to marriage without one. The only problem was, I was broke. I literally had $1.89 in the bank! I couldn't afford to throw her the kind of event she deserved—complete with erotic dance teacher on hand to show her the kind of moves that would make her husband hot. So I did what any resourceful person would do: I figured out a way to get the entire party for free.

The thing about getting comped is that in order to pull it off, you always have to give something back in return. In my case, I had one very valuable offering: press. If I could find a way to write about the escapade, which I wanted to develop into a piece about women embracing the ancient art form of the striptease, I was certain people would happily lend me their services.

My first order of business was to find the right space, a cool looking boîte that wouldn't require additional decor preparations. I had written about Isla, a funky Nuevo Cuban restaurant on a quaint block in the West Village, a few times. And I loved the owner, a fashionable woman named Diane Ghioto who was once the fashion editor of *Elle* magazine. Her place, a sexy powder blue–and-white den reminiscent of a 1950s pool cabana, is the perfect spot to play. When I contacted Diane and explained that I wanted to throw Mel a fabulous soiree, she instantly piped in, "Do it at my restaurant."

"But we can't pay anything," I said sheepishly. "And we were hoping to find a place where we could get food and drinks for, well, free." I added, "Not a lot of food or drinks. There will only be fifteen of us," to cushion the blow.

"Okay, do it here," she said. I was surprised how easy my plight was becoming. "I love having you in the restaurant," she continued. "You're our little famous friend! We read your *Marie Claire* article! We love Melissa, too! We'll feed you!"

Like a true celeb, I was getting comped just for being me. I revealed my plans to bring in an erotic dance teacher, and Diane went crazy for it. Apparently the evening of Mel's party was also Isla's debut weekly gay party. "What boys won't love to learn how to strip with you?" she squealed, before planning a tangy menu of mojitos, empañadas, grilled shrimp skewers, and yucca fries. "We'll make a whole press event out of it," she said excitedly. Three things down, one to go. Next, I needed to find a stripping instructor.

At the time, there was a lot of talk of the trend of women learning how to pole-dance. Apparently Kate Moss was into it. Pamela Anderson had a pole at home. Two of my friends actually got a pole installed and hosted pole-dancing parties at their boutique. It was the latest thing from LA to London. I researched the Internet and came across Sky London, a saucy fifty-four-year-old former stripper, who hosts a naughty show on a public access cable station and also teaches classes in becoming a goddess, giving oral sex, and dancing seductively. Due to my excellent reporting skills, I found her phone number. I knew I had called the right person when I heard a breathy voice purr on her answering machine, "Hi. This is the heaven of Sky London. My words of wisdom for the day are: after three martinis, it's okay to do someone in the bathroom of a restaurant, but don't go home and give yourself a haircut!"

Sky and I got along, for lack of a better word, famously, on the phone. She—and her crass, bold opinions and tell-it-like-it-is attitude—seemed so cool that I wanted her at the party, even as a guest. When I told her what I was doing, she wanted in on the action, especially because the night would expose her to hundreds of new people who could possibly drum up business for her. By giving me her services, she would be giving herself access to new clients. It was a win-win situation. Barter at its finest.

Stripping 101 with Sky London at Isla.

TANYA BRAGANTI

The second she walked into the restaurant, one of Mel's gay friends screeched, "Sky London in the house!" Apparently Sky has a big following in the gay community. (Who knew?) The night was out of control! We all learned arousing ways to remove opera-length gloves, how to "dip it" (meaning: our butts) while squatting to the beat of a pop song, and how to slither on the floor like true sluts! We were taught how to flutter our tongues, give ourselves proper spankings, and do all sorts of wicked things with faux pearl necklaces. We forced Mel, who's normally shy, to practice her moves in front of the entire restaurant. Sky egged her on and called out moves: "Hands in the hair. Hump the air!" Two hours later, Mel whispered, "I think I'm going to have an excellent honeymoon!" After watching her shake her booty, I was sure she would, too.

## BACK SCRATCHING
### DO UNTO OTHERS AND THEY WILL DO BACK UNTO YOU

• Say yes to all favors. Payback time is always around the corner.

• Help a new storeowner, restaurateur, artist, massage therapist, or anyone who has a service or product that you want. Get local press coverage for this person in exchange for bounty (refer to schmoozing to refresh your memory).

• Don't have medical insurance? Throw a party for the best (or better yet, newest) doctor in town. Get it catered—for free or at a hugely discounted rate, by promising the restaurant or chef that your party will bring him or her huge exposure. Convince the doctor to bestow free treatments to bring in new clients. Call a local paper and get them to cover this "hot new trend" and—voilà!—you're in swag city, sweetheart. There's nothing like a free MD!

• Invite an expert over to teach you and your glamorous friends a lesson—flower arranging, vintage shopping, reconstructing their own clothes, baking. By introducing someone who has something to sell, you'll be thanked with free stuff.

• Offer to host other people's parties and events for important organizations. By hosting, you, the famous one, will bring great cachet to the event. You will have to guarantee a certain amount of people will attend, so rope in your fab entourage, publicist(s), and new journalist friends. Make sure your generosity will be rewarded in cash or—more important—in kind.

• Call marketing and media or public relations departments of liquor companies and ask them to sponsor your birthday party. By putting them on the invitation, you're giving them ample opportunity to promote their brand to "imagemakers, tastemakers, and trendsetters" such as yourself. There's no such thing as tacky when you're in haute pursuit.

• Switch careers. Become a journalist. People send them free stuff all the time, just so they can write about it. We've gotten free hair products, moisturizers, makeup, shoes, yoga mats, CDs, denim jackets, cashmere sweaters, watches, handbags, perfume, and—ahem!—even vibrators. (Regift whatever you don't want and you'll never have to stress about holiday shopping again.)

• Blackmail. If nothing else works, get dirt on luxury purveyors and haunt them with it. Who wants cash when you can get cashmere?

# LAND OF THE FREE?

· · · · · *Melissa* and *Karen* · · · · ·

𝒴es, there's always a catch. The hidden cost of free stuff is something we learned the hard way. Take the day we got everything for free, but ended up paying through the nose anyway. To celebrate the publication of our article, we had lined up a "free day of fun." Hair salons, restaurants, and beauty spas were clamoring for our business, inviting us to try their services as the newest "famous" girls in town. We were excited, especially since, as irresponsible shopaholics, Karen and I usually had very little in our bank accounts to pay for necessities such as haircuts and food. (We lived on cheap takeout and splurged on designer shoes.)

We started the day at Just Calm Down Spa, a cute day spa in the Flatiron District, where we were given the full celebrity treatment: manicures, pedicures, facials, and Swedish massages. "Everything is complimentary." The receptionist beamed. "But I do need twenty percent gratuity for the staff." Final cost: $110. We arrived at the Prive salon, a chic downtown hair palace that caters to clients like Drew Barrymore, for our complimentary hair booking. We were cut and glossed, highlighted and styled, by Laurent DuFourg's excellent team of Ludovich (color), and Elena and Vanessa (haircuts). They even threw in makeup by their talented makeup artist, Maureen, and were nice enough to give Tanya, our photographer friend who was with us, a blow-out as well. We kissed, thanked, and tipped everyone. Final cost for ten tips at $20 each: $200. We were only halfway through the day and already we had spent more than $150 each!

Dinner that night was provided gratis at Man Ray, a super-trendy restaurant owned by Sean Penn, Johnny Depp, John Malkovich, and Harvey Weinstein (one of the brothers behind Miramax Films). Naomi Campbell had just thrown a party for her new venture there, and it was also the spot for *Saturday Night Live*'s season premiere bash, where Matt Damon, Bruce Springsteen, and Jimmy Fallon hobnobbed in the restaurant's posh lounge. Our reservation was for four, but we were quickly joined by five more people whom we bumped into at the restaurant (famous people have a habit of "collecting" others as nights progress). We were seated at the best table. We spotted Barry Diller nearby. And we feasted on roasted sea bass, oysters, and tuna and octopus sashimi, and drank copious bottles of wine. At the end of the evening, a waiter handed us a leather book. I froze, thinking, *Oh, no! They don't know it's supposed to be free!* But we breathed a sigh of relief upon seeing the large *comp* stamp on our $850 bill. We tipped a little over 25 percent, which brought the final cost to $215!

So our day of "free stuff" actually cost us $500! We barely had enough in our respective checking accounts to pay for all the tips. It brought us more into debt. But we wouldn't have missed it for the world! (Burp!)

# THE TIPPING POINT
### KNOW HOW TO HANDLE THE COMPED LIFE WITH GRACE

• Find out how much the free service, whether it's a car and driver, meal, massage, haircut, or makeup application, would have cost if you were a civilian who had to pay—and leave 20 percent (when something is free, skimping on the tip is frowned upon).

• Leave $1 to $2 per drink at parties at nightclubs and restaurants where there's an open bar. (You don't need to leave a tip at someone's private home, club, or wedding.)

• If you borrowed clothes, shoes, or accessories, send the lender a thank-you note and a thoughtful gift—an art book, candles, beauty products, journal, or something apropos from your "swag closet."

• If someone gives you a fat gift (i.e., hotel stay, vacation, cruise, tickets to a performance), you must thank them by sending a little token of your appreciation, parallel to the level of what you received. Play tickets get a thank-you note and a phone call—but a two-week trip to Aspen calls for a grand bouquet and a special bottle of wine (or your firstborn—whatever's available, really).

## NO, WE DID NOT TAKE
## THE FIRST-AID KIT

• • • • • • • • • *Melissa* • • • • • • • • •

*I* thought I had it down. I was a pro at maneuvering the gravy train. During my two weeks of fame, I ate my way (for free) through some of the best restaurants in town. By convincing publicists and restaurateurs that I was a "famous" novelist, doors opened and culinary opportunities were given to me that I could never afford on my own. Who knew you could fake stardom? Mike and I ate our way through some of the best restaurants in town: City Crab, Steak Frites, Porto Tuscana, Chango, Chicama, First, Cucina, Savannah Steak, and many others. The red carpet was rolled out everywhere we went, and it was gratifying to order $60 steak on the menu knowing that someone else was footing the bill. At City Crab, the manager had to give us an extra table for all the food we had ordered. We looked upon the diners who made do with measly plates of one or two crabs with pity and smugness.

What a difference celebrity makes! When I was reviewing restaurants for a small local paper (that could not afford to pay for my receipts) I used to shiver whenever the check arrived, fearing they'd forget I was having a complimentary "press meal." More than once I was presented with the astronomical bill at the end of a fabulous meal—and they only let us leave once the publicist personally vouched for us. "Fear and Dining," Mike called it.

The free clothes and the free meals begat bigger things. Suddenly I was fielding invitations for free hotels and free trips to luxury resorts! I thought I had hit the big time! Mike and I packed our bags and spent a heavenly weekend in a five-star resort in Arizona, where we were esconsced in the triplex penthouse suite. We spent every night ordering five-course dinners from the four-star restaurant in the lobby (much better to eat it by candlelight and a view of the desert!). It was relaxing and invigorating—we each had massages at the in-home spa, and availed ourselves of the minibar treats.

"Did you enjoy your stay?" the desk receptionist asked as we checked out.

"It was wonderful!"

"Great!" he said, and handed us a bill documenting each of our activities: the restaurant bills, the spa bills, the long-distance phone calls. I had forgotten how ambiguous accepting things for free could be.

"But I thought this was free," I argued, my heart sinking. They didn't even bother to take our credit card imprint when we checked in! We spent a good fifteen minutes battling with the desk clerk, his manager, the publicist of the hotel, and the publicist in New York who had invited us on the trip. We left the hotel in triumph—without paying a penny.

But the minute I returned to the city, the publicist in New York berated me for our behavior. "They said you guys stole everything from the room and even took the first-aid kit!" The charges they levied at us were ridiculous, and in the end, I just had to laugh it off as a casualty of "fame" and the delicate art of swag. Never look a gift horse in the mouth. The next time I accept a "free" trip, I'll make sure I know exactly how much it's going to cost me.

# TROUBLE-FREE?

## Karen

𝒥t's easy to look smashing when you're famous. Stars have personal chefs, a throng of trainers, yogis who travel with them, and personal assistants who make sure that their bosses get the right carb-free, high-protein meals while on film sets. Having a hot body comes with the fame territory. Sadly, I have always had issues with my frame (my nickname growing up was, unfortunately, Bagel because of my love handles!). If I only had smaller thighs . . . If I only had slimmer hips . . . If I only had slinkier arms. That's why I'm constantly trying to write stories about trainers, fitness, nutritionists—anything that will bring me to someone who's capable of solving all my figure woes and giving me the kind of limbs I can insure for $1 million. (Many of the Hollywood set have done that, you know.)

After my two-week mission, I had managed to work my way into so many restaurants (and one chartered yacht in the Caribbean) without having to pay for it (one place, Domicile, a groovy hot spot in Greenwich Village, owned by the guy who was once engaged to model Molly Sims, stayed open for me on Easter Sunday, when they were supposed to be closed, so I could host a small dinner party for twelve people) that all of my pants were getting snug.

Even worse, I had just received a hot gift—sexy, low-slung Juicy Couture jeans (waist size twenty-seven!)—that I could not squeeze into. And there was no way I was even going to try to put on the teeny-weeny Imitation of Christ top and $2,500 (size petite) hand-painted, one-of-a-kind vintage jacket from Language that I had received as "congrats, you're famous" gifts. After Radu kicked my butt to Timbuktu, I managed to convince an editor to let me do a "before and after" story and work my ass off with another trainer for three months to lose my bulk and find my inner "vampire-slayer body."

I showed up to this trainer's gym three mornings a week and jumped rope for twenty minutes, did thousands of jumping jacks, and channeled Jane Fonda until I could feel the burn no more. After two weeks I lost a total of ten inches. I was on a roll . . . until I injured my scapula, the muscle by the shoulder blade, so badly that I couldn't turn my head. It wasn't the trainer's fault. I had exacerbated a previous injury, but the result was: no working out. I had to stop the program and kill my story.

Well, let me tell you. This trainer was not pleased.

He began stalking me with nagging messages about the feature story I promised him. He told me I'd have to pay him back for the thousands of dollars of free services. He said he'd ruin my name. He said very mean things, including that he hopes I gain the inches back! Never once did he ask if I was okay, mind you. His calls became the bane of my existence. My e-mail account was full of nasty, threatening messages. "You promised a feature," he'd say, "and if I don't get one, there will be repercussions." I explained that I was in no shape to continue the workouts and that I was certainly in no shape to be in an "after" picture. I told him that once I healed, I'd do the story. But he was relentless with his pursuit. He wanted payback and he wanted it now!

In the beginning I planned to remedy the situation by referring to him in other stories I was working on. (In fact, I did mention him in a large feature in a fitness magazine, but that wasn't good enough.) When his publicist told me he called me the C-word (!!!), I stopped answering his calls, returning his e-mails, and trying to get him featured in any kind of story. His harassment didn't stop for weeks. In one letter, he actually promised to sue me. I was freaking out, I must admit. I hate letting people down, but in this situation there was nothing I could do. My editor assured me that he didn't have a leg to stand on. But that didn't ease my anxiety. The only solace I found was in cupcakes with buttercream icing.

I bumped into the trainer weeks later. And while we shook hands and made peace, he found the time to inform me that I looked like I found the ten inches I worked so hard to lose. That bastard! And I currently have no body insurance to speak of.

# WHAT NOT TO DO

- Don't start freeloading and asking for too much. Greed is one of the seven deadly sins for a reason.

- Don't ask for gifts for your friends or relatives. (See above.)

- Don't forget to send a thank-you note.

- Don't announce (in public) that it was free. Keep a low profile and brag in private.

- Don't take anything for granted, behave like a diva, complain, send back food, or cop a 'tude. Remember, free stuff is a privilege, not a right.

- Don't be late for your appointments or returning things to the lender.

- Don't pull the "dirty return" routine, which is when you bring back the free item to a store for either credit or cash money. Often free gifts are marked in some way or not even available in retail stores (we know people who have been busted—and it has tarnished their image).

*Two Weeks and Onward:*

# LIFE BEYOND THE FIRST FIFTEEN MINUTES

Fame is often fleeting. You can be the hottest thing on the planet one minute and a distant, fading memory the next. In New York society, there is a famous story about a no-name shop girl who became famous because she met up with the right publicists, who dressed her in designer clothes, pitched stories about her to the media, and invited her to fancy parties. She became the darling of the tony uptown subculture. She was in beautifully art-directed pages of the fashion magazines. Everyone thought her star would burn brightly forever . . . until she slept with the wrong person. She was banned from society, blackballed from parties, and completely ousted from New York life. No one has heard from her since.

If you don't want to be a flash in the pan, yet another Warholian statistic—here today, gone tomorrow—then brush up on your marketing skills and learn how to constantly surprise the world by reinventing yourself wisely and continuing to practice the fame moves we have taught you. First things first: you must never take fame for granted or else you will lose it. If you think climbing, begging, faxing, bribing, lying, crying, and schmoozing your way to the top was hard . . . get ready to work even harder to stay there.

Once you reach the limelight, you have to learn to withstand the test of time. Any celeb, celebrity manager, agent, or publicist will tell you there are a few rules to follow: Manage your image strategically. Think before you say or do anything marginally offensive in public. If you do run off at the mouth, be prepared to deliver a public apology to facilitate your return to glory. Surround yourself with the "right" people. And don't let things go to your head.

That said, this chapter includes details on dealing with the public (when you're no longer a nameless, anonymous person, life changes drastically and you'll need to know how to handle it elegantly), ideas for reinventing yourself (can you say Angelina Jolie?), comeback tips that will make your second act better than your first (Hugh Grant is so much better post–Divine Brown, don't you agree?), and all the sneaky tricks you'll need to stay in the picture, kid.

## DEALING WITH RECOGNITION— YOU'RE NO LONGER ANONYMOUS

# HERE'S MY CREDIT CARD— AND AN AUTOGRAPH

### *Karen*

*A*fter the *Marie Claire* article came out, my phone rang like crazy. Childhood camp friends called me. My parents refused to stop referring to me as "our famous daughter." A publicist informed me that "everyone" was talking about Mel and me. Invitations flooded my mailbox—a private Oasis concert, some kind of gala for the Rolling Stones in Vegas, Art Basel (the biggest modern art event in the states), a party for Kevin Spacey, charity balls, a trip to Brazil. I was even asked to host a benefit for breast cancer at a chic gallery space. ("Can we please put you on the invitation?" the event planner asked. "Anything for a good cause," I said.)

My mother's friend's twenty-four-year-old son mentioned my name to one of his friends in casual conversation. "Karen, a close family friend, had a party at Bungalow 8." When his friend heard it was me, she yelled, "You know Karen Robinovitz! The famous writer!" It was madness. On the one hand, it was amazing, as if it were a sign of universal acceptance. I had never experienced anything like it. A part of me felt like tossing my hat in the air and singing, "I've made it after all."

On the other hand, it was all so overwhelming, uncomfortable, and seemingly fake. I couldn't imagine what the "real" stars must go through. People I never met were coming up to me and saying, "I love that you did all of those things!" Old friends reconnected with me . . . to see if I could help them get things for free or reservations at certain fully booked restaurants. Someone even asked me if I'd call "my people" at Harry Winston to get her a diamond tiara for her wedding! It made me feel used. What did people want from me? I was really just the same girl from New Jersey whose favorite pastime was popping black-heads in the mirror. (Yeah, I know, I've been practicing that line.)

Months after the piece ran, I was shopping at my favorite store. While I was trying to concentrate on whether or not to splurge for a beaded tunic with kimono sleeves, two women asked me if I was that girl who did that famous article. When I told them I was, they said, "I knew it! You're so cool!" They grabbed my hand as if we were best friends, and began to fire a million questions my way. They wanted all the juicy details—how I got into parties, appeared on television, borrowed furs and Harry Winston jewels—so they could pull off the same "act." I gave them the scoop, thanked them, and bought my new favorite top. As I signed my name on the dotted line of my credit card bill, the girls came up to me and asked me for my autograph.

My autograph! Hello!

It was my first true celebrity moment. I will cherish it always.

# UNDERCOVER BACHELOR

*Melissa*

*I*n the winter of 2001, a young man tapped me on the shoulder and asked me if I was Melissa de la Cruz. Unfortunately, instead of asking for my autograph, which I was more than ready to provide, he handed me a stack of bills instead. "These were mistakenly put in my mailbox," he explained. Apparently, even if the London *Telegraph* once dubbed me a "minor celebrity" in New York since the publication of my novel, I was far from famous, and slightly delusional as well.

So when my *Marie Claire* editor asked me if I wanted to take on the challenge of "becoming famous" in two weeks, I jumped at the chance. The reality-show fan that I am, I don't even want to live off camera. What's the point? These days, you don't even have to have talent or looks to become famous. You can be famous just for being famous—like the plethora of socialites who are photographed at parties simply because they attend a lot of them.

It was a grand two weeks. From the borrowed couture to the glamorous parties, I lived the kind of life that is bestowed on only the very, very lucky. I didn't have to pay for a meal or a drink during the whole experience. And afterward, my social life transcended to a higher level. Instead of my having to fax, cajole, and beg my way into events, my mailbox is now crammed with thick, gold-bordered invitations, and my phone hasn't stopped ringing. I've been asked to the film premiere of *Unfaith-*

*ful*, hosted by Richard Gere; the Whitney Museum's annual Art Party; a private theater benefit with Julianne Moore, and openings of hotels in Paris and Sao Paolo. I was invited to host private parties in restaurants and to appear on local and national television. Not mention all the designer clothes I got to actually keep.

I got effusive fan e-mails from as far away as New Zealand and good wishes from acquaintances from high school and beyond who made an effort to get back in touch. "You were on *Extra*," a friend e-mailed excitedly the other day. Well, no, not really, but close. I never received as much notice for my novel as when my name appeared in Page Six. The story even took a life of its own. *Gotham* magazine even used our little stunt as a kicker to their fame issue: "Fabulous or frightening?" the editor's letter asked. A worthy question indeed.

I'm so famous that I got tapped on the shoulder while I was waiting for a table at a neighborhood restaurant. "Are you Melissa de la Cruz?" a young woman asked. "Why, yes," I answered, thinking she must have seen me in all the magazines and gossip columns. She just laughed. "You're the one who crashed her fiancé's bachelor party as Judge Ito!"

So as much as I wanted to style myself as the next It-girl-about-town, I realized that to achieve true celebrity, good hair, great clothes, and fancy parties are nothing next to looking like a frumpy Japanese judge in drag. In other words, Michael Musto was right. I've become famous because I've done something embarrassing. And I have the photographs to prove it.

# FACING THE PUBLIC

**NOW THAT YOU'RE FAMOUS,
PEOPLE WILL WANT A PIECE OF YOU.
GO AHEAD, MAKE THEIR DAY!**

• Be gracious and modest. Nobody likes a sulky or arrogant celebrity who punches out paparazzi photographers.

• Look your best—even if it's just for going to the supermarket. You don't want to disappoint people or hear them say, "You look so much better in your photographs."

• Always sign autographs if you are lucky enough to be asked.

• Never complain in public—it will be gossiped about.

• Have confidentiality agreements for those who are close to you. You don't want them turning on you one day and ruining your image to make a quick buck.

• Realize that your every move will now be scrutinized, from your breakups and heartaches to your tipping habits and doctors' visits. So be sure to be a good tipper! There is nothing worse than being seen as cheap. It will make people resent your success.

• Put a positive spin on everything. Not getting much attention lately? Claim you've taken a much-needed, well-deserved hiatus.

*Rewards of fame are in the mail!*

A DAY OF INDULGENCE WITH
JUICY COUTURE
AT THE CHATEAU MARMONT

COME PICK OUT YOUR SUMMER ESSENTIALS FROM JUICY COUTURE,
CHARLOTTE RONSON, INCA, CORUM, TRACEY ROSS,
DOONEY & BOURKE AND HUGO EYEWEAR. PREVIEW JUICY'S FALL
COLLECTION AND PRE-ORDER YOUR FAVORITE PIECES.
ENJOY COMPLIMENTARY MANICURES & PEDICURES BY THE BUFF SPA.
MAKE-UP BY NARS AND BLOW OUTS BY JOHN BARRETT.
BY APPOINTMENT ONLY.

WITH CHAMPAGNE FROM PERRIER JOUET.

THURSDAY JULY 26TH AND FRIDAY JULY 27TH
RSVP TO ALI WISE AT HARRISON & SHRIFTMAN 310 271 6411

HAVE A JUICY DAY,
LOVE, PAMELA SKAIST LEVY
AND GELA TAYLOR

Special thanks to Perrier, Long Life Teas
and The Coffee Bean & Tea Leaf.

JAY Z
DAMON DASH &
ROC-A-FELLA RECORDS
INVITE YOU TO
CELEBRATE THE RELEASE OF
THE DYNASTY
TO THE SOUNDS OF DJ MARK RONSON
NOVEMBER 7TH 9PM
HARRISON AND SHRIFTMAN 310.271.6411

Joel Silver & Robert Zemeckis
invite you and a guest to a private screening and party f

*Ghost Ship*

Friday, October 11 · 7:30 p.m. sharp

SCREENING
Orpheum Theatre
842 South Broadway Street · Downtown Los Angeles

PARTY
The Standard Hotel Rooftop
550 South Figueroa Street at 6th Street

Special Musical Performance by Mudvayne
DJ Mark Ronson

Robert Downey Jr.
cordially invites you and a guest

To the holiday event celebrating the
4th Anniversary of Flaunt Magazine and the
release of the W Hotels third CD,
Rhythm and Muse II.

special performance by Ravish recording artist
Deborah Falconer

Monday, December 9th, 2002

W Hotel New York–Union Square
2nd floor, Great Room
201 Park Avenue South (corner of 17th Street), NYC
8:30 PM until Midnight

Please RSVP to Plug at 212-966-7991
or rsvp to event@pluglimited.com

This Invitation is Absolutely Non-transferable

## CH-CH-CH-CHANGES: THE ONLY WAY
## TO KEEP YOUR PROFILE FRESH

# THE NEXT PHASE?

• • • • • • • • • *Melissa* • • • • • • • • • •

*I* started life as a geek. Then I was popular. Then I was a computer programmer with a serious job and real money. When I switched careers to write full time, I had to be "popular" again. I wrote a humorous novel about fashion and society. I was frothy, cotton-candy, cream-puff girl. I was a fashion journo, a glossy magazine chick, someone whom former boyfriends likened to Cher on *Clueless*. But it's time to say good-bye to the popular-girl personality, to bid *au revoir* to the cute ditz. While these personas worked well for me in my attempt to rid myself of the unglamorous stigma of actually knowing how to program in Visual Basic, they sometimes mask the real person and the real writer underneath.

Sometimes the smartest thing to do is to act dumb. I think Marilyn Monroe was the one who said that, and she should know. Playing shallow and affecting frivolity is one thing, but I want to show the world there's more to me than five-hundred-word articles about the latest Marc Jacobs jacket (admittedly, it might not be much, but it is there). I grew up in Manila, and immigrated with my family to San Francisco when I was twelve. Growing up in America as an immigrant has strongly affected how I see the world, and I have yet to write about my perspective. When I first started my writing career, I made a name for myself as "the Angry Asian Girl." I wrote rants and screeds in wonky journals and controversial local newspapers. I wrote articles entitled "Gook Fetish" (about white-man-and-Asian-woman relationships) and "Single White Female: A Second 'Banana' Speaks Out" (about my relationship with a privileged white friend). But I gave it up once I stopped being so angry, and I devoted my career to the lighter side of life.

I loved trying to become famous, and I'll always have a soft spot for fashion, celebrity, and frou-frou. I'll always be up for assignments that ask me to "figure out what it takes to get fired" or to "round up the gold diggers." Yet even as I make an effort to produce works that are maybe a little quieter, maybe a little more introspective, and, dare I say it, maybe a little more serious, I'll always remember what my mom told me: "Just be yourself!" And man, I just can't keep a straight face—even as I write this solemn and self-indulgent creed. Heh, heh, heh.

## LIFE BEYOND INSANITY?

• • • • • • • • • • • *Karen* • • • • • • • • • •

*I* have mentioned more than once that I built a name for myself for somewhat sensationalized journalism, that people knew me for being naked or doing something crazy—like injecting non-FDA-approved drugs into my body to dissolve fat and smearing human placenta on my face to clear up my skin (such a trend in Hollywood and jet-set society circles that the placenta woman actually books a suite at the five-star Peninsula Hotel before the Oscars to do celeb skin with purified placenta, shipped from Russia, for the big night)—for the sake of an article. "What won't you do?" people often asked. ("Well, I wouldn't fake my own death," I tell them.)

After a while, I got sick of being seen as "a crazy." Truth is, I may be a ballsy, brazen, bold, open-minded person who likes a bit of attention from time to time and appreciates the art of shocking others, but I am actually quite wholesome at heart. I don't booze up. I don't smoke. I don't do any form of drug. Even if some of the stories I've written about sex (the one about the orgy scene in Manhattan or my day in the dominatrix dungeon come to mind) lead people to believe otherwise, I don't sleep around. I avoid white flour whenever possible. I don't even drink caffeine. After hearing enough people say, "I cannot believe that story! It's your most insane one," I became determined to alter my image and be more than just "the naked girl who will do anything." I am more profound than that—and I have a $100,000 college degree from Emory University (where I was pre-med and interning for a neurosurgeon) to prove it!

So I began to cover more serious stories—women's issues, private anticounterfeiting investigations of Chinatown lairs where fake Chanel and Louis Vuitton bags are illegally stored and sold and often made in sweatshops, a ring of kidnappers in Mexico who peddle children for kiddie porn, the new wave of spirituality in America (and the models who subscribe to it). I turned down the kind of assignments I used to kill for—making out with someone in a church just to see how long it would take before we got in trouble, and taking an oral sex class.

Although it became relieving to stop getting calls from my father about the latest article about the clitoris, it was also a hard adjustment. I actually had to mourn for the identity I once had before I could fully embrace the new one: serious journalist. I began to get complimentary phone calls and comments from people who appreciated the change of direction of my work, but at the same time, I dealt with frustrated editors who were not that pleased with the fact that I was no longer their go-to girl, the writer who would do anything no mere mortal would attempt (i.e., walk around the city wearing a wrap dress that purposely unwrapped . . . just to see who would tell—and help—me). I didn't have as much work at first, as it took time to build a new reputation. But I got there slowly and wound up in a better place than I was before (I got this book deal, after all).

Life in the more conservative lane, admittedly, is not always as exciting. I don't wind up in strange subcultures of New York City, reporting on funky lesbian S&M parties. I haven't met a drag queen who sells Tupperware in months. There may be no more assignments that require me to be kidnapped by a company that offers abduction-experience services, but in a few more years I expect that everyone will be sick of my straitlaced self and I can go back to my wicked, randy ways.

# REINVENT YOURSELF

**PEOPLE ARE FICKLE.
IF YOU DON'T GIVE THEM SOMETHING NEW EVERY TWO YEARS,
YOU'LL BE IGNORED AND THEN FORGOTTEN**

• Change your personal style. Go from stiletto-wearing vamp to tree-hugging bohemian, or tattooed rocker to sophisticated up-town lady. If you've always been buttoned-up, let it all hang out for a change and channel Christina Aguilera's dirty spirit.

• Get on a health campaign. Eat only macrobiotic food. Hire the most famous Hollywood chef to help support your cause. Tell everyone who will listen. Eventually, when you're a svelte size four and palling around with Donna Karan's entourage of helpers (trainers, yogis, healers), they'll start paying attention.

• Drastically alter your haircolor or haircut. A new look will always give you a fresh image.

• Take up a new lifestyle. If you were a playboy, settle down and declare that you've "fallen in love" and adopted a new Cambodian baby.

• Constantly find a new cause to defend. Support PETA with a vengeance. (Try to do an ad for them if possible, but if you do, don't run around soon after wearing a fur jacket, like Cindy Crawford did.)

• And while you're at it, take up a new religion and promote the hell out of it.

• Consider changing your accent—even if you don't move out of the country.

• Remove your breast implants. You'll be lauded as a brave martyr.

• Announce that you're retiring, Michael Jordan style, or giving your very last performance, à la Babs. Have farewell parties. Make a big hoopla over the fact that you're leaving the lime-light. Change your mind six months later. You'll have been gone just long enough for them to start really missing you.

## THE SECOND ACT

# ROLLER-COASTER RIDE

*Melissa* and *Karen*

*If* you mapped out the life of a famous person, it would look something like an EKG. There are many ups and downs. You're hot one day and obsolete the next, only to return, sometimes twenty years later, because some new film director wants to take a chance on an oldie but goodie; you wind up a star again when you come out about your bipolar disorder (and the fact that you were found wandering barefoot in the desert of New Mexico); or you pioneer a suddenly popular charity, benefit, or cause. If cats have nine lives, celebrities must have a dozen.

They can go from superstar child actor to drug-addicted petty-thief leper and return to the public eye by cleaning up, getting in shape, writing a tell-all book, and posing for an ad campaign—or even *Playboy*—to get their name back on the map . . . and eventually parlaying the attention, strategically, into superstar status. This is also known as "the comeback," the time when someone who has lost their fame reemerges with a new attitude, vibe, and brand name. Just look at John Travolta, Drew Barrymore, and Rob Lowe. They've all successfully gotten famous, lost fame, and regained it again.

So before you decide to do the walk of fame, you should make sure you have a comeback plan in the back of your head, a strategy you can rely on when you lose favor in the public eye or do something awful that makes the world shun you. The key to the comeback is, you need to remain insignificant for a while. People have to sort of miss you, wonder what happened to you, and want you back by the time you return to grace. Your timing has to be perfect. If you wait too long, you might wind up like David Lee Roth, which is not good. But if you hit it right, you'll be cruising, Travolta-style (even if he hasn't made a good movie to save his life since Tarantino resurrected his career).

Luckily for us, we have not been playing this little game for long enough to speak from experience. But we can tell you this— we know exactly what we'll do if we're ousted from society. And next, we'll give you some thoughts that will do the trick for you, too.

# COMEBACK TIPS

**THINGS ARE ALWAYS BETTER THE SECOND TIME AROUND**

• Have a much-publicized accident. If you almost die, people might start to care about you again.

• Come out of the closet about a deep, dark, tragic secret in your past: an eating disorder, alcoholism, a jailbird daddy. You'll be on *Oprah*. Everyone will want to know how you survived.

• Change your sexual preference. Look what it did for Anne Heche, who went from obscure to fabulous (Ellen years), incoherent Ecstasy freak (post-Ellen rampage), to a happy working mom (Coley Laffoon years).

• Lose weight or stop starving yourself and embrace your "real" size, be it an eight or a fourteen. The public loves nothing more than a good makeover.

• Publicly apologize for any bad behavior that may have caused your star to dim. If you've been in jail, have your publicist contact Barbara Walters to offer her the exclusive interview.

• Plan to get caught doing something disgraceful, like picking up a transvestite prostitute to get the public's attention. Deny it (you were just helping someone get a ride, for heaven's sake!) and use your newfound spotlight to make an announcement (a career change), reach out to your old publicist friends, or do something positive for the good of humankind.

• Write a tell-all book and have no fears about dragging names through the mud.

# IN RETROSPECT . . .

## I MISS MY MTV!

• • • • • • • • • • • *Karen* • • • • • • • • • •

*W*hile life in the fabulous lane led me to many extreme highs— glittery parties, free couture dresses, VIP courtside seats at Knicks games, dinners with people who have said, "I'd like to thank the Academy" without irony, glorious trips abroad—it was also incredibly tiresome. I "worked" eighteen-hour days. I hardly slept. I bickered endlessly with my (then) boyfriend. I didn't have time to sit on my sofa and enjoy a little "Must-See TV," let alone go to the bathroom in peace. I constantly had to be "on" and "dressed." And I was exhausted, beat, and desperate for a full eight hours of sleep. And half of my friends wanted to fire me for being MIA. Don't get me wrong—it was so much fun. But living that way full-time . . . well . . . that's another story.

My life would have been easier with ten assistants, a personal chef, a masseuse to work the kinks out of my neck between appointments, stylists who shopped for me around the clock, a team of managers, and full-time publicists who weren't helping me as a one-time-only favor. But the upkeep of all of that is so unmanageable that I'd need a whole separate entourage to handle the business of it all. Truth is: I longed for calm days of hanging out with a friend at lunch without spending three-quarters of the time on my cell phone. I missed not being so frazzled morning, noon, and night. I craved some bonding time with my sofa! And I was ready to return to my (somewhat) mellow life behind the scenes (at least on a part-time basis) . . . even if it meant never wearing $2 million of diamonds again.

# BACK TO THE SHADOWS?

## *Melissa*

*L*iving under the spotlight is a strange thing. While I'll always feel a special thrill from seeing my name in the paper, receiving invitations to the kind of parties I never would have been invited to in the past, and the hordes of free gifts, I can live without the gossip-column brouhahas, the fake conversations with people I barely know, and the underlying resentment from the staff for complimentary services rendered. ("Who does she think she is?")

I realized one very important truth: I actually like my anonymity. I don't like being fawned over (it makes me nervous) and I don't like salespeople at boutiques to know exactly who I am and how much I'm paying. While I enjoyed getting great tables at the newest restaurants, I was uncomfortable with the scrutiny that came from such "celebrity" treatment. All the stuff can really go to your head—at one point Karen and I thought we were "too famous" to stick labels on the seven hundred-plus envelopes for our own book deal party. We were so used to people doing things for us that we sat in her kitchen, sighing and moaning and complaining about not having a team of lackeys to do the deed for us. It was then that epiphany struck: we needed a reality check!

While I'm more than happy to be invited to parties where I can guzzle free champagne, after reviewing all the unflattering photos of me in public, having to be "on" all the time was exhausting, not to mention the toll it took on my marriage (I'm still sorry I planned our gratuitous book deal party on my husband's birthday . . .). I now realize I'd rather be in a quiet corner with a lot of hors d'ouevres, and far, far away from the flash of a photographer's camera. Like Greta Garbo, I just vant to be alone. Until the next party, anyway!

# AN IMPORTANT REMINDER

The real secret to fame is more fame. It's a snowball that feeds on itself—once you convince enough people that you're "famous," more people will believe it, and the more famous you become. The cycle usually continues until the life you once called your own is hardly recognizable, albeit much more enchanting.

Fame is a many-splendored thing, but it is also quirky and unpredictable. Some seem to acquire it effortlessly vis-à-vis winning personalities, good looks, or a pedigree that fascinates the public. But for most of us to become well known, it takes elbow grease, determination, and a lot of butt kissing. Regardless of how you get there, you have to be prepared for some ugly times.

Your trainer may threaten to sue you. Your free haircuts could be abominable. Makeup artists may wind up leaving you with a sty in your eye before your big television debut. Hotels may accuse you of stealing stuff and breaking things. Significant others—and platonic friends—may resent your newfound popularity. You may have to wear something you hate just because it was a gift from a VID (very important designer). You could get hate mail, even if you're the nicest person on Earth. If you gain weight, everyone will notice (and may even secretly be glad).

But unlike skateboarding down a hill, fame is not dangerous. Nor is it life-threatening. It's a blast, and everyone who wants to do it should go out there and get their stuff together. So thicken your skin. Toughen up. Let your journey begin. Because the aforementioned disadvantages are nothing more than a luxury problem, when you think about it—a small price to pay. Just remember this: the object of the quest is not the free stuff, the fancy parties, the press clips, or the fact that you now get recognized when you buy the newspaper, but to enjoy life.

Why should celebrities have all the fun?

TANYA BRAGANTI

# Acknowledgments

So many to thank, so little time before we get shushed by Bill Conti's orchestra.

First of all, Marie Claire. None of this would have been possible without you, especially Lesley Jane Seymour, editor-in-chief extraordinaire; Stacy Morrison, who assigned us the story; Michael Callahan, who kept upping our expense account; and Sarah Eisen, who edited the piece and listened to countless hours of "oh my God" moments.

Deborah (our super-agent) Schneider! You rock. You totally believed in us, supported us, and indulged our school-girl antics and excitement. We adore you—you are such a godsend in great shoes. And Allison Dickens, our amazing editor, who got our jokes, encouraged our insanity, and (most importantly) loved every word we wrote (there's a gift bag in heaven with your name on it)!

To our families, Judi, Alan, and Jason Robinovitz, Mike Johnston (who bore the brunt of it all, patiently), Bert, Ching, and Francis de la Cruz, Steve and Aina Green, Dennis, Marsha,

John, Anji, Tim, and Rob Johnston. You are our best cheerleaders and fans. This would mean nothing without you.

Big kisses to our supportive friends: Alison Oneacre, Alix Boyer, Grace Cha and the house of Christian Dior, Alvin Valley, Amy Larocca, Amy Sacco, Ann Dee Goldin, Jacob & Co., Beauty.com, Ben Widdicombe, Bill Ford, Brad Hamilton, Brad Zeifman, Carol Brodie and the Harry Winston designers, Daniel Boulud, David Trugerman, Deborah Hughes, Desiree Gruber, Diane Ghioto, Donna Bagdasarian, Edward Tricomi, Elisa Jimenez, Elizabeth Harrison, Ereka Dunn, Foxy Brown, Gail Parenteau, George Rush, Green Air, Horacio Silva, Jared Paul Stern, Jason Oliver Nixon, Jason Strauss and Noah Tepperberg, Jeff Klein, Jeffrey Slonim, Jennifer Maguire, Joey and T., John Potamousis, Jonathan Cheban, Jonathan Shriftman, Josh Sherer, Keith Kelly, Kenneth Tepper, Kim Hovey, Lara Shriftman, Laura Branigan, Laurent d and the Privé team, Lee Carter, Leslie Stevens, Libby Callaway (our favorite fashionista—without whom we would never have met), Liney Li, Lysa Bitner, Mama Combs, Marc Malkin, Mark Silver, Marvet Britto, Matt Paco, Melissa Silver, Michael Bragg, Michael Musto, Nancy Kane, Naomi Ramsey, Nicole Esposito, Nicole Young, Norah Lawlor, Peter Laitmon, Rachel Bernstein, Radu, Roger Friedman, Sam Firer and Stephen Hall, Sally Narkis, Sarah Greenberg, Sasha Lazard, Shawn Purdy, Simon Doonan, Stephen Knoll, Sue Devitt, Tammie Rosen, Tanya Braganti, The Siren girls, Tom Dolby, Winnie Beattie, everyone at Ballantine, and our tireless interns.

We'd also like to give a little love to everyone else who has been behind us and, of course, to the "little people" (we promised not to forget you)!

# About the Authors

**Melissa de la Cruz** is the author of *Cat's Meow* (Scribner 2001), a comic novel about celebrity society, and was dubbed "the Jackie Collins of the Moomba generation." The book was published as *The Girl Can't Help It!* in the United Kingdom and spent two months on *Heat* magazine's Top 10 bestseller list. She writes regularly for *Marie Claire* and the serial fiction column The Fortune Hunters for *Gotham*, and she has penned the Celebrity Spotlight Column in *Rosie*. She lives in Manhattan with her husband.

**Karen Robinovitz** is a prolific writer who covers fashion, trends, style, celebrities, lifestyles of the rich rich and fabulous, and sex for *Marie Claire*, *Harper's Bazaar*, the *New York Post*, and *Elle*, where she writes an entertaining column called, It's My Party. In addition, Karen has contributed to the *New York Times* Styles section, *Details*, *Glamour*, and *In Style*. Her second book, *Fete Accompli! The Ultimate Guide to Creative Entertaining* (Clarkson Potter), will be released in the fall of 2003. She lives in New York City.

For more information (or fun) visit
www.becomefamousintwoweeks.com, and stay tuned
for their next book . . .
**How to Become a Fashionista in Two Weeks or Less**